MORAL TRAINING,

INFANT AND JUVENILE,

AS APPLICABLE TO THE

CONDITION OF THE POPULATION

OF

LARGE TOWNS.

By DAVID STOW,

A DIRECTOR OF THE MODEL SCHOOLS, GLASGOW.

" PREVENTION IS BETTER THAN CURE."

SECOND EDITION, ENLARGED.

GLASGOW:

PRINTED FOR WILLIAM COLLINS;

OLIVER & BOYD, W. WHYTE & CO. AND W. OLIPHANT, EDINBURGH;
W. F. WAKEMAN, AND WM. CURRY, JUN. & CO. DUBLIN;
WHITTAKER, TREACHER, & ARNOT, HAMILTON, ADAMS, & CO.
AND SIMPKIN & MARSHALL, LONDON.

M.DCCC.XXXIV.

PREFACE.

An attempt is made, in the following pages, to explain and exhibit the practical working of the Infant system of Moral Training;—at the same time we are satisfied, that a thorough knowledge can only be obtained by a long and patient inspection of a School in actual operation.

During the last few years, several publications have appeared, advocating the cause of Infant School Education; but as these have referred chiefly to the kind of lessons proper to be taught in an Infant School, much practical misconception still prevails on the subject, and inquiries, such as the following, are frequently made:—What are the peculiarities of the Infant system? How are the children taught? Why use such a variety of apparatus? This led to the publication of the Dialogue contained in Chapters IV. and V., which was intended as a mean of acquainting the Parents with the intellectual and moral training of their children. But having found its way among various ranks of society in England, as well as in Scotland, whose prejudices, in some instances, have in consequence been removed, and who may now be ranked among the warmest friends of the system, we make no apology for retaining the phraseology of our Scottish Granny.

As it is desirable to exhibit particularly the practical distinction between teaching and training, and the importance of this system, in a national point of view, we have been induced to enlarge upon these points in the present Edition.

The principal alteration, and we trust improvement, in the practical working of the system, upon the plan laid down by Wilderspin, (the chief promoter, if not the originator, of the system itself,) is the mode of daily BIBLE TRAINING, adopted in the Model Infant School, Glasgow, which at once places the system upon the only sure moral basis, and secures a daily variety and progressive advancement in scriptural knowledge.

We may here remark, that this was the first School formed in Scotland upon the system alluded to; and that in it, with few exceptions, every Infant Schoolmaster in Scotland has been trained.

In the first Edition, we recommended the introduction of the Infant system of Moral Training into every Juvenile School in the kingdom, especially in towns. Now, however, the experiment has been tried in one of the Parochial Schools in this city. It has fully succeeded, and even surpassed our fondest expectations; the practicability of its application to older children, therefore, is now placed beyond all doubt. See Chapter VII.

We have thought it necessary to add a separate Chapter, exhibiting the circumstances of the working classes in large towns, especially of Glasgow, as also the amount of the moral machinery in operation, in order to show, that something new and additional is awanting for their moral improvement, and which we conceive to consist in a widely extended system of Infant and Juvenile Training.

In the Appendix, will be found extracts from letters, received from several of the Parents of the children, affording ample proof of the efficiency and influence of the system.

The Superintendents of the Model Infant School, Saltmarket, and the Model Juvenile School, Annfield, continue to receive such persons as may be desirous of becoming Teachers, and of being practically trained to the system.

ERRATUM.—The reader will please particularly observe, that the third paragraph from bottom of page 251, ought to read thus :—
" The Gallery rises each step as follows—No. 1, 6½ inches; No. 2, 7; No. 3, 7; No. 4, 7½; No. 5, 8; and top-seat, lined at back, 9 inches," &c.

CONTENTS.

CONTENTS.

APPENDIX.

PLATES.

MORAL TRAINING:

INFANT AND JUVENILE.

CHAPTER I.

TEACHING AND TRAINING.

Training may be intellectual, physical, or moral—Teaching not training—Moral training the primary aim of all national education—
Development precedes training—Sympathy and example powerful
auxiliaries in the process of training—Power of habit—Illustrations
of physical, intellectual, and moral training—Fact regarding infant
training.

In entering upon an exposition of the principles
and plan of moral training, it is necessary, in the
first instance, that we take a view of what training
is in itself.

Training may either be INTELLECTUAL, PHY-
SICAL, or MORAL. Intellectual training may be
carried on distinctly and separately—so may physical,—but *moral* training, while it in a great measure includes the other two, yet in itself is a loftier
and more elevated cultivation than either.

The meaning of the term, TRAINING, will, per-

A

haps, be best understood by contrasting it with that which in schools is usually substituted for it— we mean, TEACHING. Teaching, however, is not training, although it is included in it.

Teaching may be stated as the infusion of principles; and training, as the formation of habits. By infant or juvenile training, is meant the development and practical cultivation not merely of one, but of all the principles of an infant or youth.

Moral Training is, or ought to be, the primary aim of all National Education,—to the accomplishment of which, simple teaching is not sufficient: there must be called into exercise the intellectual and physical, above all, the religious and moral, faculties of our nature.

Intellectual education, by some, is conceived to possess in itself the power of forming a virtuous character. But such persons seem to forget, that we also possess physical and moral natures, which powerfully influence our conduct in life, and which necessarily require a separate and distinct cultivation; and not only so, but all must be cultivated simultaneously, or else the child, as a child, is not under a complete training.

The training of a child, in its intellectual department, is not so much the affording instruction, as it is giving to the mind a habit of thinking—of thinking correctly on every subject. The same may be said in regard to the moral affections; it is that of training the child to feel aright—and also in regard to the bodily organs, that of training to the habits of acting aright.

From these considerations we conclude, that, while teaching is not training, infant and juvenile

training is just the fulfilment of the Bible precept
—"Train up a child in the way he should go"—as
a physical, rational, and moral being. And here
we observe, that the Divine command is not simply,
Teach, or show, the child how he ought to walk in
the way, but *Train* him *in* the way; which implies
personal superintendence and example.

It is proper that we now show the importance
of training, by analysis and illustration.

Our first position then, is, There must be a
development of character and disposition, ere the
process of training can be commenced. We must
actually see the habits and actions, hear the words,
and observe the bent of the affections, of the child.

Development is not sought for, nor is it necessary, previous to *instruction;* for, in ordinary
teaching or instruction, there is not any difference
made between children of large or small capacities—the heads of all are alike attempted to be
stuffed with knowledge. How much better would
it be, first to draw out and DEVELOPE the extent
and quality of those powers which the Divine
Being has implanted, and afterwards exercise them
upon those subjects which they show a capability
of acquiring, and which may render them in after-
life good and useful members of society!

Moral Training, it is evident, presupposes a necessity of being led—a waywardness—a propensity which needs to be restrained and directed to
proper objects and pursuits. Were we perfect
moral beings, such a necessity for training could
not exist, for all our thoughts, feelings, and actions, would of course move in a right and proper
direction.

As a precursor to the exercise of Training, DE-VELOPMENT must be three-fold—Corporeal, Intellectual, and Moral.

Under the first head, we have the modes of sitting, standing, walking and running—the holding of a book or slate—distinct articulation—the modulation of the voice in reading or speaking, &c.

Under the second head of Infant and Juvenile training, we have the development of the strength or weakness of mental powers, of whatever kind—calculation—reasoning—illustration—imagination—particular modes of thinking. All must be developed, ere the mind can be cultivated or directed, in other words, ere it can be TRAINED.

Under the third head, or moral affections, it has been wisely remarked, that children should be taught most carefully those things that will be longest and most constantly useful to them, and that the education of the heart should always take precedence of the head. The developments of moral character and habits are exceedingly varied and extensive. A very few only need be mentioned :—regularity—speaking truth—doing justice—showing kindness and courtesy—forgiving injuries—fidelity to promises—submission to parents and teachers—and, we may add, personal cleanliness and neatness. The negative to all these requires training ; and the palpable exhibition of any of these can be turned, by the shrewd superintendent or parent, into a powerful incentive in the way of EXAMPLE ; and the accumulation of such instances of moral rectitude, on the part of the children, will just produce that SYMPATHY, and fine moral atmosphere, which every enlightened and pious parent would desire his children should breathe in.

This naturally leads us to the next position; namely, SYMPATHY and EXAMPLE. For although development, in every department, must precede the exercise of training, and this process may be applied to a single child, or two or three in any family, yet training will want much, nay most, of its power, unless we add to it the sympathy of numbers—numbers of the same, or about the same age; example and sympathy thus becoming conjoined. The example of a parent or superior is powerful; but when to example is added the sympathy of companionship, such a union is found greatly more influential. The buoyancy of youth sympathizes not with the staidness of age, however powerfully the example of the latter may operate upon the former. Yet nothing is more important in moral training, than for a parent, or superintendent of a school establishment, to make himself on such terms with his children, or pupils, as that they can without fear make him their confident—unburden their minds, and tell him any little story or mischievous occurrence.

We find, that if parents, teachers, or other elderly persons, wish to gain the confidence of the young, they must themselves, as it were, become children—they must bend to, and engage in, their plays and little amusements; and without such condescension, neither parent nor teacher can acquire a thorough knowledge of the real character and dispositions of those under their charge.

From the foregoing observations we perceive,

that the sympathy of the children of several families, united under an enlightened superintendence,
developes a greater variety of disposition, and affords a better and more favourable opportunity of
training to virtuous habits, than possibly can be
accomplished single and alone. Example and
sympathy, therefore, operate powerfully in producing evil or good,—evil, if children are permitted to take their own way without control,—
good, great good, under suitable management and
superintendence: " Evil communications corrupt
good manners," saith St. Paul; and we believe half-
a-dozen boys or girls never meet on the street at
their usual sports, without *example* and *sympathy*
operating as a contaminating influence on one or
more of their number, nay, perhaps, to all in one
point or other, either as regards mind or manners.
This forms a powerful argument for Infant and
Juvenile Schools for moral training.

Perhaps the most powerful means, in the system
of moral training, is not exactly the sympathy between master and pupil, for a cordial sympathy is
not always attainable, but by the master keeping
up a certain spirit, and establishing certain moral
habits amongst his scholars: thus, when a child is
added to their number, he instantly finds himself
in a new temperature, and free from his old temptations—he catches the moral atmosphere of the
place—and by the influence of sympathy, he gradually, and imperceptibly to himself, imitates their
example. People of every stage in life are influenced more or less by sympathy and example;
and the younger the more easy is the impression.
Hence the superiority and importance of early

moral training; and this cannot be accomplished under any system of education, without a spacious enclosed play-ground.

If, therefore, we desire a system of moral training, we must have an *actual development* of all the faculties and principles of human nature.

Without training, the child is not fitted for the duties of more advanced life. He must acquire habits of obedience and docility—habits of justice, truth, and kindness—habits of attention, perseverance, and self-control. His selfishness, pride, or obstinacy, must be checked and overcome. Habits are of slow growth—obstinate, however, when formed—difficult, nay, often impossible, to shake off, or get rid of, especially if they have been formed in early life. How important, therefore, that mind and body be early subjected to a moral training! Moral ends must be brought about by moral means; and while we hesitate not to recommend every means of training which can improve the intellect and outward habits; yet, unless means are also taken to affect the heart, by virtue of a thorough Bible training—unless its biographic sketches, its plainest precepts, and, in particular, unless the varied announcements of God's love to mankind, contained in that book, be made to bear upon the children, with a blessing from above—we are assured, that the mind exercised on human science alone, must fail in producing a moral people.

A few simple ILLUSTRATIONS will close the present chapter.

In illustration of PHYSICAL TRAINING—Suppose a child sits in an improper manner—his feet, perhaps, on the opposite seat, chair, or form, and his elbows resting on his neighbour's shoulder. The master says, "Don't sit so,"—this is *teaching.* Showing the child, in the first instance, how to sit, is *training.* And if the offence is repeated, the training is continued by simply making the inquiry, in an audible voice, "How ought children to sit when in school, or at table?—look at the other children; see how well they behave." There is, however, this distinction, that the former, being merely an act of the body, is Physical Training, while the latter is Intellectual; the former is the training of man as an animal, the latter of man as an intelligent being. And when the offence is repeated, it becomes disobedience; and then, of course, requires a distinct exercise of moral training, by a reference to the law of God—to their feelings, and to conscience.

If a child comes to school with dirty hands, the master says to the child, "It is wrong to come to school so—you must wash them properly before you come here." This is teaching. To make the inquiry, audibly, in the hearing of all, "How ought children to come to school?—ought their hands to be dirty or ... *clean?*"*—at the same time holding up the dirty hand, and comparing it with the clean hand of another child,—is training. The instruction or teaching may, or may not, be attended to, but the intellectual perception brought out by the question, and the comparison of the clean hand with the dirty one, along with the sympathy of companionship, never fails, in any case, to produce the habit of cleanliness.

* Elliptically.

Suppose a child presses his thumb on the centre of his book, in a particular way, while reading, the master says,—"Don't hold the book so, child; the perspiration will soil it." This is teaching. Showing the child how to hold it, and afterwards asking, "How ought children to hold their books when reading?" or, elliptically, "Children ought to hold their books this...*way*," is training,—the children filling in the word, way. The same process in regard to shutting the eyes during prayer—the reasons why and wherefore are all developed, so that the children have an intellectual perception, as well as a moral feeling, of what is right and wrong, added to the physical habit of shutting the eyes in a devout manner, to keep the attention more fixed, it may be, and from wandering, while addressing their great Creator.

A child may be told to make a bow on entering or leaving a room, and every plan of making it graceful may have been fully laid before him; but, without training, he makes a pitiful exhibition on attempting his first obeisance.

A person destined for a public speaker may have read much, and been taught much—he may know most critically all the rules of elocution; but he will make a poor figure, unless he has applied himself practically to the art—until, in fact, he has been trained to public speaking.

Saying to a child, or children, Put your books, slates, bonnets, or caps, in their proper place, is *teaching*. Seeing them do it, and showing them how to place them properly, is *physical training*. Asking them, How ought children to do so and so? —ought they to leave every thing topsyturvy?—

this would be *intellectual* training. The same plan may be gone through in every process of physical training, which, in a rational being, ought not, and cannot long be kept disjoined from reason and conscience.

We shall now content ourselves with one additional illustration.—A master may teach or show me how to make a pin, or a nail, or a shoe, or how to weave a piece of cloth; but I am not trained, nor is the teaching of any practical use, until I put my hand to the work, and acquire the habit.

INTELLECTUAL TEACHING may be stated as the storing of the memory and understanding with knowledge; but habituating the mind to reflect upon and to digest the subjects presented, is TRAINING.

Suppose a particular word is used in a book, I am told the meaning of the word,—that is *teaching*. If I am not told the meaning, but my intellectual powers are called upon to find it out by analysis, root, construction, &c. and thus determine for myself what must be the meaning of the word,—that is *training*. The same may be said regarding objects: the height of a hill—the size of a nut—the quality of an apple. Telling is *teaching*; not telling, but compelling the mind to exercise itself by comparison, is *training*.

A child may commit to memory the whole rules of English or Latin grammar, and may be able to repeat every example, and answer any query, contained in the book itself, thoroughly and correctly; and thus far he proves the extent of his instruction or teaching. The child is only under *training*, however, when he is put to the work of applying these rules to the formation of a sentence in speaking or writing; and it is evident, that the person well taught in the rules, may be exceedingly ill trained, or not trained at all, to the practice of speaking or writing good grammar. Ere the child, therefore, is a trained grammarian, his mind must be made to bear upon it—he must understand it, and actually apply for himself the rules of speaking and writing correctly. The same may be said in regard to music. Knowledge of any kind, on the memory alone, is like bread on a shelf; it is only useful when used and digested. Examples might be multiplied without end, in every department of education, whether purely physical or intellectual, or a mixture of religious and moral. There is the training of the understanding to the meaning of every word read in a book, or used in conversation; the training of the mind and habit to what books ought to be read; the training also to the comparative size, quality, use, and value, of every object the child sees, and the real meaning and tendency of every sentiment he may express.

MORAL TRAINING.—The most important of all yet remains : the training of the Religious and Moral Affections ; for out of these really are " the issues of life." At the same time, a single example or two is probably all that is requisite in this department ; for the same principle holds true in these, as in physical and intellectual training. The proper object of religious worship is God, as he has revealed himself in the Scriptures of the Old and New Testaments ; and the proper standard of morals, therein inculcated by precept and example, ought to be held up to the understanding, to the love, and to the practical habits of the child.

As religion affects, in the most powerful degree, our moral conduct here, and happiness hereafter, it ought therefore to hold, not simply a prominent, but a pre-eminent place in every national system of education. And in this, as in the physical and intellectual departments, we proceed upon the principle, that man has by nature a religious power or faculty; in other words, that he naturally possesses within himself a disposition to be religious, more or less active or strong; and that this disposition, from ignorance and other causes, needs to be directed and trained; and which may be directed to one or more objects of worship, true or false. Whether true or false, however, man's darkened understanding and perverted will cannot of itself discover. The entire history of mankind proves the truth of this fact. Even a false religion, it is well known, has a strong influence on the minds and morals of its devotees; and according to the purity of the religion embraced, so in exact accordance would we expect that the moral conduct of its recipients will be affected. This we find literally true; for in every country and clime, if cruel and impure rites characterize the religion of the inhabitants, there do we find the people proportionally debased; but wherever the pure and simple religion of the Bible is clearly known and received, there do we find the people the most moral, virtuous, and happy. Consequently, if pure morality is to be promoted and widely established in our land, it must be by training up the **young to** pure religion; in other words, to the plain and simple truths of the Bible.

In regard to the plan of communicating religious knowledge—upon our own principles, we therefore cannot approve of the ordinary mode of instruction or teaching; namely, committing large tasks to memory, and storing the mind, as it is called, with truths, with little or no understanding. We prefer a development, and a training of the mind and affections upon the obvious truths presented in the pages of the word of God.

How delighted, in the act of acquiring religious knowledge, would children in a family be, or in a Sabbath or week-day school, provided only training—a training of the understanding and affections—was substituted for instruction or teaching! Great, however, as would be the pleasure, greater still would be the profit, to the young ones. This, upon trial, in every case, has been fully proved.

I tell a child not to quarrel or fight with his companions at play,—that is *teaching*. I impress the child's understanding and conscience with the impropriety, and even the sin of it, by asking, How ought children to do when provoked? Ought they to ...... ?—(bringing the Scripture precept to bear upon him)—" Be not overcome of evil, but overcome evil with...*good*." And, if I farther superintend him while at play—that is *moral training*.

Suppose I select several passages from the Bible which inform us that God is love, and I require the child to commit them to memory without explanation, this would be the lowest kind of *teaching.* I proceed to explain the literal meaning of the passages, as they occur, or as they are repeated by the child,—this is what may be termed, *intellectual religious teaching.* If, however, I gave proofs of God's love, from his ways of dealing to patriarchs, prophets, kings, apostles, and holy men mentioned in Scripture—presenting such passages as the following to the attention and practical consideration of the young :—" If God so love you, how ought you to love one another ?" "God so loved the world, that he gave his only begotten Son, that whosoever believeth in him should not perish, but have everlasting life." Also, the melting tenderness of Him who took little children in his arms, " and blessed them." And if I still farther draw out the mind, to consider, God's love to themselves in their daily experience, the food they eat, the clothes they wear, the air they breathe, the kind parents who care for them. All this we would term, *religious training.* And when we add the idea, that this good God, as he is both revealed and experienced, is at the same time omniscient, almighty, holy, and cannot look upon sin but with abhorrence, invisible, yet constantly watching over our conduct,—we, in this way, are not only training to religious sentiment, but establishing *moral* habits; and this moral training must of course be practical, as all training must be. Teaching may be accomplished in a school-room, but training can only be so in real life— in an enclosed play-ground—amidst companions freely at play, and under the moral superintendence of the master. A race-horse is not trained in a stable : he is put on the course—not alone, or without superintendence, but with a rider on his back. So is it in regard to children; if we expect them to do well, and act well, we must superintend them well—we must educate and train them well, —not merely physically as the horse, but as intellectual, religious, and moral beings. The master of a *training school*, while he maintains a strict moral superintendence, yet he must so deport himself, as that the children feel at liberty to play and enjoy themselves, except in what is wrong. If the master cannot manage so, then he is not a proper superintendent. It is true, God alone can change the heart; but our duty is to use these and other appointed means: not simply to teach, but " train up a child in the way he should go;" and the promise will assuredly be fulfilled, that " when he is old he will not depart from it."

Respect for private property, even to the value of a pin, or the principle of *mine* and *thine*, the children should not only be *taught* to understand, but *trained* to practise.

We may here state, as a result of this system of training, that, during the present season, above 200 children daily and freely enjoyed themselves in the play-ground of the Model Infant School, Saltmarket, (the St. Giles of Glasgow,) in which black currants have been allowed to ripen, the bushes being within reach of the youngest child. Similar facts might also be stated in regard to fruit remaining untouched in the play-ground of other Infant Schools in town, during this and former seasons.

CHAPTER II.

ARGUMENTS IN REGARD TO THE ESTABLISH-MENT OF SCHOOLS FOR INFANT AND JUVENILE TRAINING.

The practical difficulty of training infants discovered the system of moral training—Children ought to be first exercised, not on signs, but on things—Present system of school education inefficient as a moral training—Dame Schools—Under the Infant School system alone is the whole man trained—Training less efficient above six years of age in Juvenile Schools, than below it, in Infant Schools—Exposed condition of children in large towns—Parents engaged all day in factories, or at other out-door work in towns, cannot train their children—House of Refuge—Sabbath Schools, extent of influence—Parochial Schools only part of the machinery which morally elevated Scotland—Volun-tary contributions insufficient to provide education for the poor—Prussian system of education—French system—Grammar schools—Fact regarding Factory Bill on Education—What this country ought to do for education; and, in the first instance, for large towns.

THE practicability of teaching and training very young children, is now no longer disputed; facts having put to silence all scepticism on this point; while, at the same time, they have proved, that infants are not so incapable of being taught, as masters are of the method of teaching them.

It is to the destitute condition of infants in large towns—to the difficulty of arresting their attention for any length of time, on any subject, and of teaching or instructing them,—that we are indebted for one of the greatest modern discoveries in the science of the schoolmaster. Legislators and philanthropists have puzzled themselves in solving the important question, How can an entire people, or nation, be morally elevated? and the general conclusion they have come to, has been, *at least in theory*, that education is the best, if not the only proper mean, for accomplishing the object.

But the question is, What is usually meant by Education? Why, simply learning to read, and perhaps to write—committing rules and tasks to memory. A few intelligent teachers, no doubt, go a little farther, and teach the children the meaning and construction of words; a very few go farther still, and exercise their understandings upon *things*. And although in most of our schools the Bible is read, and sometimes even explained, yet still, at best, while there is *teaching*, there is unquestionably not yet a *moral training*.

Notwithstanding the great improvement, of late years, which has taken place in school teaching, it has not accomplished, and is not now accomplishing, the important moral, as well as intellectual purposes, for which it was designed. And why? Simply because children have been educated not agreeably to nature, but as if composed purely of memory and understanding. We see children physically fixed to their seats, or confined, at least, for hours together, within the walls of a school-room, and their memories stored, and their understandings, if exercised at all, exercised upon subjects they feel no interest in.

If the understandings of children are to be improved and cultivated, they ought to be exercised principally, in the first instance, not on signs, not on mere letters, but on natural and visible objects. They ought also to be at liberty,—physically free, but morally restrained,—their hearts ought to be appealed to, as well as their heads,—the sympathy arising from numbers, and the power of example, must be made to bear upon them,—their consciences, too, must be cultivated and kept alive,—they must be taught and trained to know their duty to God, to their parents, to themselves, and to society at large; and all this founded on the plain revealed will of God, as contained in the Old and New Testaments, and brought to bear upon them, practically, both within the schoolroom and at play.

In fine, when we look at our schools, we see they are neither, in machinery, nor in plan of operation, fitted to accomplish a moral training. In these observations we include the whole range of our Parochial, as well as Private and Charity Schools; but we must particularize some, which ought not even to have the name of schools—which have no pretence even to the name, *intellectual;* and only deceive the public, as to the amount of education; and we are sorry to say, these form too large a proportion of our private adventurers.

What can be expected from old pensioners, raw lads, and old women, as teachers of youth, whose extent of information, often, is not such as to enable them to explain the meaning or construction of words? Fear of punishment, is the coercing principle on the part of the master; and when not one moral sentiment is imparted, except on the memory, or practical habit formed, need we wonder, that when actually freed from their cage of confinement, these rude untrained children should exhibit such scenes of riot, quarrelling, and wickedness, as are daily witnessed in our streets and alleys.

The high importance of education, and even of early education, is generally acknowledged; but the necessity for establishing Schools for Infants, under six years of age, is not so apparent. It may be proper, therefore, that we state some of those arguments and facts which have appeared conclusive, and which are drawn from a survey of the real state of society in our cities and towns,—especially in reference to Glasgow; and as this system of moral training is equally applicable* to juveniles of the ages of six to twelve or fourteen, as it is to infants of from two to six. Conceiving, also, that its general adoption in towns would greatly diminish crime, and powerfully tend to improve and elevate the moral condition of the whole community—we trust we shall be excused taking a glance, not merely at our infant population, but at the relative and moral condition of parents, their natural guardians, as well as at the amount of the moral machinery now in operation for their improvement; thereby the more fully to show the necessity for some new, additional, or more powerful influence, in regard to the training of youth, than exists at present. From the complexity and

* When we say equally applicable, we do not mean that the system is equally powerful above six, as below it; that is impossible, for every year above the age of two, increases the difficulty, and raises a barrier to the application of moral training. Better, however, late than not at all.

importance of the subject, however, and in order not to divert the attention of our readers from the explanation of the Infant System itself, and the plan of operation, a separate chapter is appropriated;* from which we see the sad condition of our city population.

Before proceeding farther, we must here enter a caution in regard to the formation of Juvenile Schools upon the infant system. They are necessary, of course, for carrying forward the child of six years of age in his moral training; but if the training is only commenced at that age, we have not simply to bend the wayward inclination of young children of two or three years of age, as in Infant Schools, but to break up habits, often wonderfully obstinate, even at the age of six. Besides, the younger the child is, the more capable is he of being impressed by sympathy and example. Again, therefore, must we return to the text, *the primary moral lever*, INFANT TRAINING.

And here we remark, that we have not any schools for children under five or six years of age, but Infant Schools, if we except Dame Schools, common in England, which are a burlesque upon the infant system,—very generally kept by old, ignorant females: they are schools for children whose parents are out at work all day, and cannot attend to them—schools, or confined rooms, for the reception of infants, but not for moral training. In them it is all art and constraint, and to the little ones, therefore, a positive weariness. Moral training, of course, they cannot have without a play-ground—the rod is in frequent use, and still

* See Chap. VIII.

more frequently needed—and fear, *not love,* is the governing principle. And whilst we recommend the establishment of Infant Schools in every town, as an addition to the existing moral machinery, or rather, as the primary moral machine, we also desire to see every existing school for teaching altered into a school for training.

Let us bear in mind, that it was necessity which first discovered the system of infant or moral training. If infants could have been taught otherwise, the schoolmaster would never have condescended to the simplicity and naturalness, found to be absolutely requisite in the teaching, or rather in the training, of infants. In fact, it was the impossibility, under the old system, of teaching infants, or keeping them quiet by art and bodily restraint, (as may possibly be done in the case of older children,) which developed the necessity, and led to the discovery, of this system; and which, although simple and natural, like the steam in the tea-kettle, will be found, and is destined, we trust, to be equally powerful in the moral world, as the steam-engine is now in the commercial.

Except Infant Schools, we have no schools for moral training, such as the Bible commands: "Train up," &c.—and this simply because there are no schools but these, where man, *as a man,* is educated as at once a physical, rational, and moral being. Other schools are content with the cultivation of the head, or rather the memory, alone; which, like a cupboard, is too often stored, or stuffed, with useless lumber, or materials which the child has never been taught to use.

We recollect of meeting, a few years ago, a *blind idiot*, in one of our county towns, who could repeat every and any verse in the Bible; and not only so, but on our repeating, or reading in his hearing, some passages in the Prophets, Psalms, and books of Moses, without our saying where, he almost instantly particularized the book, chapter, and verse.

On the system under review, we first begin with the understanding, and through it enter into what is usually termed the memory: what is therefore lodged there, is not likely to be forgot, so long as the understanding exists.

We farther remark, that if necessity discovered the Infant School system, and if it should be generally applied to juveniles of the ages of six to twelve or fourteen, which we now beg warmly to recommend should be forthwith done, at least in towns—we say, that the Juvenile Training School can only be kept up in life and vigour, and upon the real infant system, by its being placed alongside, or in the immediate vicinity, of a school for Infant Training, with which the comparison may constantly be drawn; for necessity will keep the infant schoolmaster, who has himself been trained to the system, right, if he trains children of the ages of two to five or six. But as teaching is generally fancied to be so much easier than training, and withal there is so much a greater demand for memory or intellectual instruction—reading, for example, than for morals. The former exercise is much more obvious to the senses than the latter: the child who can repeat the 119th Psalm, is a vulgar wonder, compared to the one who is trained to practise the virtues it recommends and exhibits,—and pride, prejudice, and love of ease, are certain to break down the system of *entire* training, in any Juvenile School, where the model of an Infant School is not constantly in the eye, and subject to the comparison, of the master himself, the parents of the children, and the managers of the school.

We much fear that many will say, Why take children so young into school, as two or three years of age? Why have Infant Schools at all, since the system is applicable to juveniles?* Learning to read, they say, is the grand thing. Let us apply the system to children somewhat younger than usual—let us begin, they may say, at four or five years of age. Let these mix with the older children—and let the schools be all termed *Juvenile;* which is a much more magnificent name than *Infant.*—In answer, we ask such to remember, that prevention is better than cure,—that early impressions are powerful impressions, and that they are either for good or evil,—that from the moment a child is two years of age, nay much earlier, he is every day acquiring good or bad habits; learning what is right, or what is wrong,— and farther, that even children of four or five, cannot sympathize with those of nine or ten years of age; either the one or other must suffer. And we know, from experience, it would be the youngest and weakest. It would very soon be said, such are *fully* too young to learn to read— don't send them *quite* so early. Let this be but the case generally, and then we shall have an end

* See Chap. VII.

of the system itself. The love of ease is of course natural, and teaching is much easier than training. And when children are permitted to ask questions, and exercise their minds upon every thing, and any thing, that is presented to their attention, as is the case under the training system, much knowledge, as well as tact, is absolutely necessary on the part of the master. We are glad, however, to find, that of late, amongst teachers, as well as the public at large, to mention the idea of training upon the infant system, instead of producing a smile or a laugh, as formerly, is now felt to be the strongest term of recommendation.

The proportion, in point of numbers, in every parish or town district, ought to be one Infant, to every two Juvenile Schools,—the former, of the ages of two to six; the latter, from six to twelve or fourteen.

We take it for granted, that every individual, in the habit of visiting the poorer districts of cities, and who simply exercises his eyes and ears, must be fully satisfied, that much open vice and profligacy prevails—and that children, from carelessness on the part of some parents, and from want of suitable accommodation at home, in almost all the houses of the working classes, are permitted to amuse themselves, and ramble in the streets, lanes, and filthy closes, unprotected, and without suitable superintendence. Infants, of the very tender age of three and four, and even younger, are not exempt from this demoralizing exposure: they are to be seen at every corner, in groups—learning no good—oftentimes much evil—at all events, they are a prey to every random influence.

What an undisturbed harvest does the wicked one generally get in this the spring-time of human life! How plentifully are the tares sown in this fallow ground, amidst the weedage of this uncultivated garden! How often are mere infants on the street, who know not their right hand from their left, heard lisping oaths, obscenities, and even blasphemies!

Apart from parental instruction, we know not of any antidote or check to this evil, which can be applied to children under six years of age, except Infant Schools—a period the most interesting and important, because the most impressible portion of the life of man. Who can tell the permanency of those impressions which are made at this, as it were, our entrance into life! And the question is, Do we now endeavour early to bend the wayward twig?—Do we actually direct its onward course? Young children are capable of learning much evil—why ought they not to be trained to what is good? And if vicious habits can be formed at a very early period, why not, on the contrary, those which are proper and right? And we may remark, that every parent is bound morally to train up his child, either personally or by proxy.

This unshielded and unguarded situation is too much the case in regard to infants, even of parents of good and respectable character, who being necessarily almost all day out at work, are really prevented, and have not the opportunity of morally training their children. Teach them, no doubt, occasionally, they may; but train them, certainly they cannot. And even were both parents quali-

C

fied and willing to teach and train their children, small, inconvenient dwellings, and densely-peopled city lanes, are not only unfavourable, but render the task of bringing " up a child in the way he should go," almost impossible. Out into the street to play, the children must and will go; and the most attentive mothers, who have their ordinary work and household duties to perform, are positively glad to get rid of their children for a little while. These infants, indeed, are occasionally put under the care of some one, but it is more generally under that of a child very little older than themselves.

Hitherto we have spoken only of those parents who are willing, but have not the opportunity or convenience for training their offspring; but what shall we say of the sad and deplorable condition of those infants whose profligate parents are neither able nor desirous of setting before their children a good example—of whom it may be said, they drink in evil with their mother's milk; who listen to no songs of Sion, although they do so to those which ought not to be named, and with which they are too familiar; and as their opening minds expand, expand chiefly amidst scenes of drunkenness and profligacy, or at best of utter carelessness! This is no overcharged picture of the state of Glasgow, and other large towns, whose population has quite outgrown the means of improvement provided for them, as hundreds can testify.

There are at this moment in Glasgow, we have reason to know, full 5000 to 6000 infants, from two to six years of age, the offspring of the third or lowest class in the moral scale, who are growing up, and from day to day breathing, out-doors and in-doors, such a pestilential atmosphere,—from whose ranks, at a future period, our bridewells, jails, and convict-ships, will be replenished, and whose fermenting and growing immorality, even a House of Refuge cannot reach. What philanthropist would not desire to see the establishment of a House of Refuge, as a check to the growth of crime! But it can, even in its most extended sense, be nothing more than a check, and a limited one. Something earlier, something more of a preventive, something more thorough and extensive, must be applied, ere we can hope to have a moral people. We must not deceive ourselves with false expectations; for although, unquestionably, a House of Refuge will do much good, and will be the means of throwing a handful of salt into the stream, still the polluted source remains untouched. Independently of these 5000 or 6000 infants, the offspring of the third, or lowest, in the moral scale,—there are double this number, or 10,000 to 12,000 infants under six years of age—independently of juveniles from six to fourteen—children of the more decent and church-going; but who, except in-doors, are equally exposed on the streets and lanes to the contaminating influence of evil example, and also standing in need of suitable superintendence. The truth is, nothing short of a system of week-day schools for Bible training—infant and juvenile—each with an enclosed play-ground, and a moral superintendence, can possibly accomplish the all-important object. And such seminaries must be co-extensive with the population, and brought within reach of their earnings, by means of a Government endowment, upon the principle of our Scottish parochial school system.

Mere intellectual education or training, we beg to say, will not accomplish the object; neither can the simple elements of reading. A thorough knowledge of the Bible, and practical moral training, alone can do it.

Sabbath Schools will very naturally occur to the mind of most of our readers, as an excellent antidote. And so far, certainly, they are. They afford what may be termed a religious instruction, but not a moral training; and although they are, in a certain sense, substitutionary to week-day schools, they ought never to be so in regard to parental instruction. But we fear they afford the only religious education which thousands of children at present receive.

Sabbath Schools, however, even though more generally embraced than they are, come in decidedly too late as a preventive. Habits are formed very early, and the conscience, too, is often deadened and distorted, ere children reach the age suitable to attend. Besides, excellent as Sabbath Schools are, we have to put in comparison, as an antidote, the instructions of one day, with the contaminating influence of a whole week—the religious and moral training of two hours on a Sabbath, with the same process, in scriptural Infant Schools, for five or six hours each day, during the other six. It is important not to be deceived on this point; for although several thousand children and young persons, in Glasgow and suburbs, are in attendance on Sabbath Schools, yet it is a fact, which from actual survey we know to be true, that full two-thirds of that careless and neglected class, for whom Sabbath School instruction was primarily intended, have not been brought out. And why? Simply because in infancy they have not been *trained.* It was the experience of this fact, and the almost impossibility of bringing out such children, or at least of retaining them any given time under instruction, even with the powerful influence of the *local** system, that was the impelling cause, why some earlier system of training was sought for, and which, when found in the infant system, was of course very naturally embraced.

We may here notice, that Sabbath Schools differ very widely in their tendency and results. In England, the object is twofold. First, To give the children a religious instruction. Secondly, Teaching them to read.

In most of the Sabbath Schools in the South, however, the former, or chief object, is too much swallowed up in the latter. Teaching to read on Sabbaths, instead of week-days, has this sad effect, that the smattering of reading which is often given in these schools deceives the public mind, not only as to the amount of education, but in regard to the amount of real influence Sabbath Schools have, in a religious and moral point of view; and causes some even of our talented statesmen to imagine, that we are pretty much an educated

* See Appendix, No. IV.

people; whereas, the truth is, the mass are actually in ignorance.

If England had a complete national system of education, no child ought to be taught their letters in a Sabbath School. Who could imagine that in Manchester, for example, the state of education is such, that, except in Sunday Schools, only 3000 children of the working classes last year were at week-day schools, out of a population of above 200,000!

In Sabbath Schools in Scotland, teaching to read is not practised, except in very rare cases, and we trust never will be the practice. Teaching to write is of course uncalled for. The exercises are wholly religious, and the teachers in both countries are, it is well known, gratuitous.

The drudgery of teaching to read, when practised, causes a frequent change of teachers, so that from this shifting and changing alone, much less good is actually done in Sunday Schools than we are apt to imagine.

We thus see, that our Parochial and Private Schools teach, but do not morally train; leaving the children for a great portion of the day, in towns, completely at random, and without superintendence either at home or at play. Our Sabbath Schools, except when mere reading schools, teach or instruct in religious doctrine during one day, and leave them (necessarily we know) to practise what they choose during the other six. There is thus, in consequence, what may be termed a feast and a fast. Neither our Week-day nor Sabbath Schools, therefore, are schools for moral training.

What, then, is the course we ought to pursue,

seeing our schools are not constituted so as to meet the condition of a town life?

Are we to be content with the few training schools we have—six Infant Schools, for example, for Glasgow—when the infants of the most careless and neglected portion of the population require above *fifty;* and this independently of nearly double the number for the children of the more respectable among the working classes, who, when out of doors, are exposed to the same contaminating influence with their degraded neighbours?

These institutions do attain the object in view, or they do not. Sufficient proof,* we believe, already exists, to show that, according to their limited number, they have done, and are doing, much good; and if this system is not calculated to raise a city population, we know not of any other means which can. It remains with those therefore who object, and think otherwise, to prove the reverse.

But say some, and they say truly, Our Parochial Schools worked well in olden times. We answer, Our Parochial Schools were only part, not all, the machinery which morally elevated Scotland— they formed only one spoke of the wheel. The master of the Parish School *taught,* and the parents *trained* at home. The parent engaged in agriculture *then could,* but the parent in the factory *cannot now,* morally train his children. The truth is, *the schoolmaster taught, the parent trained, and the minister influenced all by his pulpit ministrations, his household examinations, his juvenile catechising, and his frequent visits to the parish*

* See Appendix, No. I.

school—not one, but *all* of these, formed the moral machine; the Bible itself being the spring of the whole.

This same machinery may be applied in towns as they are at present constituted. We may have the minister, and the elder, and the schoolmaster, but, at the same time, in the altered circumstances of society in towns, we cannot, and we actually have not, *the training.*

These parochial teaching schools must, therefore, be turned into training schools—schools for moral training. The schoolmaster must not supersede, but he must make up for the want of training at home—in fact, he must, during a considerable portion of the day, take the place of the parent, who is not with, and therefore cannot, although willing, train his children.

Our plain and simple statement is this, If our towns are ever to be placed in like moral circumstances with the rural districts of Scotland, we must establish Infant Schools for children of from two to six years of age, and Juvenile Schools for those of six to twelve or fourteen; each, of course, with an enclosed play-ground for moral superintendence: and our Parochial and other Schools must adopt the system of juvenile training, as Infant Schools have done that of infant training—both being formed on one and the same system—at the same time, advancing the children in knowledge as we proceed.

The friends of Infant Schools court inquiry; they solicit every one sceptical on the subject, to call on the families in the immediate neighbourhood of any one of our six Infant Schools, and inquire of the parents what idea they have formed of the effects of the system upon their own children; and we promise that no one, who has an understanding to conceive, and a heart to feel, will return from such a survey otherwise than fully convinced, that schools upon Bible principles, for infant and juvenile training, in conjunction with other means for those more advanced in life, are just the very thing for morally elevating an entire population. We say nothing here of other ranks of society, one and all of whose children might be much improved by their attendance a few hours a-day under this system.

For want of due investigation, therefore, or proper attention to the subject, shall these several thousand children be allowed to grow up, from infancy to youth, and from youth to manhood, without a helping hand being put forth? The last eight years' experience in this department proves the melancholy fact, that private contribution is altogether insufficient to accomplish the object; for every one of the Infant Schools now in operation have been getting into debt, and some of them, for want of funds, are even at this moment well nigh being given up; nay, had not two of the Schools lately been taken under Parochial care, the general public would have allowed both to have gone down. The public tire of the annual subscriptions, and also soirées, and musical entertainments, which have been resorted to for their support. Institutions for the religious and moral improvement of the people, ought not to be dependent on such uncertain means.

Our duty, we conceive, is to petition the Legis-

lature on the subject; and if the request is general
on the part of the people, it will no doubt be re-
sponded to. Let us prove the extent of the evil
in towns, and that the happiness and even the
stability of the empire depend upon their deci-
sion. Let us show, that Bible knowledge and
moral training alone is the remedy, and that too
applied early in life, ere children can have acquired obstinate and vicious habits—keeping the
maxim constantly in view, that *prevention is better
than cure.*

It must not however be denied, that Infant
Schools will succeed only partially in bringing out
the neglected children of a crowded city, unless
we have, what would be felt a very unpopular
measure, a compulsory legislative enactment; or,
until the whole surface of the population is covered
with an efficient parochial agency. For want of
this thorough parochial agency, even the present
limited number of schools are not filled—few, very
few, of the neglected, careless class, for whom we
plead, are brought out—the greater proportion of
those in attendance are children of the better or
middling classes, who value the system, and desire
the good of their offspring. Such as these uniformly come out first; the others will not attend
school, unless " compelled " (we mean morally
compelled) " to come in."

Our first established schools get out the best
children, and the worst or most neglected come
out last. For instance, if six schools will do the
work of a parish of about 14,000 inhabitants, the
first two schools which may be established will
generally bring out the middling class—the second

two schools, the lower—and the last two schools, the lowest grade of the population. We therefore perceive, that a vast many schools for infant and juvenile training may be formed, even to two-thirds of the requisite number, and yet public crime remain undiminished.

Just imagine one hundred infants in a school play-ground, clean, cheerful, and happy—learning no evil, but much good—and suppose these same children on the streets and lanes, there listening to much evil, and acquiring many bad habits, from day to day,—and it will be impossible not at once to perceive the national importance of collecting the children of the poor into such seminaries, especially in towns.

What have other Countries done for Education?

This is a very important question. We shall, however, notice only one or two of those countries which have signalized themselves, by establishing a national system of education. And it is not our intention to enter into a minute detail of those branches of education which are taught, it being more particularly with the moral results which have accrued, or which are likely to accrue, from any of them, that we have to do. We beg however to remark, that we are far from disapproving of an Intellectual system of national education; indeed, upon our own principles, we could not approve of any which was not actually so, in every department. Let Science, Religion, and Morals, go hand in hand, and we fear not to look upon the truth, that " Knowledge is power."

One of the chief objects in the present publication, is to show the fact, that true morality must
be founded on the plain and obvious truths of the
Bible—that a Bible education, on the training
system, must be Intellectual—and that it was this
Bible knowledge which, in a very few years, raised
Scotland from being a bigoted, ignorant, and rude
country, to one which, for a century and a half,
has attracted the attention of foreigners, both for
its intellectual and moral character.

Prussia.—The Prussian system of education
has been deservedly praised for its intellectual
character—for the varied information which it
imparts—for the thorough provision it makes for
the education of every child within the Prussian
dominions—and for the mode of securing it in life
and vigour, by the admirable system of Model or
Normal Schools for training teachers—but, above
all, for the public acknowledgment, by the state
provision itself, that all national education must
be founded on religion and morals.

Although the system was in operation for several
years before, yet the Prussian law for National
Education, or Primary Instruction, is dated 1819,
about the same period that in England the important system of *direct* moral training was first applied in Infant Schools.

There are generally at least two schools in every
parish—one for the children of the Roman Catholics, and one for those of the Protestants. Each
small religious sect in a parish, if large enough, is
bound by law to establish a school, and may
choose a master of their own particular persua-

sion; but if not able to do so, they must either prove that they are educating their children properly at home, or send them to the public school of some other sect. The Jew can have no share in the management.

The Prussian schoolmaster, or priest, who is of the particular persuasion with the parents of the children, may teach religion to such in school, but not to any belonging to a different persuasion. " The instruction shall always be adapted to the spirit and the dogmas of the church to which the school belongs." The turning of all these into schools for training, and adding the infant system of moral training in towns, would be a great improvement on the Prussian system.

Children ought to go to school at five years of age; but the law compels the attendance of every child from the age of seven to fourteen inclusive.

All are taxed for the support of the schools, according to their property and circumstances, by the public functionary, namely, the minister of instruction, whether they are Jew, Roman Catholic, or Protestant.

The population of the Prussian monarchy, by last census, was 12,726,823. Of these, 2,043,030 are between seven and fourteen, the school age in Prussia. The actual attendance at school in 1831, was 2,021,421; leaving only 21,609 short of one-sixth of the whole population, for, we may suppose, schools for the rich.

According to the Prussian system, every complete elementary school for the working classes necessarily comprehends the following objects:—

" 1. Religious instruction, as a means of forming the moral character of children, according to the positive truths of Christianity.

" 2. The German language; and in provinces where a foreign language is spoken, the language of the country, in addition to the German.

" 3. The elements of Geometry, together with the general principles of Drawing.

" 4. Calculation and practical Arithmetic.

" 5. The elements of Physics, Geography, General History, and especially the history of Prussia. ' Care must be taken to introduce and combine these branches of knowledge with the reading and writing lessons as much as possible, independently of the instruction which shall be given on those subjects specially.'

" 6. Singing—with a view to improve the voices of the children; to elevate their hearts and minds; to perfect and ennoble the popular songs and church music or psalmody.

" 7. Writing and Gymnastic exercises, which fortify all the senses, and especially that of sight.

" 8. The simplest manual labours, and some instructions in Husbandry, according to the agriculture of the respective parts of the country."

No particular books are fixed upon, or mode of teaching; so that full power may be left to adopt any improvement in either.

The masters have frequent conferences for the improvement of their schools.

The law requires, that each school have a master and mistress; " that, except in Schools of Industry, the management of every school shall be under a male teacher, the female to act as assistant, and specially to take care of the little girls, and conduct the singing, which is much more touching than when conducted by a man."

The Prussian system, upon the whole, while it is decidedly intellectual, and drawn up with much fine feeling, yet it is much too complicated, and in its machinery not adapted to the religious taste or moral habits of this country. It is best suited for rural or country districts, and could not attain the primary object we have in view; namely, the moral elevation of large manufacturing towns.

Prussian Schools for the middle or richer Classes.—Although the Burgher Schools, or those intended for the children of the upper classes, do not so immediately come within the range of our object, still we may enumerate the various branches :—

" 1. Religion and morals.

" 2. The German language—reading—composition—exercises in style—study of the national classics.

" 3. Latin is taught to all the children within certain limits, as a means of exercising their faculties and their judgment, whether they be or be not to enter the higher schools.

" 4. The elements of Mathematics, and especially, a thorough course of practical Arithmetic.

" 5. Physical Science, as far as is sufficient to explain the most remarkable phenomena of nature.

" 6. Geography and History combined, in order to give some knowledge of the earth, of the general history of the world, of the people who inhabit it, and the empires into which it is divided,—Prussia, its history, laws, and constitution, shall form the subject of a special study.

" 7. The principles of Drawing shall be taught to all concurrently, with the lessons in Physics, Natural History, and Geometry.

" 8. Writing must be carefully attended to, and the hand trained to write distinctly and neatly.

" 9. The Singing lessons shall be attended by all the pupils—not only with a view to form them to that art, but to qualify them to assist in the services of the church, with propriety and solemnity, by singing the psalms or choral music with correctness and judgment.

" 10. Gymnastic exercises, adapted to the age and strength of the scholars."

Whatever sort of education the richer classes in Great Britain may choose for their own children, we think it would be found an improvement, of no ordinary value, if, in addition to such sciences and arts as are taught in the Burgher Prussian Schools, each master had his school-house and dwelling-house placed in the centre of a tolerably-sized garden, and as near as possible to our great cities, where the children might add the pleasing and enlivening science of Botany and Zoology, not forgetting a daily course of Bible training,—giving full ten minutes, each hour, to play. And, at the same time, to be under the moral superintendence of a well-trained master, for at least five or six hours a-day, during the hours their fathers are engaged in business, and their mothers attending to household and other duties. Thus training the children to what is at once cheering, instructive, and highly elevating, and keeping them also from acquiring many bad habits.

The truth is, instead of the schoolmaster, or rather the present system of education, operating as an assistance to parents in the moral training of their children, it, on the contrary, generally proves a powerful counteraction; thus diminishing the great advantages which otherwise might be derived from a public education.

Let any one but remember the practices in Grammar and other large public Schools, where there is no moral superintendence at play, and where children move from school to the street, and from the street to the school, and say whether some decided alteration ought not to take place in the rearing of boys of the richer classes. Some parents, who are unacquainted with the facts, or may not have reflected upon the importance of a moral superintendence, such as we here recommend, would no doubt be shocked, were we to mention such things as go on without the walls of these seminaries, where they are taught, but not trained: for example, the petty thefts and schemes resorted to by many of the boys, in order to procure money to spend in mischief.

If the present talented and highly accomplished masters of our Glasgow Grammar School had each a separate enclosed play-ground, and made himself the companion and superintendent of his own class while at play, such would unquestionably be a great improvement on the present system; the want of which is now felt to be a positive grievance. In the Grammar School,

Latin is taught, which fits for the college ; but there are no classes for fitting a young man to be a merchant—unquestionably a desideratum in such a place as Glasgow.

To return to our subject. It is an important question, What has this system done, or what is it likely to do, for Prussia, in a religious and moral point of view? We know what the old Scottish Parochial system, *in its complete form*, accomplished (even without the late improvements in the mode of teaching) in about twenty years after its establishment in Scotland. The Prussian system has existed for an equal period, and *we wish much to know what are the moral results.*

France.—The French Government, in June 1833, passed an Act of Assembly, ordaining a school for every commune, or parish : certainly, one of the most magnificent acts of any legislature in the history of the world—outstripping in splendour even the British grant of twenty millions, for the emancipation of 800,000 slaves in the colonies. The French Act is intended to emancipate from intellectual slavery, a population at home of nearly thirty-two millions.

The French Act in regard to Education, is nearly verbatim that of Prussia, with this exception,—that whereas in Prussia it is imperative on parents to send their children from the age of seven to fourteen—in France, the duty is simply recommended. Mankind will not provide instruction of their own accord ; facts sufficiently prove this position ; and even when provided for them, they will not all, or nearly all, embrace the opportunity thus afforded, unless it is also pressed upon them by law, as now in Prussia, or by the moral suasion of parochial agency, as in the country parishes and small towns in Scotland. Under these circumstances, we much fear, therefore, that France may fail in accomplishing her benevolent intention, of having every child properly educated. Although the attendance of the children is not imperative, yet as the law provides the funds, as in Prussia, no doubt France will approximate nearer to the point of educating her whole people, than if, as in this country, the establishment and keeping up were principally left to voluntary contribution.

We may state a fact, of home occurrence, in order to show the necessity for some sort of compulsion, ere parents will send their children to school. It is in reference to the working of the late Factory Bill, as regards education.

On the first of January last, (new-year's-day,) in a factory in this neighbourhood, where a few children under twelve years of age are employed, it had been announced some days previous, that an examination, in regard to this point, would take place on that particular day; and that those who could not read, must either go to school two hours each day, or they must, by and by, leave the work. Accordingly, they attended, and the children were called in one by one. The question was put, What is your name?—age? &c., and can you read? At first, there seemed a disposition to say, Yes, when they could not read words of more than one syllable. But having been provided with a New Testament, each was asked to read three verses of a chapter; this at once destroyed the possibility of deception, and out of forty, fine, well-dressed children, it was found, that nineteen could not read at all—that five read very imperfectly, three imperfectly, and thirteen only were good readers. We were surprised to find, that fourteen, out of the nineteen who could not read, were at school; and on asking them alternately, when they had entered school, one child said, Yesterday evening, Sir—another, last week—another, the week before—another, three days ago—and so on. And how comes it, we inquired, That you are all at school? The children uniformly replied, that their mothers had sent them, because they were afraid of their being 'put out of the work.'

France leaves the religious instruction of the school to the priest or clergyman of the particular sect to which the parents belong. Such an arrangement in this country would amount to an exclusion of religious instruction altogether from our Parochial Schools, and destroy the only sure means of giving moral training. Simply reading the Bible is of little use, unless children are also made to understand it. In every elementary school, Bible training, on the simple method here recommended, we conceive, ought to form a part of the schoolmaster's daily duty.

We have met in one Sabbath evening school, with twenty-eight Protestant children, from the age of nine to fourteen, who had been brought out from contiguous families, all of which could read the Bible, and nearly all were possessed of Bibles, and yet, on their first admission, twenty-three of this number knew not the name of our first progenitor, nay, were ignorant of almost every sentence contained in the Bible.

We have already endeavoured to show the necessity for a change and improvement in our educational system, so as to meet the condition of the population of a town life. The following will show the great deficiency there is of even elementary education, such as it is. Our readers will bear in mind, that a sixth of the whole population (independent of infants from two to six) ought to be at school :—

There are of children in attendance at school, out of the population of

Old Aberdeen, ... only one child out of every	25.
Paisley, Abbey Parish, ... ~~~~ ~~~~	18.
Dundee, ... ~~~~ ~~~~	14.
In large Districts in Glasgow, ... ~~~~ ~~~~	15 or 16.
Smaller Districts in Do. ... ~~~~ ~~~~	24.

In 132 Parishes, in the counties of Aberdeen, Elgin, and Banff, in 1832, there was only one in every 11.

By a survey lately made over the whole town of Paisley, it appeared that, independent of a vast number of adults, nearly 3000 children above six or seven years of age were unable to read; and that much of the education received, was merely a smattering at evening schools, after being fatigued by the day's work. Except in cases of very urgent necessity, children ought not to be taught at evening schools. One thing is certain—although they may be taught, they cannot possibly be morally trained. What can be expected from a child, in the way of education, after the fatigue of a day's work? What can be expected, but lassitude, weariness, and disgust? Such time ought rather to be devoted to refreshing bodily exercise, or reading—something or other that will improve body or mind, and not burden either, so as to make learning a drudgery.

Since putting to press, we have received Report, of date May, 1834, of the French Minister of Public Instruction, upon the execution of the Educational law of 28th June, 1833. Each commune, or parish, according to the law of 1833, was to have one primary, elementary school, to teach Reading, Writing, Grammar, Arithmetic, weights, measures, and Religion. Each commune of 6000 souls was to have a primary, superior, or Burgher school, for the middling classes, to teach, besides these, Geometry, Surveying, a little Natural Philosophy, Natural History, Civil History, Geography, Music, &c. There are in France 37,187 communes; of these, 20,000 have already established, entirely or partially, elementary schools, in obedience to this ordonnance. Only six communes have voluntarily established superior schools —45 are established—54 are in preparation—and 184 are delaying. Guizot considers that schools of adventure cannot answer in country districts; but he thinks in towns they may, " where the number of pupils is great, and the circumstances of parents easy;" that is, for the schools of the rich alone.

The Normal or Model Schools in 1830 were 13. There are now 62, and 15 are projected.

The Normal Schools are at present attended by about 2000 pupils.

The Communes laid out on school-houses, in 1833, £120,000; and the Municipal Councils, £93,000. There will be required of outlay, £2,880,000. Guizot is of the opinion, which Dr. Chalmers has so often enforced, that separate buildings for school-houses are of great importance, for fixing the attention of the neighbourhood. For the endowment of the masters, ten and a half millions of francs, or £420,000, annually, will be required. An examination of all schools in France took place in 1833. The number of boys attending primary schools was, 1832, 1,200,000; 1833, 1,654,000. Of these 1,654,000, 1,277,000 pay fees; 377,000 do not. The rich departments, as might have been expected, have most at school; the poorest least, and therefore require most aid. As soon as the law of the 28th June, 1833, was passed, M. Guizot sent a circular letter to the schoolmasters, pointing out to them the nature of their duties. He requested them individually to acknowledge the receipt of this letter, and only 13,850, out of 39,000 schoolmasters, sent any reply: the greater number of those who gave no answer being, probably for want of proper training, almost wholly illiterate.

The first great improvement called for in Scotland, as in England, is Model Schools, on which depends the success of all other schools which are or may be established. Already 73 of the departments of France have joined in the support of 62 Model Schools, attended by nearly 2000 future teachers; of whom, 1308 are supported at

their education by the departments—345 are
bursars on the state—118 bursars on the communes—and 293 are supported at their own
charges. And from these schools will emanate
the future schoolmasters of France. May we
soon rival our great ally France, not only in the
extent, but in the quality, of our national education!

England, last year, voted for national education,
£20,000.

France, for her first instalment, voted £600,000.

What ought this Country to do for the Education of her Children?

What ought to be done for England, and for
Ireland, and for Scotland? We shall commence
with the latter, with its population of 2,365,807,
for the amount requisite for the two former, with
inhabitants nine times in number, will no doubt
to many appear frightful. But why should we
startle at a sum, when the nation could and did
freely vote twenty millions for the noble object
of slave emancipation? Why not vote half the
amount for the extinction of slavery at home—
the slavery of mind and morals? Such would be
a nobler achievement far than Waterloo itself,
which cost the country forty millions sterling.

What is national wealth, without national intelligence, piety, and virtue! The former may
rapidly increase, yea, even tenfold; but destitute
of the latter, it will only accelerate our ruin.

We live in a new and eventful state of things.

Towns are the great sources of wealth, the centres of political power, and the seats of vice and profligacy. The question is, How can this wealth and political power be properly directed? how can crime and ignorance be diminished? If this is to be accomplished at all, whatever other means may be necessary, we are fully satisfied, that the *primary* antidotes to these evils, are Schools for Infant and Juvenile training, and in such numbers as to embrace the whole community.

By Dr. Cleland's Tables for 1831, it appears, that the number of infants between the ages of two and six years, is about one in eight of the whole population. Provided Infant Schools were established in every village and town of from one to two thousand inhabitants and upwards, Scotland would require 603 in all. As the formation of these in the smaller towns, however, is not our immediate object, and can be formed at one-half the expense, we present the following, in order to show the cost of establishing Infant Schools in twelve of the largest towns in Scotland, comprising full one-fourth of the whole population, calculating that, were proper schools built, with enclosed play-grounds attached, a master and mistress could train 150 children; but as, from several causes, the whole infant population could not be got to attend at any one time, or might be provided for privately, we have made a deduction of one-half; say one-sixteenth, instead of one-eighth :—

Schools for INFANT Training.

	Population.	Requires for one-half of the Children between the ages of 2 and 6,
Glasgow, .	202,426,	84 Schools, 150 Scholars each.
Edinburgh, .	162,156,	67 〜〜 〜〜
Aberdeen, .	58,019,	24 〜〜 〜〜
Paisley, . .	57,466,	24 〜〜 〜〜
Dundee, . .	45,355,	19 〜〜 〜〜
Greenock, .	27,571,	11 〜〜 〜〜
Perth, . .	20,116,	8 〜〜 〜〜
Kilmarnock, .	18,093,	7 〜〜 〜〜
Dunfermline,	17,068,	7 〜〜 〜〜
Inverness, .	14,324,	6 〜〜 〜〜
Montrose, .	12,055,	5 〜〜 〜〜
Dumfries, .	11,606,	5 〜〜 〜〜

TOTAL, . . . 267 Schools.

Supposed Cost of PLAY-GROUNDS *and* SCHOOL-SITES.

	Schools.				
Glasgow, .	10,	at £100 each,	£1000	
〜〜 . .	25,	at 200 〜〜	5000	
〜〜 . .	20,	at 400 〜〜	8000	
〜〜 . .	14,	at 600 〜〜	8400	
〜〜 . .	15,	at 1000 〜〜	15,000	37,400
Edinburgh, .	10,	at 100 each,	1000	
〜〜 .	20,	at 200 〜〜	4000	
〜〜 . .	15,	at 400 〜〜	6000	
〜〜 .	11,	at 600 〜〜	6600	
〜〜 . .	11,	at 1000 〜〜	11,000	28,600
Aberdeen, .	8,	at 80 each,	640	
〜〜 . .	10,	at 200 〜〜	2000	
〜〜 . .	6,	at 300 〜〜	1800	4440

Carry forward, ... £70,440

Brought forward,		. . .	. .			£70,440
Paisley,	.	. 15,	at	£80 each,	£1200	
	.	6,	at	200 ―	1200	
	. .	3,	at	300 ―	900	3300
Dundee,	. .	6,	at	80 each,	480	
	.	6,	at	200 ―	1200	
	. .	7,	at	300 ―	2100	3780
Greenock,	.	3,	at	80 each,	240	
	. .	4,	at	200 ―	800	
	.	4,	at	300 ―	1200	2240
Perth,	. .	4,	at	80 each,	320	
	. .	4,	at	200 ―	800	1210
Kilmarnock,	.	4,	at	80 each,	320	
	. .	3,	at	200 ―	600	920
Dunfermline,		4,	at	80 each,	320	
	.	. 3,	at	200 ―	600	920
Inverness,	.	3,	at	80 each,	240	
	. .	3,	at	200 ―	600	840
Montrose,	.	. 3,	at	80 each,	240	
	.	2,	at	200 ―	400	640
Dumfries,	.	. 3,	at	80 each,	240	
	.	2,	at	200 ―	400	640
TOTAL,	.	267 Schools.	. .		Cost,	£84,840

Paisley, from its being wide-spread, and almost
every house having a garden, affords peculiar
facilities for the training system; and from the
now very early employment of both boys and girls
at the work of " drawing," in weaving shops, it is
also peculiarly necessary. With the exception of

Dundee, perhaps, no manufacturing town in Scotland has so decidedly sunk from its former high moral elevation as Paisley.

Ground, in Edinburgh and Glasgow, is extravagantly high; and in some parts of these and other densely-built cities, where the moral superintendence of the play-ground is most needed, and sites most difficult to be had, some back-houses would require to be purchased, and pulled down, for this purpose. Although, therefore, we must expect such play-grounds to be extremely costly, yet they will be cheaper in the end than jails and bridewells; besides, the alteration, in whatever quarter, will have a salutary influence upon the health and morals of the neighbourhood. We also observe, that although it may be possible, in one or more of the towns, to procure single sites for school-houses, and play-grounds large enough, and airy enough, even for less than the lowest sum specified—yet we believe there is not one of the towns enumerated, where the ground, upon the whole, will not cost considerably more, on the average, provided the schools are properly placed—we mean, where they are mostly wanted, in the centre of the population.

Supposed Endowments of £50 a-year, to the Master, say 267 Schools, ... £13,350

The remainder of his income, as well as that of the Female Assistant's, to be made up by school fees, or private subscriptions. For the sake of the proper spirit it imparts, we prefer that every child pay the master a small wage, although it might be even as low as 1s. or even, in some cases, 6d. per quarter.

Salaries for five Model Teachers, at £150 a-year, £750.

Towns.—Edinburgh, Glasgow, Aberdeen, Perth, Dumfries.

Cost of 267 School-houses, with conveniences, small class-room, and enclosing wall, say £350 each, ... £93,450

Some persons may imagine, that the Model Teacher of an Infant School ought to have a less salary than that of a Juvenile. But the talent for training infants, intellectually and morally, in a proper manner, is more rare, and requires a greater combination, than for a Juvenile School, where more of the time and attention is taken up in infusing the elements of reading, &c. The materials composing an Infant School being more tender and delicate, of course more varied information, shrewdness, and finer tact are required. The information communicated to infants, no doubt, may be less profound; but it must be, at least, equally minute and pointed. Besides, in addition to the system of training itself, much of the knowledge which infant schoolmasters, in a general way, must acquire, in order to fit them for their duties, may be expected to be learned from the Model Teacher; and, also, the life and continued vigour of the training system rest more particularly with them than with the Juvenile.

Schools for JUVENILE *Training.*

Although 1200 of a population, will yield one school of 150 infants, from about two to six years of age, yet as we have, for reasons already assigned, proposed schools for only one-half, (say a sixteenth of the population, instead of an eighth,) we therefore make the calculation from 2400. Taking the Prussian standard, of a sixth at school, independent of infants, every 900 inhabitants of a town would yield a Juvenile School of 150 children,—the same 2400 inhabitants, therefore, which yielded one infant school, of 150 children, after deducting one-half of the number, will yield twice the number between the ages of six and fourteen, by deducting one-fourth for the richer classes, or private schools, say two schools of 150 each. Although nearly 1300 training schools would be required for Juveniles, if all the towns from one to two thousand inhabitants and upwards were provided with them, yet, for reasons already mentioned, we shall confine our statement to the number required for twelve of our largest towns.

As the training school and play-ground of the Juvenile, ought to be at least as large as those for the Infant, and the proportion in towns being one Infant to two Juvenile Schools, the following will be the result:—

Ten Model Juvenile Schools in the principal Towns of Scotland, with a Salary of £150 a-year to the Master,.....................................£1500

Towns.—Edinburgh, Glasgow, Aberdeen, Dundee, Perth, Dumfries, St. Andrews, Inverness, Kirkwall, Ayr.

Proper masters, under any system, but more especially in the one under consideration, are the very life and essence of the school. No school ought to be left to the chance of having as a superintendent one who has not been properly trained. Hence the absolute necessity for Model Schools for training teachers.

According to the above arrangement, each Parish of 2400 inhabitants, will require the establishment of one Infant and two Juvenile Schools, of 150 scholars each; leaving one-half of the former, and one-fourth of the latter, for private and other schools.

PLAY-GROUNDS *and* SCHOOL-SITES *for Juvenile Training.*

(Supposing, according to our calculation, that they ought to be as two to one, and each, on the average, the same cost.)

	Schools.		
Glasgow,	168,	of 150 Scholars each,	£74,800
Edinburgh,	134,		57,200
Aberdeen,	48,		8880
Paisley,	48,		6600
Dundee,	38,		7560
Greenock,	22,		4480
Perth,	16,		2240
Kilmarnock,	14,		1840
Dunfermline,	14,		1840
Inverness,	12,		1680
Montrose,	10,		1280
Dumfries,	10,		1280
TOTAL,	534 Schools,	Cost,	£169,680

Supposed cost of 534 Juvenile School-houses, with conveniences, small class-room, and enclosing wall, £350 each, ... £186,900

£350, we believe, will be found fully too low a calculation, for a school-house, with class-room, play-ground-enclosure, master's small parlour, and other out-door conveniences, which are absolutely requisite in every school for training. We mean this sum for each school, or double the amount, say £700, when an Infant and Juvenile School are built under one roof, (each with separate play-grounds of course.) The process of training, however, will be best conducted when the Juvenile, as well as the Infant School, is upon the ground-floor, as it is in the Parochial Model Juvenile School. See Chapter VII.

Endowments of £50 a-year, to 534 Masters or Superintendents, annually, ... £26,700

The remainder of the master's income to be made up of small fees from the children.

TOTAL COST *of Infant and Juvenile Schools.*

INFANT SCHOOLS.

Five Model Schoolmasters, . . £750
267 Teachers' Salaries, ... 13,350

Annual Grant, ... £14,100

Cost of Play-grounds, with School-sites, ... } 84,840
Do. of Building School-houses, 93,450
Building 5 Model Schools, with Master's House, suppose at £600 each, ... } 3000

Government Grant, ... £181,290

JUVENILE SCHOOLS.

Ten Model Schoolmasters, . .	£1500
534 Teachers' Salaries, . . .	26,700

Annual Grant, ... £28,200

Cost of Play-grounds and School-sites, ... }	169,680	
Do. Building School-houses, .	186,900	
Do. Building 10 Model Schools, with Master's House, suppose at £600 each, . . . }	6000	

Government Grant, ... £362,580

Of course, the whole of this amount would not be required the first year; at the same time, if, for such important good, why lose a moment in its completion? The expense the country can very easily bear, and soon would be returned manifold, in actual comfort, in the saving of poor's rates, building of jails and penitentiaries, nay, in national security. It may be proper here to say, that the training system, and moral superintendence at school, are equally necessary in such towns, as Sheffield, Birmingham, Newcastle, Liverpool, Leeds, Manchester, Coventry, Dublin, Belfast, and the grand emporium, LONDON, which is at once the most religious, most enlightened, wealthiest, and, in too large a proportion of its inhabitants, most ignorant and depraved. Here the poor are actually smothered with charities; and yet, more perhaps than any other city, does it stand in need of an enlightened, systematic, parochial influence. Is it really a fact, as has been publicly stated, that 500,000 human beings are there living in practical heathenism!

As there are few schools in any of our towns, large enough, or otherwise suitable for training children, or with play-grounds attached, after making the large deduction of one-fourth for private schools, from the number of juveniles, we think the full complement of schools will require to be erected, and also play-grounds purchased, at the public expense; and as, at present, there is not much above one-half at school which ought to be in attendance, (which may be seen by reference to the General Assembly's and other Reports, received from every part of the kingdom,) the erection of the whole of these schools, infant and juvenile, would scarcely displace one respectable private teacher.

Had the requisite number of schools been very small, we should have said, let Government provide the endowments, and the cost of play-grounds, and let the school-houses be built, wholly or half, by private subscription. But the remedy required is too immediate; we cannot with safety wait on the operation of such a distant and slow process. If we continue to sleep on as heretofore, without putting forth a thorough healing system of education, there is an under-current of profligacy and vice, in all the large towns of the United Kingdom, which, ere long, will overturn the happiness and social order of society.

Large towns, at this crisis of the country's history, ought to be specially looked to by the British Legislature; and we would recommend the above, as an instant and preliminary measure, to one which may pervade every parish in the land; at the same time, as forming a part of one great national system of intellectual and moral training.

We must, however strange, talk as familiarly of millions for education, as we were wont to do for war. And if these sums are objected to for preventing crime, and adding intelligence, comfort, and happiness, to the mass of the working population, we ask such persons to reflect on the following amount expended for the purposes of *punishing* crime:—

Cost of Glasgow Jail,	£34,800
Do. Bridewell, which, it is feared, from the rapid increase of crime, must soon be increased,	27,000
Sums raised, by private subscription, for a House of Refuge,	10,500
Annual expense of Glasgow Police Establishment,	14,000
Do. of London, for 1832,	223,160

This last, alone, reaches nearly to the funded annual interest of eight millions sterling!

CHAPTER III.

INFANT TRAINING—PECULIARITIES OF THE SYSTEM.

Play-ground—School-gallery—Objects and pictures of objects—No spelling books used—Teaching to read, although partially acquired, forms no necessary part of the system—Bible training—Infant Schools have a powerful reflex influence upon parents at home—The power and influence of music—Clapping of hands, and its use—Punishments—Monitors—Geometrical lines, why taught—Age of admission—Comparison between the effect of family and school training—Boys and girls ought to be trained together—Each Infant School ought to have a master and mistress—Necessary qualifications in an infant school-master—Necessity for Model Schools for training Teachers.

THE chief peculiarity of the Infant School system, we have already seen, is that of its being a system of moral training. A few of the other peculiarities, more especially the requisite machinery, will occupy the present chapter.

We shall commence with the play-ground, without which all attempts at moral training must prove abortive.

PLAY-GROUND.—An enclosed play-ground, *not less* than 50 feet by about 60, or 42 feet by about 70, with a flower border, in which also there ought to be planted a few shrubs and small currant bushes, wherever the air in towns will permit such to grow, and even although the greater proportion of them might require to be renewed every year. Even in those places most closely built round, geraniums and other flowers in pots may be introduced. The flowers and small fruit are a temptation which the children are likely to be exposed to in after-life; and being constantly within their reach in the play-ground, such, consequently, afford the master an opportunity of training the children to habits of self-denial.

Parents or masters may teach children in-doors not to steal fruit or flowers, but in this, as in every branch of moral culture, teaching is not training. The play-ground also affords an opportunity for healthful exercise and recreation, and while it refreshes the body, it also invigorates the mind. No child, we conceive, ought to be longer than fifty or sixty minutes within the walls of a school-room, without having at least ten minutes to play in the open air. And under the system for which we now plead, such recreation, with attendant circumstances and development of character therein, forms a prominent and most important part of the child's education. In an Infant School, especially full one-third of the children's time ought to be spent in the play-ground, in which the master or mistress, or both, exercise a constant superintendence at play; and where each boy and girl finding a number of companions of their own particular age, the natural, and therefore the true dispositions of every child are fully developed. There is a humanizing influence in boys and girls being trained together. The girl who falls, is most probably raised by a boy; and should a boy accidentally dirty his face at play, a little girl is sure to be the first to run and offer her pinafore. Children ought to have varied, though not continued or severe exercise. Confinement of mind

F

or body is not proper for young children,—they are constantly in motion, if left at liberty; and without liberty they are never happy. Two gymnastic poles are also placed in the middle area of the ground, at suitable distances from each other—one for girls, and one for boys. For the particular use, see Chapters III. and IV. Wooden bricks are also introduced.

An infant play-ground is a little world of real life, where nature and the force of principles are exhibited; and when found in fault, it is the duty of the master, on the children's return to the school-gallery, and as circumstances may occur, to endeavour daily to awaken the conscience to a sense of the evil, and to impress the understanding and heart, by a reference to their duty to God and to one another. We shall suppose that one boy at play gives another boy a box on the ear —a very common occurrence no doubt among boys—of course, however highly vexed the party receiving the blow might be, yet, if he has been properly trained to the principle and habit of " Render not evil for evil," but " overcome evil with good"—and if, in addition to this, he is in the presence of fifty or a hundred children equally well trained with himself—a *battle* is at all events prevented. This offending boy may perhaps be a new scholar, not yet broke into order; or he may be one of a furious, and even a vindictive disposition; but he is to a certain degree under a moral restraint—he is now breathing a more moral atmosphere than he did, or would do, elsewhere, on the street. But the affair does not stop here; the master, perceiving the offence, *takes no notice of it at the moment,* but waits a favourable opportunity, when passion has cooled, and reason is uppermost. On the return, as we have stated, to the gallery, in order to convict the boy in the face of the whole scholars, it is only necessary for the master to tell a story of a little boy, whom he saw in the play-ground, giving another little boy a box on the ear. Was this right? my children, he will inquire. *No, Sir,* they will, with *one* exception, give for answer. Can you tell me, the master proceeds to say, who might be guilty of such a thing? It is unnecessary to mention *who;* for the flushed, downcast countenance of the silent individual, at once discovers the guilty conscience.

Without multiplying words, it is evident, that such a lesson will prove not simply one to the guilty, which is the case in individual training, but to all; and when to this conviction is added the moral lesson, which may naturally be deduced, not only the culprit, but all the scholars, in this way, from day to day, and on account of any acts of petty thefts of playthings, overreaching, cheating, or lying, are brought within the sphere and influence of an enlightened moral training. Sympathy arising from numbers, if not absolutely necessary, at least greatly facilitates the training system. A transient visitor must not always expect to witness such occurrences, or the consequent process of training. He sees the result, however, in the order, obedience, and self-denial, of the little ones.

The master, under this system, in a single month, may bring the children under his care to the habit of an outward and eye obedience; but nothing short of the training to such religious impressions, as, " The love which God bears to us,"—" Thou God seest me," &c.—can possibly secure a permanent principle of moral obedience.

The enormous expense of suitable play-grounds, in the densest portions of large towns, is frequently brought forward as a great objection to the establishment of Infant Schools. Now, we answer, it is just the existence of large and closely built towns, and the consequent difficulty of properly rearing young children, that render *enclosed* play-grounds so peculiarly necessary, and the sacrifice, in some quarter, so imperiously called for. If such a great national good is desired, we must make up our minds to a great national expenditure.

School-Gallery.—The next peculiarity is, a Gallery, capable of seating the whole children; which increases the power of sympathy, and enables each child to fix his eye more easily upon the master, while he narrates a story, or presents an object or picture to their attention. When we say, *peculiarity*, the gallery is only so in regard to schools for Infants, for all our halls in colleges are so fitted up. If all schools had a gallery, so as to allow the children to be placed, *en masse*, before the master, and if, in addition to mental development, the Infant School plan of story, comparison, or illustration, took the place of committing so many tasks to memory, how would the understandings of children be improved, and weariness avoided. Nothing more facilitates in-

tellectual training, than placing the children in
front upon a gallery—the attention of the eye and
the ear are thus at once secured and arrested.*

The next peculiarity is, OBJECTS, and PICTURES
OF OBJECTS, animate and inanimate, to arrest the
wandering eye of the child, and, in union with
oral narrative, to inform his understanding. A
master may talk long enough upon the colour and
shape of an article to a child, without his understanding it; but simply present the object, and
instantly he acquires a knowledge of both. A
child's attention is first caught, and continues to
be occupied, with natural and artificial objects;
and when exercised upon such, on a mixture of
the *elliptical* and *interrogatory* plan, the mind is
uniformly interested, instructed, and improved.
And this may be commenced from the earliest
dawn, up to a considerable age in childhood.
In the department of objects, the Ball-frame is
found to be a powerful auxiliary, not only in
calculation, but in exercising the powers of
observation and individuality. The Pestalozzi
plan of objects, as beautifully arranged by Dr.
Mayo, to a certain extent is introduced: but,
except on common objects, the sustained attention requisite is fully too much for infants.
They ought, however, to be fully carried out in
all their variety in the Juvenile School. Without
these three accompaniments, namely, *Play-ground,*
Gallery, and *Objects,*—schools, such as Dame
Schools, may be formed for the reception of in-

* For size of School-houses, see Appendix.

F 2

fants; but, destitute of these, no school can be conducted under the Infant system.

In the Glasgow Model School, spelling and other books are not used by the children, the more especially as learning to read forms no necessary or constituent part of the system.

It is a great mistake to suppose, that a child's education should commence with learning to read. His mind, like his body, is too volatile, to be long fixed on any subject, especially one so dry, and to him so unmeaning, as the A B C. A child at five or six, beginning to learn his letters, and who has not been previously trained, as in the Infant School, has no conception of the use or advantage of such an exercise. Parents, however, state the fact, in regard to their own children, that after being so trained two or three years in an Infant School, the elements of reading, &c. have been acquired in less than half the usual time.

In the Infant School, of course, the children acquire a knowledge of the letters, and even the names of animals, and other objects, containing one or more syllables, which are presented to them on the Lesson Boards. This they acquire, first, by the acquaintance they have of the geometrical lines of which the letters are composed, and also by brass figures. Thus, letter A, is for Adam or Apple; B, for Book or Boy; C, for Cat, Comb, &c. Also, the Italic letters are sometimes taught by means of slates. Thus *d*, for *dog*; *e*, for *elephant, egg*, &c. This last, however, has not been at any time much practised in Glasgow, except on wet days, when the children require in-doors a greater variety, and cannot be better employed.

While, however, no school-books are used by the children, a large Bible is placed on a stand, in the centre of the floor, from which the master daily selects a passage as a new lesson, according to the plan laid down in Chapter VI. This plan secures a variety and progressive advancement in Bible knowledge. Thus the "milk" is first given, not the "strong meat." The master reads sentence by sentence, and, as he goes along, developes the children's ideas of the subject, upon a mixture of the elliptical and interrogatory system. The fact of reading, *in the first instance*, every new lesson from the Bible itself, and not from a collection, has this important effect, that they acquire a reverence and love for a book which contains so many very interesting and instructive stories, and which are rendered so, by this system, quite as attractive as some of those fables with which the minds of children were wont to be filled. They observe this is God's book, and therefore God's book must be true.

The system of BIBLE TRAINING, which in a measure is peculiar, aims at affording to the children a clear understanding of the historical parts of Scripture; the relative position of the countries narrated; the nature and qualities of the animals spoken of or used as illustrations in Scripture; every illustration also drawn from inanimate nature; sketches of good and bad characters, the one held up to be shunned, the other to be followed. This, therefore, necessarily brings their minds and

understandings within the outlines of almost every
art and science. And the following quotations
will show, that it is impossible for the children
to understand the meaning and quality of every
term and object referred to in Scripture, without
at the same time entering, to a certain extent,
upon those which are usually conceived more advanced sciences. What human science is there,
the outlines of which must not at least be entered
upon, ere we can have a full understanding of Bible
illustrations? For instance, in regard to the ani-
mated creation, we have " the Lion of the tribe
of Judah." " Like as the horse or the mule,
which have no understanding." " Out of the
mouth of the lion, and the paw of the bear."
" Like an owl in the desart." " Swifter than
eagles." " Pelican in the wilderness." We have
here not merely the pelican, but the wilderness.
What is a wilderness? A wilderness is a ......,
and so on. In regard to inanimate nature—" Ye
are the salt of the earth." " As iron sharpeneth
iron, so," &c. Why does iron sharpen iron?
" Now we see through a glass darkly." Why a
glass darkly, for our present glass is pretty clear?
Why was the ancient glass dim? We have
mountains, hills, valleys, trees, brooks, seas, wood,
hay, stubble. The sun, moon, stars, &c. with an
innumerable variety of other objects; all of which
are interesting and improving to the mind of children, and a knowledge of which is essentially necessary to the understanding of Scripture.

We have also in regard to the subdivisions of
nature into *animal, vegetable,* and *mineral.*

Animal kingdom.—Stork, owl, dove, raven,

sparrow, fish, bear, wolf, ass, sheep, dog, camel, locust, serpent, worm, ant, moth, &c. With many combinations. Parchment, for example. The book of the prophet Isaiah written on parchment —Joseph's coat, &c.

Vegetable kingdom.—" Lily of the valley," " Rose of Sharon," " grass of the field," cedars, briers and thorns, wheat, tares, olive oil, and several combinations, bread, linen, &c.

Mineral kingdom.—Brass, gold, silver, precious stones, iron, clay, &c. With many combinations, in furniture, or workmen's implements, candlesticks, plough, hook, spear, &c.

To how many objects in nature is Christ Jesus compared! and until intellectually understood, such passages as the following are perfectly sealed. Christ is " a morning Star." Why a morning star? We have here, in order to elucidate this metaphor, to revert to the time when the sailor had no compass to guide him save the stars; and when the morning star appeared, the mariner knew his position, and hailed, with rejoicing, the approach of day. So, &c.——" As the hart panteth after the water-brooks, so panteth," &c. We have here the nature and situation of the hart—the water-brooks—the climate—the heat—the dust— the distant brooks—the panting. " What is panting?" " Why pant?" &c. And, (elliptically,) " Panting is ......?" It is unnecessary to magnify words. Bible training, in its simplest form, is a most magnificent and enlarged science; and while human science receives an impress from the heart, divine science changes the heart.

Almost every lesson in an Infant School may, if

we choose, start from the Bible. We must remember, that, until the use and importance of all these objects are known, the illustrations themselves are of no value to the individual; the book, in so far as these illustrations are concerned, is sealed; the children might as well read a foreign tongue. As a matter of course, the connecting passage of Scripture, in which such illustrations are found, is uniformly read at the time, and forms a part of the daily exercise.

To this Bible training, is added a knowledge of every article in common use, and of every object, natural and artificial, by which they are surrounded. The outline of the picture is, as it were, first fixed upon the understanding; the minuter points are afterwards taken up progressively.

Bible, or religious education, is too frequently conducted, not on the Bible plan, but as if revelation had little or nothing to do with the things and ordinary affairs of this life. Animals, vegetables, minerals, arts and sciences, are seldom included. The sea, sky, fish, land, and human habitations, appear to be left out. The Divine Author himself has not done so; for when we look into the sacred page, we see it enriched with references to all these; and that by the familiar illustrations they afford, God has revealed a large portion of his will to man. Let but a labouring man know all the objects, natural and artificial, alluded to in Scripture, and, independently altogether of its moral influence and sublime hopes as to eternity, that man, we say, cannot be an ignorant man. Is it not a fact, that much of what is delivered from the pulpit is lost, for want of previous training to Bible knowledge in early youth?

In regard to the plan of communicating Scripture narrative and Scripture illustration in Infant Schools—while we move steadily onwards to a distinct point, yet we hesitate not, childlike, to peep at many things as we pass along, not however too tardily, lest we lose the object in view. For example—were we to sail up the river Clyde, while the surrounding scenery would naturally engage our attention, yet, in passing along, we might glance up the tributary streams, the Leven, Cart, and Kelvin—not to seek their sources, but to survey, for an instant, their interesting and fertile banks.

The acquirement of useful knowledge, and the formation of correct habits, are certainly the ultimate aim of all infant training. At the same time, one primary object of infant school establishments, is to enable the closely-confined labourer or artizan, in a crowded city, to bring up his child as free from evil example as his forefathers did, or as his brother, the farmer perhaps, now does, in the scenes of country life.

The infant school is found to have a powerful reflex influence upon the parents at home. Formerly the uncultivated child excited but little interest higher than instinctive affection, in the worn out father, fatigued with the previous day's toil. But the interesting Bible and other stories awaken in the infant mind a desire for farther information, which is exhibited in the evenings, by his begging the father to take down his large Bible, and read to him about Samuel, *the good boy;* for that had been the Bible lesson in school on that day; another evening the father will be asked for that of Jonah, sitting under the gourd, and *being very angry;* or *cast into the sea.* A third evening, that of St. Paul riding to Damascus, and of being spoken to by Jesus in the way. Thus the Infant School stories find their way to the parents, in a way formerly unknown, and add to the natural affection between parents and children, that of rational and moral beings.

Music is known to possess a powerful influence over the affections, and even the memory. Hymns, Psalms, and moral songs, therefore, form an important part of each day's exercises; and as these are generally adapted to the lesson immediately under consideration, they stamp the impression more deeply on the thoughts and feelings; and from what we have learned regarding those children who have long left school, we believe the essence of such rhymes will never be forgotten.

So delighted are the children with the singing lessons, that, in passing the neighbourhood of an Infant School, after the school is dismissed, the infant scholar is frequently distinguished by his chanting the simple rhymes.

The alphabet and the geometrical figures are each set to music. A favourite air teaches the pence table; and, " Ye banks and braes," a moral lesson. The dog—the cow—and little pussy— have each their appropriate air; and the hymns and psalms in use, are all set to animating and suitable tunes. An excellent selection of hymns, songs, and other lessons, will be found in the Glasgow Infant School Magazine.

Mountebank Shows, children ought to be trained to avoid; not so, however, exhibitions of wild animals. By the kindness of Mr. Womb-well, the children attending the Model Infant School, in number about two hundred, were lately admitted, gratis, to witness his noble collection of wild animals. So perfect was their confidence in their Master, that but one child, out of the whole, hesitated to go, or cried from fear. On approaching the dens, the children, in *full chorus*, greeted the lion, monkey, elephant, &c. each with its appropriate air, which threw some of the animals into most amusing attitudes. This infant band, for the first time in their life perhaps, had now come in contact with these real objects in nature—the character and dispositions of which they had been familiar with, but whose forms they had only known through the medium of coloured prints.

The clapping of hands, marching, beating of feet, singing, swinging, and running, to which so many object, and which are so peculiar to the Infant School, do in fact promote the most important purposes, namely, amusement, so as to keep from mischief, bodily health, mental vigour, and development of character.

The first lesson in an Infant School ought to be obedience, *instant obedience ;* next, that of giving a direct answer, in their own words, to every question. If so, "Mr. Nobody" would soon vanish. A parent or master may adopt a very simple method of training children to obedience, and of strengthening their perceptive powers, by requiring of them a clear description of any occurrence.

For example:—Make a child walk from his seat a short space, then order him to run—to sit down—to run again—to walk out of the room—to walk or run in again—to sit on his former seat, or any other to which he may be ordered. After which, require him, or some other child, or several children, alternately, audibly to state, in distinct language, every particular movement the boy has made, in exact succession. This may be varied many ways, and will be found an excellent exercise.

There ought to be a frequent reversion to first principles, and every observation by the master expressed in language nearly as plain as if the children knew nothing of the subject spoken about. This is good for the older scholars, and absolutely necessary in regard to the young ones. The teachers of more advanced schools acknowledge that children transferred to them from Infant Schools are instantly discovered by their ready answers, and by their superior docility and cheerfulness.

The master opens and closes the school each day with prayer and singing a hymn. After the morning prayer, the children simultaneously repeat the Lord's prayer, audibly and distinctly.

In prayer the master ought to use only simple words, which the children understand, and can easily follow.

We may here state, that the rod, or taws, in the literal sense, is not in use in the Model

School, being found unnecessary. We do not say that in every case they can, or ought to be dispensed with in a family, where, from the variety in age of each child, the power of sympathy is comparatively weak. In a school for training, however, they are unnecessary, if the master does his duty. A severe punishment to a child, is to order him out in the middle of the floor, with his face to the children, they taking no notice of him. The severest of all, is to make him turn his back to the children, seated, *en masse*, in the gallery; *for he has behaved so bad, that, for some time at least, he is not fit to look his companions in the face.* Punishment, it is evident, is very much in idea, and may be inflicted either through the body or mind : the latter ought always to be preferred, in reference to a rational being. Still, however, it is said, that if we "spare the rod, we hate the child;" and we cannot say otherwise; but it is only when other means, more rational and gentle, fail, that corporeal punishment ought to be resorted to. All we say is, let such be the last resort; and when absolutely necessary, do not spare the child " for his crying." At the same time, from experience, we find that the literal rod, in a properly conducted training school, is unnecessary. It may be so where children are simply taught, but we have not found it so where they are properly trained.

One great evil attending the use of the rod in Infant Schools, is the easy use it is put to in many instances, to save the trouble of convincing the judgment, or impressing the conscience, as to the impropriety of any action or line of conduct.

A great defect in our present system of education is, that the affections are not cultivated: it is all head—no heart; all teaching—no training.

Those who imagine that taking infants five or six hours a-day from their parents, and training them in school, has a tendency to weaken the tie between parent and child, we refer to the testimony of parents themselves: see Appendix.

Monitors are in use. (A portion of Bell's, or the Madras system.) One child is a monitor for singing; another for counting; several for objects; for marching to time; for Bible biography and history. No one child can be a monitor in every thing: each child in school, therefore, has an optunity of exhibiting his or her own peculiar bent of mind and natural capacity.

The following short rules may be attended to by every master of a training school:—

1. Never to punish or correct a child in anger.
2. Never to deprive a child of any thing without returning it again.
3. Never to break a promise.
4. Never to overlook a fault.
5. In all things to set before the children an example worthy of imitation.

The teaching of the simple lines of geometry is seriously objected to: these, however, the children very soon gain an acquaintance with, and are trained to use with great facility in regard to every object which is presented. Such objectors may be asked to state, how, without some knowledge of these, a child can describe the shape of a chair, or the position of a pole or seat.

Whether generally acknowledged or not, it is nevertheless true, that it is easier to train a number of children than one. Three children, for example, from two to six years of age, cannot by any possibility make the same progress, as if there were thirty; and the reason is obvious—each one of the thirty sympathizes with those of the same age, and the example of each operates mutually. Whereas, in the case of the single family, or three children of different ages, the child at six sympathizes not with the one at four, and far less with the child at two. This principle operates equally in regard to children of whatever rank in life. Sympathy, therefore, is a powerful auxiliary of the Infant system.

Nothing certainly is more beautiful, nothing more natural, than for a parent to teach and train his own children. But all parents are not capable; few, if any, have the opportunity of being constantly with their children. Every judicious parent, therefore, calls in some assistance to his or her own exertions, in the way of tutor, schoolmaster, or domestic servant. The only question then is, What portions of this time for teaching and training must or ought to be left to others? At what age ought it to commence? Is there a single child, it may be asked, poor or rich, who has attained the age of two years, who is not left, during some portion of the day, to the care of some one or other than the parents? And we ask, Are the persons *so instructed always* well qualified to superintend?

Whether is it better that fifty infants should be placed under an equal number of guardians, perhaps children, or household servants, forty-five of which number possibly cannot impart one enlightened or moral idea—sometimes, however, the reverse—or that these same fifty children should be, simply for the same length of time each day in an Infant School, under the eye and care of an enlightened and suitably qualified master?

The system of moral training in an Infant School, like that in a well-regulated family, cannot be exhibited during a transient visit. In the latter case, ere this can be rightly ascertained, we must witness a father and mother's daily care in bending and directing the moral affections of their tender offspring.

As in a family, so in an Infant School, boys and girls ought to be *trained* together; it being apparent that the energy of the one, and the gentleness of the other, under such circumstances, must afford great mutual improvement. On the other hand, we believe, that some of the evils chiefly feared do follow when they are taught separately during childhood. On these points, and one or two others, which might be noticed, we conceive we cannot do better than quote the words of a practical lady, eminently qualified to judge, and which we beg to extract from a letter lately addressed to the Secretary of the Glasgow Infant School Society, signed, " A Mother."

" To educate the boys and girls separately will be injurious to both, because it deprives the girls of the benefit of the concentrated answers produced by the stronger minds of the boys; and it deprives the boys of the quick perception, and sometimes deep feeling, evinced even by very little girls, particularly when Scripture narratives are under consideration.

"The boys require to be educated with girls, in order to soften the boisterous manners consequent on their exuberant animal spirits; and the girls require to be educated with boys, in order that they may set more value on intellectual and moral qualifications, and less on frivolous show. It follows, of course, that if boys and girls are trained together, there must be both a Master and Mistress; for it will be readily granted, that there are very few women who possess fine tact, varied information, delicate feeling, and a natural love of children, joined to great physical strength; all which are absolutely requisite for conducting an Infant School.

"Female instructors alone have been tried before now, but the schools conducted by them have never succeeded, any more than they would do without them; the one founded by the Bishop of London was superintended by two females, perhaps as well qualified for the task as any that could be found, yet, to any person visiting that, and the one on the opposite side of the street, conducted by a master and mistress, the superiority of the latter was very obvious. The voice alone of the master commands the attention of the giddy; there is a formality in all schools conducted by females alone, which is totally destructive of the liberty so essential towards the development of the infant mind. *In the hands of a woman the reins of discipline cannot be loosened, because she feels the effort of again curbing them would be beyond her physical powers.*

" The next point is the idea of introducing knitting and sewing among children of three, four, and five years old. Let any picture to themselves the delight and intelligence displayed in the countenances of infant scholars whilst filling up the pauses in one of the beautiful parables of our Lord, given on the elliptical plan; and then figure to themselves those same little beings sitting pale and listless over some bit of sewing or knitting which their little fingers are mechanically trying to perform, without use and without interest.

" I believe any sensible mother will allow that it is quite impossible, except in peculiar instances, to fix the attention of a volatile child of four or five years old to needlework. And suppose it done, what will be gained? Nothing; for the child trained in the true Infant system until six years old, and then commencing in a Juvenile School to learn needlework, knitting, &c. will be fully as forward at eight or nine years of age, and take much more delight in her work than the one who had begun at three or four without proper training."

If our whole people are to be educated, all past and present experience proves, that private or voluntary contributions will not accomplish the object. Much no doubt is doing, but still a very large proportion of the children of the poor, are left out and untouched. Even as regards the elements of reading, hundreds who have left school

cannot put words together of more than two
syllables. A private society, in a large town, may
provide and support gratis, or at a cheap rate,
one, two, or even three schools, and one here and
there may be sprinkled over the country, but
nothing short of a Government grant, and partial
Government endowment, or, which amounts to
the same thing, Parochial support by Legislative
enactment, can supply the educational wants of
an entire people.

Education, in order to be valued, ought not to
be given entirely free of charge; and that it may
be embraced by the many, it must be brought
within the compass of their small earnings. One
shilling or eighteen pence per quarter, as in some
of our country parochial schools, is quite as much
as a poor man can possibly afford to pay for his
children: this state of things, of course, cannot
be brought about but by an endowment. A partial government endowment, and partial payment
on the part of the scholars, in addition to a moral
superintendence, is the only mode which can at
once secure the attendance of every child, and
the perpetuity of a vigorous system of national
education. In the Glasgow Model, and several
other Infant Schools, the wages are payable in
advance, which we decidedly recommend, in order
to secure a regular attendance; for what is paid
for, we find people are determined to possess.
Two shillings for one child, and half price for
every other, if from the same family, is charged;
or half the sum for six weeks. Such sums, however, do little more than defray half the annual
expense, even when the building is free. If pro-

per endowments, however, were given, 1s. per quarter for one child, or 1s. 6d. for two, would be a preferable charge for children of the working classes.

A common objection urged against the extension of the Infant School system, is, that the necessary qualifications of a master are so varied, that, even though money was forthcoming for the establishment of schools, a sufficient number of persons could not be found capable of becoming teachers. Of course, they must have a natural fondness for young children—they must be cheerful in disposition, and condescending in manners—they must be possessed of general information, and have a facility of narrating stories —above all, they must have sound moral and religious principles. Well, all these are certainly requisites in an Infant Schoolmaster; but are these uncommon? By no means; many there are who, at least, possess the natural qualifications, and who, by a suitable course of training, would become admirable teachers; and if, instead of the small salaries now given to Infant School Teachers, suitable encouragement was held out to young men to prepare themselves in MODEL SCHOOLS, under experienced professors, we would find little difficulty in providing a sufficient number of suitable masters. Without a certificate from such professors, no person ought to be allowed to take charge of any school.

The intelligent and successful Master of the Model Infant School, (Mr. Caughie,) independently of his training a considerable number of

teachers, male and female, has, during the last
seven years, at the request of a number of Gentlemen, been deputed, by the Infant School Committee in Glasgow, to several of the larger towns
in Scotland, accompanied by ten or a dozen of
his pupils, in order to excite an interest in behalf
of Infant training. One Model School in Glasgow we already have; but we want a partial endowment, not merely for the Master, but for an
able assistant, whereby to enable the Infant School
Society to continue this practice; (which want of
funds now renders impracticable;) also of allowing
their Model superintendent to move from home,
and remain two or three weeks on the opening of
a School; and also to train the Master, in concert
with the new, raw, and uncultivated mass, among
which he is for the first time to be introduced.
For however well trained this young master may
have been in the Model School, amidst well trained
children, he is apt to lose confidence, or to commit sad mistakes, which may injure, if not ruin,
the future prosperity of the school, unless he is,
during the first few days, guided at almost every
step, in the mode of treating the dispositions and
moral sensibilities of his infant pupils; and this,
of course, can be accomplished only by the assistance of an experienced practitioner.

During the first two or three weeks after the
opening of an Infant School, if any parent or
manager attempts to visit it, even for five minutes,
a decided injury to the discipline of the school
must be the consequence. Nay, if even the
Secretary should feel it necessary to look in, regarding the arrangement of any portion of the

requisite machinery, his visits ought to be both seldom and short; and, at the same time, he ought not to interfere with the Master, in the slightest degree, in the presence of the children.

The Master and an experienced superintendent, who ought to be at the opening of every school, should be allowed to maintain, for a time at least, undisturbed and uncontrolled authority.

We require, therefore, not merely a minister of instruction to direct, but several experienced superintendents, who might travel from town to town, to establish schools, and watch over their progress.

MODEL SCHOOLS are indeed well worthy the attention of a parental Government; and till such are established, it will be vain to expect that our schools, generally, can attain any height in elementary, in natural, or in moral science.

CHAPTER IV.

THE INFANT SCHOOL—PRACTICAL WORKING OF THE SYSTEM.

THE DIALOGUE contained in this and the following chapter, was intended to exhibit, in some degree, the practical working of the infant system, and to supply a desideratum, in regard to those who have not the opportunity of witnessing an Infant School in actual operation.

Grandmother's observations are, perhaps, as slightly tinged with Scottish phraseology, as, in her circumstances, might well be expected. Her character, twenty or thirty years ago, was a common one; now, however, more rare. And as these have died out, we find their places filled, at the best, by such conformists as her daughter-in-law, Leezy.—The object of this system is to implant in infancy and youth, such principles and habits, as may, with the Divine blessing, stem the torrent of immorality, and turn the tide into that channel, whereby our country may yet produce *many such Grannies.*

After calling upon her daughter-in-law Leezy, and expressing surprise that her two young grandchildren should be sent so early to school, especially to one, the constitution and plan of which was so opposed to her ancient prejudices— Grandmother visits the school herself, for a portion of two successive days, in order to search into this *newfangled* system.

H

GLASGOW, *9th January.*

Leezy. How are ye the day, Granny?

Granny. Gayan frail, woman; but what can be expected at my time of life. Deed, Leezy, when a body turns seventy-three, the crazy tabernacle finds the cauld gayan sair sic weather as this. But we shouldna complain, when we hae sae mony mercies and sic hopes ayont the grave. This comforts and supports me, Leezy, in my weak state o' nature.

Leezy. O ay, ye're aye talking that way, Granny. I wonder what mercies ye hae to boast o'—I'm sure ye're ill eneugh aff; and although my ain Sandy, puir fallow, is very fond o' his auld mither, it's unco little that a weaver lad, now-a-days, can spare out o' his winnin', when he has three hungry bairns such as we hae to feed.

Granny. Deed, my ain laddie is willing eneugh, gin he had it to gie. But how are the weans, Leezy? I have na seen them these twa-three days but ance, just for a minute or twa, the night before yestreen; and little Mary then tauld me they've gaen to the school; gin I mind right, they ca'd it the Infant School. What kind o' school is that, Leezy? Ye're surely daft to think o' sending Geordie to a school—what can he learn, woman? Puir man, he's only twa year auld last Mairt. Would it no be better to keep him at hame in the house, and bring him up in the fear o' God, and learn him his Questions?

Leezy. Deed, his father learns him the Mother's Catechism every Sabbath night afore brose time; but what wi' keeping the wean, cawin' the pirns, and ae thing and another, I have na muckle time to look after him thro' the week, let alane instruct him. But he'll no amaist be instructed by me. He wouldna bide in the house a minute after his porritch in the mornings, but out he gaed wi' the neebour laddies down the wynd a' day, wading in the burn, and biggin' glaur dams.

Granny. Weel-a-weel, puir fallow, steerin' healthy weans canna be expected to be very clean. But, mind ye, Leezy, see that nane o' the laddies that he gangs wi' swears or tells lies, or else Geordie will grow up in ill ways, and, may be, ere lang gie ye a sair heart.

Leezy. Deed, I rather think the maist o' them baith swear and tell lies too, for I whiles catch Geordie and Mary baith, at a time, just saying what they shouldna just say.

Granny. Tak' tent o' that, Leezy,—that's aw-fu', woman.

Leezy. Now, Granny, ye're aye sae muckle in the preaching way whene'er ye meet a body, that ane can scarcely get in a word o' plain truth about ony thing o' importance for ye. Ye speired at me what school the weans were at. Now I'll tell ye, gin ye like. It's an Infant School, whar they learn hymns and sangs, counting wi' balls, and clapping o' hands, swinging on ropes, and biggin' brigs wi' bricks, and heaps o' these kind o' things.

Granny. And ca' ye that a school, Leezy?

Leezy. Weel, our ain man wasna very sure about it himsel'; but I wadna let him tak' them out for a wee till we saw. Indeed, Geordie, wee lad, wadna come out. He's now been there amaist a fortnight. He gangs half afore ten in the morning, and comes back at ane—then he tak's a bit bread, and aff like a whittrit again afore twa, syne back at four-hours, just at the gloamin' time.

Granny. Leezy, Leezy, are ye acting right to let Mary and Geordie be sae muckle out o' your sight, and gang to a playing place like that, and ca't a school. What gart ye send them there, .ken ye?

Leezy. Weel, I'll tell ye, Granny. Ye see, twa-three o' the neebours' weans were at that school, and enticed them to gang ae day, and they plagued and deaved my head a' the next day for siller, just to let them gang, for they got sic grand fun, they said, marching, and swinging, and singing, and I canna tell ye what a', that I was just obliged to let them gang their ain way,—and when they gaed wi' the baubees in the morning, I was like to gang clean gyte wi' anger at the maister, for he sent them back wi' word to me to wash their faces cleaner gin the afternoon; and now they daurna big ony dams, for they maun aye gang with clean hands and faces, and their hair weel kamed, neebour-like, ye ken. But atween us twa, Granny, I have na muckle objection to the change, for their bits o' legs and coat-tails are no sae often draigled as they used to be.

Granny. Ye have tauld me how ye sent them, but what gart ye send them to a place to be sae lang out o' your sight?

Leezy. Didna I tell ye, Granny, that they were amaist a' day playing down the wynd, and they're nae mair nor that at the school? and our Sandy, who has mair sense than me, speired about things the other day, for twa minutes, and he finds they learn heaps o' things about perpendiculars and horizontals, which the weans sing, and point wi' the fingers, first straught up, syne straught afore them. Sandy found out as weel that there was nae leein, nor swearin' in a' the school, and that the true religion was learned there. At first, when he looked at them, he thought it was a gentle school; but the maister said, Wait a wee, and ye'll perhaps see your ain just like the others. Syne the maister said, (and Sandy thought it wasna far wrang,) that cleanliness was next to godliness.

Granny. I'm no just sure o' a' this wark, Leezy. The school canna be the right sort, I'se warrant, when they hae sae muckle fun. Ye talk about religion being taught in't. Waesuck! what connection has swinging ropes and clapping hands wi' religion? Na, na; and as to the perpendiculars and horizontals ye speak about, and pointing wi' the fingers, as if that would mak' the truth mair visible, they're clean out the question. My lassie, sic a school canna be the right sort. But I'll gang and see't mysel', that will I, gin my rheumatics let me walk, the morn or next day. I'm really frighted my ain Sandy is beginning to be spoilt wi' some o' thae newfangled notions. I'll awa' then, Leezy—this is my stick, is't? May the Lord gie ye mair grace, and may you and my bonny Sandy, and my three braw oes, [grandchildren,] be a' lambs o' the flock o' Christ. This is my prayer for ye a' every day. And gin ye be that, ye'll be a' that's worth the being. To be children of God is infinitely afore being children o' kings. Mind ye that, Leezy.

Leezy. Tak' tent o' your feet, Granny; there's a door step, mind. Lean on my shouther—that's it now—keep the crown o' the causey, Granny. Gude morning—gude morning, Granny.

GRANDMOTHER'S FIRST VISIT TO THE INFANT SCHOOL.

TUESDAY MORNING.

[*Granny raps at the outside door, which is opened by the Children at play.*]

Granny. Weans, is this the school?

Weans. The Infant School do you mean, Mem?

Granny. Ay, to be sure—let me in, my braw bairns. Whar's the Maister?

Weans. There he's, Mem, at the other end of the play-ground, near the school; he was just swinging a wee with the laddies.

Granny. Swinging—Swinging—Maister an a'! —A fine school to be sure—let me see him.

Weans. Tak' care, tak' care, Mistress, or the boys will knock ye down, for they're swinging.—— Twenty-eight—twenty-nine—thirty.*

Granny. What's that they're saying, Weans?

Weans. They're counting their turns, Mem.

Granny. Counting their turns! what can that

* Those who are not engaged in swinging stand around the gymnastic pole, and sing and count from one to forty, when the others instantly let go the ropes.

mean?—Let me out o' the road, Weans. Ye're just like a skep o' bees, ye wee tots—tak' care my staff disna hurt your taes, ye wee bits o' things—stand a' back but ane—now, ane's eneugh to let me see the School Maister.—Is this you, Mary, my bonny thing?

Weans. Mary says this is her ain Granny.

Master. Come in, Mistress, you seem fatigued —you had better take a chair near the fire, and rest a little.

Granny. Deed, I hae muckle need to rest, there's sic a crowd in this place; it's just like a cried fair. Deed, I was amaist like to be knocked down, gin it wasna for the flock o' weans, who were gayan civil, puir things, taking me out o' the road.

Master. Just rest a little, if you please, while I call in the children from the play-ground. After each half hour's lesson or so in the school, we generally allow them a few minutes out-doors to play.

Granny. Weel-a-weel, play's a' right, but what's half-an-hour to do in the way o' perfecting in reading. In my young days we sat hale three hours at a time in the school, and durstna turn the side o' our head a' the time, for fear o' the taws whiskin' past our lugs, and maybe a loofie or twa to the bargain—but we'll see, Maister. Now, to be honest wi' ye, I hae just come this morning to search to the bottom o' this thing; for I hae twa oes in this school contrary to my will, and I hae their spiritual welfare constant at heart;—and frae a' I hae heard, I canna say that I'm just o'er weel pleased wi' what I hear.

Master. Well, Mistress, I like candour, and if you will have a minute's patience till the children are all in, I shall be happy to——

Granny. Stop there, Sir,—stop. I see by your een ye're gaun to bring me o'er wi' a word o' flattery; but mind ye, lad, that'll no do.—— School Mistress, stop the weans frae coming in at the door there, till I get my breath out, that maun I. Maister, steek the door gin ye please.

Master. Well, Mem, the door is shut. What important matter is now to be brought under discussion.

Granny. Discussions, or what ye like; I want, Maister, to speir a plain question. Whatfor do ye, as I'm tauld ye do, bring down a maister's dignity, and condescend to play wi' weans, swingin' and lampin' round a big stab like a muckle gawky? What command can ye expect to hae after sic pranks?——Answer me that, Maister, and tak' care what ye say, for they tell me there's nae leein here, and I'll be a witness to the truth o' the observe, that will I.

Master. Now, Mistress, when you stopped me so abruptly, I was about to have said, that I shall explain every thing to you; and it will afford me much pleasure showing our plan to a person of the venerable age you appear to be.

Granny. Nae glamour noo, Maister,—to the point gin you please.

Master. Well, Madam, respecting playing with the children, you know the first and most important object, in rearing up children " in the way they should go," is to gain their affections.

Granny. O ay, that's true, but what syne?

Master. And we think this important point more easily and more effectually gained, by being quite at ease with the little ones, rather than by keeping at a distance, and awakening fear in their tender breasts, instead of love. You will acknowledge, I believe, that the service done to a person you love is more heartily performed, than when fear is the animating principle. You will recollect Madam, it is said,

> "Love still shall hold an endless reign,
>   In earth and heaven above,
> When tongues shall cease, and prophets fail,
>   And every gift but love."

Granny. Ay, man, I see ye hae gotten some o' the Paraphrases by heart—that's sae far to be sure; but swinging on ropes—whatfor that, Maister, ken ye?

Master. Well, I was about to have said, that we conceive one most distinct method for parent or teacher to gain the affections of children under their care, is to enter into all their little amusements, at least occasionally. Children highly value this condescension on the part of their teachers, and the contrast in age is so great, that no child will respect a teacher the less on account of having had a game at ball with him, or even a swing, to which you seem to have such mighty objections; but, on the contrary, I would say, to offend such a master would be a matter of regret on the part of the children. Under such circumstances, he is an object of love, but never an object of terror. You know that God in Christ has condescended to many of our weaknesses and infirmities, in order to gain our affections—though never to our sins. With these God could have no sympathy.

Granny. Sins, sins—na, na,—God couldna do that. I was amaist fear'd ye were gaun wrang, lad—but ye brought yoursel' out no that ill at the hinderend—tak' tent o' thae kittle bits: na, na, God never can look at sin but wi' the outmost abhorrence.

Master. Madam, I find the children must be let in. They have been quite long enough in the play-ground, and I fear it begins to rain. I shall ring the bell, and my mistress will call them all in.

Granny. Come awa, come awa, ye wee tots— what a flock! I'se warrant there's twa hunder amaist.—I say, School Mistress, speak a wee: Does ony o' thae weans *greet* when they're sae lang frae hame? They're wonderfu' quiet, puir things, enow.

School Mistress. Scarcely ever, except the first day or so after they are entered as scholars; when the mother, after paying the quarterly or half-quarterly wage, is about leaving the school-room, we have sometimes such a stamping and roaring as you never saw.

Granny. And how do you silence them: do ye cuff them weel?

School Mistress. No, no, we never cuff them —that is unnecessary; but we commonly, after much entreaty, prevail on the child's mother to leave the school-room. She, however, generally keeps a sharp look-out after her boy, by peeping in through the windows on the outside—my stormy gentleman, in the meantime, sprawling on his back, kicking with his heels, and bawling with all his might.

Granny. And what then, Mistress?

School Mistress. Why, my husband takes no notice of him whatever for a little, but goes on with some amusing lesson or other, such as singing or clapping hands. Shortly the heels will stop beating. He listens to the music with his thumbs pressed tightly into his eye-sockets: all the while his mother outside in *twenty minds* to come in and take him away; but no sooner does the master march two or three classes past the *little stormant*, singing and beating time to the tune of " Ye banks and braes," or such like, than up he gets with the fourth or fifth class, todling after them the best way he can, wishing, no doubt, not to lose all the fun——But, Mistress, the children are in the gallery; I must run to see the girls all properly seated.

Granny. Half a word, Mistress——How do ye do wi' the weans when they're ill wi' the measles or kinkhost, ken ye?

School Mistress. Of course they stay at home. We could not, with propriety, allow an infected child to remain for a moment in school. We sometimes have ten or even fifteen absentees, dependent, no doubt, on circumstances, and the particular season of the year.

Granny. Syne, when they've got *the turn*, they'll no be in a great hurry coming back, I'se warrant——at least my Sandy used to mak' feint o' a sair head for a day or twa, for fear o' being sent back to the school; but I aye fand him out by the gleg o' his ee, and I whiles had to promise to gie him a baubee or sae next Saturday-teen, just to gar him gang a wee bit.

School Mistress. It is quite the reverse with us here, for so anxious are the children to get back to school, that it is with difficulty their parents can keep them at home a whole day, except when very sick. Indeed, they are obliged to promise them a little book, or some other gift, if they be good children, and stay in till they be quite recovered.

Granny. One word, Maister, afore ye begin— I dinna just understand your ways in this place. What I cam' for, was to look after and see gin my twa oes were under right guidance, and no brought up in ne'er-do-weel ways, but the wife and you are sae muckle in the fleiching way wi' me, that ye were amaist garrin' me forget the errand I cam' for.

Master. Why, Mistress, although you seem so afraid of flattery, I must still say it will afford me pleasure to show you the whole of our plan, if you will have patience to listen and look on. It would be well, indeed, if all mothers and grandmothers took such a lively interest in the religious and moral education of their children; for you may know Infant Schools ought to be assistants to parents, but never to supersede their exertions in rearing their tender offspring. Don't let us imagine, that when children are taught to read, and perhaps to write, they are then perfectly instructed, and fit to be sent out into the world; forgetting, that although they may be acquainted with the art of reading, that this is merely the power of acquiring useful knowledge, and cannot be said to be knowledge itself; for although young people do acquire a deal of knowledge, unless it be properly directed, it will not serve them in after life. Now, Mistress, in this school there are many things the children may be taught, but unless they are taught the truths, the plain truths contained in the Bible, they can have no proper wisdom or saving knowledge to direct them.

Granny. Say ye sae; really ye speak no that ill, gin your practice corresponds. My sight's no that gude, Maister, but just since I put on my spectacles, what kind o' pictures are these on the wall next us—a monkey, and syne a teeger, and then another board wi' L's and C's, and black scores scartit hither and thither, like lines in a wean's first copy. How can ye reconcile monkeys, and sic like trash, wi' religion, and teaching weans right ways, as they tell me ye do? And gin ye stock their heads full o' sic nonsense, what room will there be for the great and important truths.—Man, I'll be plain wi' ye—I am very angry; but I ken that's no right, for patience is a virtue, they say—Is't no?

Master. I shall shortly explain these pictures, and the use of them; but I must run to the gallery, else the children will get into disorder; for you know children are children.

Granny. Deed ay, that's truth.

Master. My dear, be so good as go on with the children for a few moments, while I am engaged with our visitor.

LESSON ON CLEANLINESS.

This is the way we wash our hands,
We wash our hands, we wash our hands,
This is the way we wash our hands,
To come to school in the morning.

This is the way we wash our face, &c.
To come to school in the morning.

This is the way we comb our hair, &c,
To come to school in the morning.

This is the way we brush our clothes, &c.
To come to school in the morning.

This is the way we show our hands, &c.
Whether they are clean or dirty.

It is a shame to come to school, &c.
With dirty hands or faces.

Clean children like to come to school, &c.
But not with dirty faces.*

Now, Mistress, I must just say one word. Whether, think you, is it preferable to keep the children, as you say you were kept, three hours at a time fixed to your seat, and perhaps only fifteen or twenty minutes of which you were employed saying your lesson, labouring away at a dry subject like the A B C, or, as these children are, employed every minute at something improving either the body or mind, learning the proper use

* In Infant Schools, the utmost attention is paid to cleanliness. The Teachers regularly inspect the children every morning, while chaunting the above lines—the effect of which is, that he seldom has to reprove any for being uncleanly.

of every thing, and even what monkeys and tigers are in their nature and dispositions. Allow me to say, Mistress, our object in Glasgow is, to render the Infant System A BIBLE EDUCATION; and this is not a difficult task, if we but consider the wideness and extreme variety of the range, embracing as it does the foundation and elements of every thing we see or require, nay, even of arts and sciences. It's true we amuse the little ones, for what child will learn much, or attend to any instruction, without amusement; frequent exercise and activity, you know, add to the children's health; and I believe you will grant, that the promotion of cheerfulness and health is perfectly consistent with the Scripture precept, " Train up a child in the way he should go."

Granny. Ay, ay, Scripture education to be sure—bears, and lions, and girnin' wolves, and a' these kind o' cruel beasts; there's a heap o' Scripture in them, I'se warran'.

Master. Well, Mistress, can you say these animals are not spoken of in the Bible? Is their creation for the use of man not made a distinct subject of Scripture narrative? And are the names and dispositions of both wild and tame animals not often used there to illustrate moral and religious subjects?

Granny. Weel, I'll no say, but I think, Maister, the less ye teach the weans about sic beasts the better, at least in a school. I aye thought they were kept in dens in a show-box. Let every thing gang to its right place, Maister; wha e'er heard o' a school for teaching about wild beasts?

Master. I entirely differ from you, Mistress; for, as animals of various kinds, not only lions, bears, and wolves, which you particularly mention, but other beasts, birds, reptiles, insects, and even fishes, are frequently noticed in Sacred History, in reference to their peculiar qualities, why then should not these children be made acquainted with their nature, dispositions, and use? For example, " Be wise as serpents, and harmless as doves." Unless children first know the peculiar character of the serpent, and also of the dove, this passage to them is of no practical use. The same may be said of fifty other passages in Scripture. But, independently of these considerations, if you don't employ the children's time in learning good, they will employ it themselves in learning evil. Why, then, not occupy a portion of it in exploring the power, wisdom, and goodness of God in the animal creation, as revealed in the Bible? Never forget this, Mistress, that except when asleep, the mind of a child, as well as his body, is never idle—all is activity. Our object, therefore, in either case, is not to curb, but to direct. Suppose, for example, I wished to give a lesson on the bear, introduced in some Bible story, I would select the picture of a bear—the picture lesson in which the bear is represented. I would then ask them, or rather draw from them, its general appearance and colour, its character and dispositions, its height, size of body, peculiarity of paws, and whether a biped, quadruped, or what. I would then ask, where are bears spoken of in the Bible? One child will give one passage; another, another passage; or many will

respond in one voice. All, however, hear wha.
is going on, and all, therefore, are learning; and
to them this kind of exercise is so positive an
amusement, that when liberty is granted by the
Master, the children eagerly call out for a Bible
story. In reference to the Bear, which is the
particular Natural History Lesson of this day,
what a variety of interesting and useful lessons
may be drawn from that passage, 2 Kings, 2d
chapter, where the two she-bears are represented
as tearing forty-two children from limb to limb,
who mocked the aged Prophet. We have the disposition of the bears which God employed to
punish the little children—the character of these
children, and the character of the Prophet Elisha.
You see the lesson, Mistress, which from this history children may receive—Respect to aged superiors, to mock no one on the streets, even though
an idiot, for they are God's workmanship—the
power of God in using these animals to fulfil his
will—his justice in punishing the little children—
and his goodness and love in protecting from in-
sult his aged servant the prophet Elisha. In this
manner, we can make Scripture the groundwork
of most of our lessons, and improve every part of
Bible narrative, without even entering into subjects or doctrines too difficult for their young
understandings to comprehend.

Granny. Weel-a-weel; but ye're aye keeping
among the beasts, Maister. I'm sure it's no beasts
the Bible was written for; was it no the glad news
of a Saviour provided for puir sinners, like you
and me?

Master. Very true, indeed; and we do repeat and enforce, in the simplest manner, such beautiful statements as these:—" Jesus Christ came into the world to save sinners." " God so loved the world, that he gave his only begotten Son, that whosoever believeth on him should not perish." At the same time, is He not often revealed to us by metaphors well suited to arrest the attention of the young mind, nay, to affect the heart? Is Jesus not compared to a Lamb, in meekly submitting to suffering; and to a Lion, in destroying his enemies, and protecting his people—" the Lion of the tribe of Judah;" in other parts to a Shepherd—a Rock—the bright and morning Star—a Sun—a Shield, &c.—a Light to lighten the Gentiles? *Of course, we are Gentiles.* Who are all the nations of the earth? *Now,* they are Gentiles; formerly there was one nation not called Gentile. Who were they? and so on. Thus the analyses of this and twenty other Scripture stories, necessarily afford to the little ones the outlines of Geography. I ask you, then, Mistress, ought not the whole of these allusions to be made clear to the capacities of children, so that in reading the Bible, or hearing it read, or spoken about, they may be able to understand, and fully apprehend, the true meaning of the terms applied? Such lessons, also, of necessity bring us to teach Infants the outlines of Natural History, and even Astronomy. *The Sun stood still at the bidding of Joshua, and was darkened at the crucifixion of the Redeemer.* Do not suppose, Madam, that it is only lofty and sublime

subjects that the Bible unfolds; we have every
variety of illustrations borrowed from ordinary
life, so that, in truth, we find " the foot cannot say
to the hand, I have no need of thee."   Our blessed
Saviour is compared, not simply to a Foundation
Stone, which all must understand supports the
building, but to its " Chief Corner-stone." Now,
the illustration is stripped of nearly all its beauty,
until the manner of building and securing the corners of ancient temples is known; for without this
we don't see the beauteous comparison, " Fitly
framed together, and growing into a holy temple
in the Lord."   You see, therefore, Mistress, that
the revelation of the word of God, is at once intellectual and religious.   And you will please
observe, that while we desire to interest, amuse,
and instruct the children committed to our care,
the purpose of all our lessons is to impress their
understandings and hearts with a love for the
Bible, and the God of the Bible.   And who will
restrain the operation of the Divine Spirit upon
the heart of even a little child, whilst thus dealing plainly in regard to the simple statements of
his own word?   A story is the great outcry of
all children, and not unfrequently stories please
big children too.

Granny. What's that the bits o' weans are
singing noo?

Master. Oh, just singing a rhyme with their
Mistress.

London is the capital—
The capital—the capital;
London is the capital—
The capital of England.

Here we go to Paris—
To Paris—to Paris:
Here we go to Paris—
    The capital of France.

Berlin is the capital, &c. &c.*

Granny. Ay, but, Maister, ye maun excuse me
ance mair, for atweel-a-wat I'm but a poor doitit
body, and maybe no sae weel learnt as my son,
or the like of you—but the prayer, man—I was
amaist gaun to be as graceless as yersel'—ye hae
forgot *it*, hae ye na? Can ony blessing be expected to come out-owre this, or ony thing else,
gin ye dinna look up and ask a blessing?

Master. Now, Madam, I find you are really
very sharp with me, but I excuse your anxiety,
and must respect those sturdy principles by which
you, unlike some of our younger matrons, appear
to be actuated, and therefore I shall also explain
this matter as you desire.

Granny. Thank you, Sir—ye're very discreet,
considering.

Master. You must know, Madam, that we always open as well as close the School by prayer
and singing a hymn. We also teach the children to repeat the Lord's Prayer; and, of course,
having explained its meaning to them, it must,
we conceive, be important that these children,
in the dawn of their reason, use that comprehensive prayer, which the disciples of Christ, in
their little more than infant knowledge of its

---

* Moving the feet, while singing this little rhyme in regard to the principal capitals of Europe, is not only a good
in-door exercise in a wet day, but it impresses the fact indelibly on their memory.

great meaning and comprehensiveness, were commanded to use. I say this, Mistress, lest ye be one of those who say that children ought not to be taught to pray.

Granny. Na, na, ye mustna think that o' me, Maister.—No learn weans to pray! I wonder wha would say that! Is na prayer ane o' the ways the sinner gangs to God? and, gin we dinna teach them to pray, how can we train them up " in the way they should go?" Na, na, dinna think that o' me, Sir.

Master. You'll excuse my being particular; for although my attention is not of course taken off so much as it has been, by every one who pays us a visit, yet you seem so sharp, that I am obliged to be very much on my guard what I say before you without explaining it. The prayer, goodwife, was at ten o'clock, precisely; after which, and previous to going out to the play-ground, the children had half an hour's lessons on Objects at the picture-posts. It is now half-past eleven; and as you did not enter the school till twenty minutes before eleven, of course the prayer was over.— Now, children, let me see if your little hands are all out of mischief. Up both hands—down again —clap hands—twist hands quickly—that's right —now get on—*sing away*—and afterwards whirl them—and afterwards whirl them—and afterwards whirl them—thus quickly about.

Granny. Now, Sir, in my opinion, ye're beginning at the wrang end; for, when our Sandy was at the school, they learnt first, and then played.

Master. Allow me, Mistress, to explain this matter. You know the attention of infants must be caught, and kept up in some manner or way; otherwise, in attempting to train them, no good can be done; for you may speak, but they don't hear. Now, this attention we acquire by making the children, when all sitting in the gallery, first stand up, then sit down, then up, then down again; or by clapping hands, as you see we have been doing. This exercise, for a time, keeps their hands out of mischief, and quickens their attention. Feeling themselves thus not only amused, but actually at liberty, and under no restraint, save a moral one, they are predisposed to receive any lesson we may see fit to impart to their tender and impressible minds.

Granny. Ay, man, ye hae a very explanatory way o' speaking, to be sure; but maybe their hands will just gang to mischief after that; will they no?

Master. No doubt they will; but we just repeat such exercises at proper intervals: and you see how delighted the children are with them. Look at your grandson, George; he is as brisk as a bee clapping his hands.

Granny. This is a wee mysterious to me; for at hame, his mother (my gude-dochter, I mean) tells me that Geordie 'll no do ony thing but what he likes. He's been ae fortnight here, I understand—I wonder what another fortnight will do! The way may be right eneugh for ony thing I ken. I thought human nature was the same in a' times; but the chiels now-a-days tak' a foolish way o' answering ony o' my observes. They say, 'Auld Lucky, ye ken naething about it; this is a far more enlightened age than the ane you was born in.' Now, in my opinion, Maister, it's a very dark ane; for the light o' the gospel is very faint, and the works o' darkness are very manifest. What think ye, Maister?

Master. I believe what you say is too true; but we must have a chat upon these subjects some other opportunity, or after the school is dismissed, if you please.

Granny. Weel, that's gude enough as far as it gangs; but ye have nae Questions, hae ye?

Master. What questions do you mean, Mistress?

Granny. O—"Man's chief end." My ain gude-man, that's dead and gane, honest man! used to catecheeze the weans every Sabbath night frae end to end, and ne'er missed ane o' them, petitions an' a'.

Master. Your daughter-in-law, or your son, I understand from Mary, catechizes her and little George every Sabbath night, which I am happy to hear.

Granny. Catecheeze—O ay, my son does it sae far, to be sure, honest lad!

Master. My little children, what shall we begin with? Shall I tell you a story, or what shall we do first?

Granny. Stop, Maister, I thought it was the Catechism ye were gaun to begin wi'.

QUESTIONS.

Master. Well, I shall ask a few questions as you desire it; but of course you know, Mistress, in our Infant Schools we use no printed books except the Bible, nor do we use any catechisms.

Using catechisms, we fear, might just be burdening the memory of very young children with answers, which, without knowing the exact meaning of words or terms, they cannot understand; at all events, we find that what they are capable of understanding, is better accomplished by our simpler and more natural method of reading a Bible story, statement, or precept, repeating it upon the elliptical plan, and also cross-questioning the children on the subject. This is done when they are seated in the gallery as they now are, and all are allowed to answer, and even assist in proposing the questions; in other words, their juvenile powers of mind are exercised and developed, without, in the slightest degree, attempting to force them. Hence the great extent of valuable information the children soon acquire—the distinct perception they have of right and wrong, of objects and things. Thus, you see, although we use no catechisms, yet we abound in questions.

Granny. That sounds a' very weel, Sir; but wha e'er thought o' a school without Question Books? Na, na.

Master. I will, with great pleasure, ask the children any question you choose; still, however, I repeat, that we leave the committing of the Shorter Catechism to memory till the children are sent to a Juvenile School. And, Mistress, I promise you, that if they have been previously trained for two, three, or four years, under our system, they will perceive, with a clearness and correctness of understanding, many truths in that truly valuable book, which were quite dark and mysterious to you and me, Mistress, under our old system of a well-stocked memory without understanding.———Well, children, to satisfy our worthy visitor, I shall ask you one or two questions. Do you know what questions mean? *Yes, Sir; askings—speerings.* Can any of you answer me this question? "What is the chief end of man?" *No, Sir.* Well, I believe few of you have yet learned the Shorter Catechism. Is there any of you can repeat any Catechism? *Yes, Sir; I know the little questions.* What little questions do you mean, child? *The Mother's Carritches.* Who learned you them? *My Mother.* Is not she very kind, to take such pains to instruct you this way? *Yes.* What should you give to your mother for this? *I have nothing, Sir, to give her.* Well, although you have nothing to give your mother, is there nothing you can do to her, for such attention? Ought you to be inattentive and disobedient, when she asks you to do any thing? *No, Sir; I should do her bidding.* Can any of you, little children, repeat the little questions? *No, Sir; but Jeanie and Mary know them.* Well, since so very few of you seem to know any questions, will you all promise to ask your mother, when you go home, to learn you the Mother's Catechism? *Yes, Sir,—Yes, we will.* Now, tell me what you will say when you go home. *We'll say, Please, mother, the Master says you'll learn us the ' wee Questions.'* Very right, children. Now, remember you must not ask rudely; you must ask prettily. You should never speak rudely to your parents, nor to any one. Don't forget this, children;—will you remember now? *Yes, Sir.* Now, children, re-

K

peat after me, " Man's chief end,"—*Man's chief end*—is to glorify God—*is to glorify God*—and to enjoy him for ever—*and to enjoy him for ever.* Repeat it again. Very well. Now, the first word of this answer to the question, children, is " man." What is a Man? *You're a man, Master.* Is that person sitting on a chair near the fire a man? *No ; she's a woman—an old woman.* Should you despise an old woman? *No, Sir.* What ought you to do then? *Respect her—you* ought to ... *respect her.* Very right. Tell me, then, what paying respect to a person is. *Honouring,* and thinking ... *well of him.* Well then, children, you say I'm a man, and the answer to the question says, " Man's chief end:" does it include women as well as men? *Yes, mankind.* Mention what you mean by mankind; are boys and girls like you included? *Yes; it means every body—a' the folk.* Does that mean young and old? *Yes, Sir ; every body.* Now then, children, we go to the next word—" chief." What is the meaning of " chief,"—is it the lowest or the highest?———

Granny. Noo, Sir, I'm really out o' a' patience at this way o't. Do ye no ken that it's the glory of God that's the first thing the weans should understand? What's the use o' saying sae muckle about men, and chief men, that ye was just beginning to talk about? gang to the point at ance, man, as my ain gude auld man did on the Sabbath night at Question time. He speered them frae end to end, and ne'er missed ane o' them—Na, na.

Master. Now, Mistress, if you are to hear, you

must have a little patience; but suppose I were, according to your plan, to leave out the meaning of words altogether, and at once to ask the children what is meant by glorifying God—what answer would they give, think you? Would it not just be this—To glorify God, is to glorify God? leaving no more lasting impression on their minds than the sound of an empty kettle :—and, in order to show you the truth of this, I shall for the present miss the meaning of words altogether, and repeat the question. Now, my children, can you answer me this question? What is it to glorify God? *We don't know, Sir.*——You see, Mistress, their answer.

Granny. Ay,—but that's no the answer ye promised they would gie.

Master. Well, I must confess, the answer is not exactly a repetition of the question, which every child would give, who is accustomed, like a parrot, to repeat, without understanding the meaning of what they commit to memory ;—but, you will observe, that, under the infant system, when a question is put, if the children don't know the answer, they instantly say, 'We don't know :' and this has the effect of encouraging openness and candour, also keeping the understanding alive and in activity. Always bear in mind, Mistress, that what passes into the memory, as it is called, and not understood, is frequently lost, being merely a tinkle, or sound—exciting no interest, and void of use : but what passes into the memory through the understanding—for some folks say the understanding, like every other power of the mind, has a memory of its own—will remain so long as the understanding exists.

Granny. Ye're far ayont my comprehension noo; wha e'er heard o' the understanding having a memory?

Master. We'll talk about that again. But here come the elder boys and girls marching from the class-room, where they have been putting the lesson-boards in order; we shall see what they say on the subject.

Granny. Noo, I'm glad to hear that ye're to get on; for I was just gaun to say, after ye stopt me last, that gin ye get nae faster on, ye may keep the weans here till they are auld men and women, afore they get through the Mother's Carritches, let alane thinking to get through the Shorter Catechism; and as to the Proofs, they needna be printed at a'.

Master. Come, make haste, my little children, strike up and join the tune, till this class is properly seated at the top of the gallery. Now, get on—all is silent.——Children, answer me this question, How can you and I glorify God? *By doing every thing to please him.* Mention any way by which you children can glorify God. *By doing what our father and mother bids us—and your bidding, Master.* How do you know that God will be glorified by your doing what your father and mother bid you? *Because God says, " Honour thy father and mother."* Now, Madam, we might proceed and lengthen the conversation upon this point for hours, if we pleased. Plain duties, we may say, are plain. But it might be asked, for example, How can you or I, in taking a walk, glorify God? Children, how can we do this? *That we may get health, in order to do all that God wishes us to do, Sir.*——You appear, I think, Mistress, a little tired, and the younger children will, by and by, get restless; suppose, previous to their getting out to play, that we sing a hymn.

Granny. Weel, really that's no that ill sayings, na, poor things! they've behaved extraordinary weel: they've just been as quiet as if they were frightened for twa or three loofies. Where's your taws, Maister, to correct the weans?

Master. We use none here, and we need none; for the little ones are always fully engaged, whether in the play-ground or in school; and when at play, the Mistress or myself is always present, watching their movements——checking them when disposed to quarrel, and animating them in all their little games and amusements.——Now, then, my little children, what hymn shall we sing? *Master, sing* "Holy Saviour, now before thee." *Master, please sing* "I'm not too young for God to see." *Master, sing* "Thou Guardian of our infant days." We shall sing three verses of the last one, which this very little girl has chosen. Who will be the Monitor? Come, my little fellow, mount the rostrum, and let me see how nicely you can lead the tune.

THOU GUARDIAN OF OUR INFANT DAYS.

Tune—" *Oldham.*"

" Thou Guardian of our Infant days,
   To Thee our prayers ascend—
To Thee we tune our songs of praise—
   To Thee—the children's Friend.

" Lord, draw our youthful hearts to Thee,
    From every ill defend ;
Help us, in early life, to flee
    To Thee—the children's Friend !

" Let all our hopes be fixed on high ;
    And when our lives shall end,
Then may we live above the sky,
    With Thee—the children's Friend !"

REVISAL OF YESTERDAY'S BIBLE LESSON, AND
OF THE PREVIOUS TUESDAY'S.

Master. Now, children, we must get on with
our lessons. What is the first thing we usually
proceed with? *Yesterday's lesson, if you please,
Sir.* What was the particular lesson of yesterday? *It was a lesson about Peter.* Very well.
What sort of a lesson do you call it? *Biography.*
Do you know what biography means? *It means
an account of the life of a person.* You know,
children, there are several distinct portions or
incidents in Peter's life; what was the particular
part of it that we were upon yesterday? *It was
denying Christ at the fireside of the judgment-
hall.* Now then, children, I shall see what you
remember of the story; be very attentive, and
repeat all you possibly can; shall I begin for you,
children? *If you please.* Well, Peter was one
of Christ's chosen ... *disciples ;* * and he was a very

* Throughout the whole of this dialogue, every word in
Italics may be considered as supplied by the children. In
addition to the mode of questioning, the master, in the
progress of the story or explanation, pauses for an instant,
and affords the children an opportunity of filling up the

bold ... *man*, and very much attached to ... *Christ;* that is, he loved him very ... *much;* and when Jesus said, that all his disciples would be offended because of him this night, that is, what, children? *That they would be afraid to follow Jesus that ... night*, when he was to be ... *crucified.* No, children, not crucified—when he was to be betrayed by ... *Judas.* Well, and what said Peter? *Though every one be offended, I'll not be offended,* and I will lay down my ... *life* for ... *thee.* Very well, children, and did Peter lay down his life for his Master? *No, Sir.* Well, what answer did Jesus make to Peter? This ... *night*, before the ... *cock crow twice*, that is, ... *two times*, thou shalt ... *deny me thrice.* And did that take place? *Yes.* Go on, if you please; tell me all about what took place? Jesus was first betrayed by ... *Judas*, and taken away by the ... *Jews*, and the ... *soldiers.* What kind of soldiers? *Roman soldiers, Sir*— to the judgment ... *hall*,—and Peter was warming himself at the ... *fire*, for it was night; and one of the ... *maids* of the high ... *priest* said ... *that he was one of Christ's disciples*,—and another maid saw ... *Peter also*, and said, that he had been with ... *Jesus.* Now, what answer did Peter give to these two maids? did he appear very bold, and say he was willing to ... *die* for ... *Jesus? No, Sir; he denied and told a lie, and said, that he did not understand what they were saying. Yes, and he*

obvious meaning. The stimulating power of this mixture of the elliptical and interrogatory plan of teaching must be self-evident; and at the same time, we believe, it cultivates quite as correct feelings as any other principle of emulation.

swore too, and said bad words. Yes, children, it was shocking, indeed. Peter did swear; but it was not at the time we are speaking about just now that he said bad words; it was a little after, when they that stood by said to him, the third time, that he was one of them, and that he was a ... *Galilean,* for his ... *speech,* that is, his tone of voice, was like what, children? *Was like the Galileans.* And during this time what did the cock do? *It crowed, Sir.* What did Jesus say? Before the cock ... *crow* twice, thou shalt ... *deny me thrice.* Well, did this happen? *Yes; after the cock crowed the second time, Peter was sorry* for denying ... *Christ.* What made him sorry? *It was Jesus turning and looking* upon ... *him,* and Peter remembered what ... *Jesus had said to him,* and Peter went out and wept ... *bitterly;* that is, he was very ... *sorry.* Did Peter fall into sin because he was one of Christ's disciples, do you think, or did he deny him because he trusted in his own strength? *You told us yesterday, Master, it was because he forgot to trust in God,* that he did all these ... *bad things.* Now, children, what lesson does this story of Peter teach us? It teaches you ... *not to be proud,* nor too confident of ... *ourselves.* What commandment did Peter break when he denied his Master, and said he did not know him? *The ninth.* And which commandment did he break on account of swearing? Don't you remember, children? The oldest class, at all events, ought to know. Well, repeat the words of the commandment itself, if you don't know the number of it, for the meaning is the principal thing. *Sir, it is, " Thou shalt*

not take the name of the Lord thy God in vain."
Now, I'll tell you, children, which it is,—it is
the third commandment. Remember that again,
if you please. *Yes.*

Master, was Peter a bad man? I am very
glad this little boy asks such a question; some of
the scholars will please answer it. You know,
children, I told you yesterday what the Bible said
about Peter. Girls, please answer this little boy's
question. *Peter was not a very good man once,
but afterwards Jesus made him a very good man,
and a great preacher too, and there was*—shall I
help you my dear—three thousand converted in
one day by one of his... *sermons.* Very right, my
little girl; you see the power of God in changing
the bad... *heart*, and making it... *good.*

Children. Please, Master, yesterday you promised to give us a lesson to-day about the fire
that Peter warmed himself at.

Master. Very right, children, I promised to
give you a lesson on the fire; but as the Bible
does not say what the fire Peter warmed himself at
was made of, suppose we explain the school-room
fire, and then you will have a better understanding of what is meant by a... *fire.* I did not,
however, mean it for this day's lesson, but for
a Natural History lesson on Friday next;—
however, as this is a very cold day, and some of
you seem to expect it, we shall have a lesson on
the fire, and we may return to it on Friday, when
we shall, also, notice some other parts of the Bible
which speak about... *fire*, as well as the fire at
which Peter warmed himself. Now then, children, look where our worthy visitor sits, look at

the fire-place, and tell me what a fire is. *It's coals, Sir.*——Let me see; is this piece of black coal I have got in the tongs a fire, children?

Children. No, Sir; that's a piece of coal.

Master. Well, did you not say to me just now that a fire was coals? if so, this piece of coal must be a fire.

Children. It's coals burning.

Master. Very right, children, coals burning make a fire—then the fire at which the old lady now sits is made of what? *Of coals.* Are fires made of any thing else, children?

Children. No, Sir.

Master. Think now, if you please, and see if fires are made of nothing else but coals. Last year, children, during our short vacation, I remember being in the Highlands with Mrs. —— and my little children; and when we entered a Highland hut or house, on the middle of the floor there was a nice fire burning. What was it made of, think you, children? *Peats, Sir, peats*——*My aunty lives in the Highlands, and she burns peats*——*Master, my mother whiles kindles the fire with a bit peat.*——Then, it appears, from what you say, that a fire may be made of peats as well as of coals? *Yes.* Well, can any thing else make a fire, children? *No, Sir.* What, can nothing else be used to make a fire? You recollect the other day little Andrew Watson, when he was made monitor for the first time at a counting lesson, did a very naughty trick. Instead of walking up the steps into the...*rostrum,* as he ought to have...*done,* he took this...*chair* for the purpose, and being in a great...*hurry,* knowing he was doing...*wrong*, he...*tumbled* it over, and broke the...*back of it*, so I was obliged to go to the...*wright's shop*, to ask him to...*mend it*, and when I was there I saw the glue-pot on the fire—what was the fire made of, think you, children? *Of sticks, Master; shavings, bits o' wood.* Then you say, children, that a fire may be made, not only of coals or peats, but also of wood or shavings? *Yes; any thing that burns will make a fire,—any thing bleezing is a fire,—— Master, the sun's a fire,—a tawnle* [bonfire] *is a big fire.——Master, I once saw a house on fire in the Gorbals, and I was frightened.* Well, children, although a house on fire is very dreadful and destructive, yet in cold winter weather like this, a small fire is a very comfortable thing: is it not, children? *Yes, Sir.* To whom are we indebted for coals and peats, and what else... *wood,* to make fires of? *To God.* Ought we then to forget God, and never think of him, when he gives us so many good things? *No, we should be very thankful.* For what? *For a good fire,* and for every...*thing else.* It is God who gives you, how much, children? *Every thing.* Now, children, although this is the first lesson on the school-room fire, and what substances a fire may be made of, yet, perhaps, you may remember some of our Bible stories which speak about fire? *Yes, Sir.* Mention one or two. *Fire and brimstone rained from Heaven on Sodom and Gomorrah.* For what, children? *For their great wickedness.* Well, another passage. Go on, if you please. *Isaac carried the fire up the mountain, where his father, Abraham, intended making him a sacrifice, and burning him up with fire.* And was Isaac actually sacrificed and burned? *No; God sent a ram in his place, and his father took it.* Any other passage, children? *Yes. At the last day the earth will be burned up with fire.* Will not that be an awful day to thoughtless, bad children? *Yes, awful—very awful.* Will good children, those that love Christ, and hate sin, be afraid? *No. They'll be very happy, and aye singing.* How singing? *Singing praise for being saved from the bad place, and for getting into the happy place.* Who will have saved them from that dreadful place? *Jesus Christ.* What did He do? *He died for sinners.* Like whom, children? *Like us.* Your parents are very kind to you, are they not, children. *Yes, Sir, very kind.* Ought you not, then, to love them for being so kind, and doing so much for you? *Yes.* Can Jesus Christ do as much for you as your parents? *Yes. He can save us from the bad place, and raise us to Heaven.* Can your parents do that for you? *No, none but Christ.* Well, if none can do as much for you as Christ, whom ought you to love above all things? *We ought to love Christ above all... things.* Above all things! for what? *For what he has done and suffered for us.*

You know, children, we were speaking about the fire; every thing in nature is divided into— what? *Three kingdoms.* Mention these three divisions. *Animal, vegetable, and mineral.* To which of the three does coal belong? *Mineral, Sir.* How do you know that? *Because it comes out of the ground.* Is every thing mineral that comes out of the ground—potatoes, for example?

*No. Potatoes grow, and are vegetable ; but coals
are got far, far below the ground, in a pit, and don't
grow.* Do minerals grow? *No.* Do vegetables
grow? *Yes, they have life.* Wh) causes the
vegetables to grow? *God.* What means does
God use to make them grow besides the earth?
He makes the sun to shine, and sends rain. How
then do you think the coals are mineral? *Because they have no life, and are found too far
below the ground to grow.* Can you tell me to
which division peats belong—are they vegetable
or mineral? *We don't know, Sir.* Well, I will
tell you about peats. It is thought peats grow in
some such way as the following: Large forests of
trees—you know what forests are? *Yes, great
big heaps of trees together.* Well, then, large
forests have been cut down, or have fallen down
with age, or from other causes, and after lying
many years, perhaps many hundreds of years, a
kind of moss grows upon them, and mixes with
the water and rain, every year growing higher
and higher upon the large trunks of the fallen...
trees, until it gets to be many feet...*deep,* oftentimes, and when cut with spades, and shaped and
dried, that mossy substance forms—what, children?
Peats, Sir. Of what shape are peats, children?
*They are oblong. They must be vegetable, Sir,
when they grow.* Now, which way will the trunks
of the trees be lying, think you, children? *Horizontal ; straight along the ground, and the moss
at the top, above them.* Coals, then, are...*mineral,*
and peats are...*vegetable.* Very right. Now you
say minerals don't grow, but vegetables...*grow.*
What is it that both grows and feels too? *An*

animal, Sir. Mention the name of an animal.
A dog, a horse, a cat, a mouse, a duck. Any
thing else ? *Yes, man is an animal.* Is man a
mere animal ? *No, he has reason.* Then man
both...*lives,*—what next...*feels,*—and what next
...*thinks.* Yes, thinks or...*reasons ;* then man is,
or ought to be, what, children ? A reasonable
...*being.* Now, children, I hope you will make
out what is meant by a fire, and what uses may
be made of it ; and when we talk about God's
works, or the nice things we are told in the ... *Bible,*
that we 'will think about...*them,* and use our ...
reason, for you know all that God says and does
is right and ... *reasonable.*

Master. Now, children, for a little exercise—
Clap hands——Look at me, if you please——
Move elbow-joints—shoulders—wrists—finger-
joints. Go on smartly,——that's right——now
then—hands on knees——silence. Who'll be
monitor at a song ? Suppose we have

THE SHEEP.

TUNE—" *Ye Banks and Braes,*" &c.

Hark now to me, and silence keep,
And we will talk about the sheep ;
For sheep are harmless, and we know
That on their backs the wool does grow.

The sheep are taken once a year,
And plunged in water clean and clear ;
And there they swim, but never bite,
While men do wash them clean and white.

And then they take them, fat or lean,
Clip off the wool, both short and clean ;

And this is call'd, we understand,
Sheering the sheep throughout the land.

So then they take the wool so white,
And pack it up in bags quite tight;
And then they take these bags so full,
And sell to men that deal in wool.

The wool is washed and combed with hand,
Then it is spun with wheel and band;
And then with shuttle very soon
Wove into cloth within the loom.

The cloth is first sent to be dyed;
Then it is washed, and pressed, and dried;
The tailor then cuts out with care,
The clothes that men and boys do wear.

Master. Well, children, be very quiet while we go over yesterday afternoon's lesson, on

BIBLE GEOGRAPHY,

In connection with the Israelites journeying from —where, children? *Egypt, to the land of Canaan.* Well, let all answer in one voice, answer me quickly, and whenever I stop a single moment be sure you help me with the words as you are accustomed to do. What was the particular part of the journey? *The Children of Israel crossing the Red Sea.* Yes, the particular part of that history was their walking through the... *Red Sea,* on... *dry land.* Now, give me some account of this nice... *story.* You know who the children of Israel were? *Yes, descendants of Jacob.* And all about the reasons which induced them to leave Egypt, and flee into the wilderness? *Yes, we do.*

Where is the Red Sea? *It joins Egypt——You told us that it divides Egypt from Arabia.* In what quarter of the globe is Egypt? *In Africa, where the black folks live.* Why is the Sea called the Red Sea, and not the Black Sea? *Because, you told us, Master, that the sand or rock at the bottom is red,* and the water being very... *clear, the bottom is seen,* and makes the water appear... *red.* And, therefore, it is called the... *Red Sea.* Well, who passed through the Red Sea? *The Israelites.* Who parted the Red Sea? *Moses.* Do you say Moses parted the Red Sea? *No, Sir, God did it.* Yes, my little children, God did it. Could any man divide a deep sea, and make the water stand like a wall on each side, till you walked through on dry land? *No, Sir, no man could do that.* Who pursued the Israelites? *Pharaoh and his army.* Had king Pharaoh any thing else with him besides fighting men in his army? *Yes, a heap of coaches.* Were the coaches like ours, covered in at the top? *No, they were open chariots, that the men could fight in.* Did the Egyptians overtake the Israelites? *No, they were all drowned in the sea, every one of them.* Who thus delivered the Israelites, when they were in such distress? *God.* Who can deliver you when in danger, and to whom should you pray for assistance? *God.* Never forget, then, my little children, that God can deliver you from every difficulty, and He loves when little children ask His assistance. But, at the same time, always remember this, that it is only when we are seeking to do right that we can expect God to help

us. Tell me what that pretty hymn says about
little children praying :—

> " Satan trembles when he sees
> The youngest child upon his knees."

How do you know that God loves little children
to come unto Him? *Because Jesus, when on earth,
said, " Suffer little children to come unto me, and
forbid them not."* Well, I see you remember so
far; but as our time is now short, we must leave
the many particulars of this beautiful story till our
next lesson on the journey through the wilderness. You will perceive, Mistress, that Scripture
stories are almost inexhaustible, and he is not
ignorant who is acquainted simply with what the
Bible contains in its various and interesting history—in its precepts—its plainest announcements,
and innumerable metaphors.

Granny. Deed ay, Sir, a' very right, to be
sure, but ye'll deal cannily, nae doubt, wi' sic sacred things.

Master. A very proper precaution, certainly,
Mistress; but in this, I believe, we will agree, that
Scripture is only useful to us in as far as it is understood, and rendered applicable to the purposes
of this life, and the foundation of our hopes in
regard to the life which is to come. We shall
sing two verses of a hymn, children.

O GOD OF BETHEL! BY WHOSE HAND.

> " O God of Bethel! by whose hand
> Thy people still are fed;
> Who through this weary pilgrimage
> Hast all our fathers led :

"Our vows, our prayers, we now present
Before thy throne of grace:
God of our fathers! be the God
Of their succeeding race."

Master. Now, when you are all quiet, and comfortably seated, we shall revise the lesson of last week on NATURAL HISTORY, and see if you remember it. You will please observe, Mistress, we must recur again and again to every story, and every division or incident in a story, until the children are thoroughly grounded in every particular. Bible knowledge is not to be obtained at a single glance, or simply by reading a chapter. No, Mistress, it must be studied; and it can be made, even to children, a most pleasing study. What was the story about, children? *It was about Christ riding into Jerusalem upon an ass. No, Sir, it was Balaam's ass.* Yes, children, this little boy is right—the last story we had upon the ass was in Balaam's history. It was the week before we were upon Christ's riding into Jerusalem. What picture is this I have in my hand? *Balaam riding upon an ass.* Now, look at the ass, whilst I point to it;—what is this? *The head.* And this? *The eye.* Which eye? *The left, Sir; the other's turned away, we don't see it.* And this? *The right ear.* This? *The left hind hoof.* This? *The left ear.* Are its ears long or short? *Long.* Tell me what this is: go on quickly as I point. *Mouth—neck—chest—back—tail—shoulder.* How many feet has it got? *Four; it is a quadruped.* What sort of an animal is the ass; is it a very gentle, affectionate creature, like the dog? *No, Sir, it is a stupid beast.* Animal, you ought to say, children. Yes, certainly it is much more stubborn than the horse or the dog, but still it is a useful animal. *Yes, Master, the tinkers use them to carry things.* Who rode upon an ass, meek and lowly, though a King, and King of kings? *Jesus.* And who employed the ass to speak to, and reprove, the false prophet? *God.* Mention the name of the false prophet. *Balaam ; he was a bad man, and he was going away on the ass to do a bad thing against the Lord ; and he struck the ass.* Well, and what then—why did Balaam strike the ass? *Because there was an angel on the side of the road, with a sword in his hand.* Did Balaam see the angel? *No, Sir.* Who saw the angel? *The ass.* And, therefore, Balaam struck ... *the ass.* Well, and what then? God made the ass ... *speak*, and reproved his cruel ... *master.* Who was Balaam going down to see? *Balak.* What object had Balaam in going with the princes of Moab down to Balak? Was it to do the will of God, whom Balaam professed to serve, and was it to tell what God desired him to say? *No. He was fond of money, and wanted to get some,* even though at the expense of displeasing ... *God.* Yes; what a sad thing covetousness is! You know, children, what covetousness means? *It is wishing very much to have what other people have,* and what we have no right to ... *get.* Covetousness, also, is loving—what, children? ... *money*, and making it a chief ... *good.* Now, I hope none of you, my dear children, will ever think money a chief good; otherwise, the love of it may lead you to do many bad ... *things*, like ... *Balaam*, the bad ...

prophet. Well, I see the most of you remember so far pretty well. We must go on with the

LESSON FOR THE DAY—(TUESDAY)—

Which was, children, ... *the Bear.* Yes, the bear; but in order to cheer you up, you may go to the play-ground for a few minutes, and it will circulate your blood nicely this chilly weather.

Here's a fine little boy who came to the school yesterday morning, and he does not know much yet of what is going on; come here, my little boy, and sit on this chair, and we shall have a lesson together—don't be frightened, sit down like a good boy. Give me your hand; how many hands has this boy, children? *Two, Sir.* How many fingers? *Ten.* How many little fingers? *Two,* How many feet? *Two.* Who was it that got a new coat from his mother once a-year? *It was little Samuel.* Yes, it was Samuel, that good ... *boy,* who always came when he was ... *bidden.* Yes, when he was called he always ran ... *quick.* What is this little boy's jacket made of? *Master, was Samuel's jacket like that little boy's?* The Bible does not say what it was made of, whether linen, like the ephod, or what it was. *That boy's jacket is made of wool, Master.* What kind of wool, children—is it cotton-wool? *No, sheep's wool.* Who cuts the wool off the sheep's back? *The shepherds.* Now tell me what is done with the wool after that, before it comes to be a jacket, children? *It is first washed and cleaned—then spun into yarn—then dyed by the dyer*——Well, go on. *Then the winders and weavers get it, and then it is sent to a mill, and splashed backwards and forwards, and squeezed until it becomes thick.* Thick enough for what? *For coats and jackets.* And then it is made by a... *tailor,* into ...*jackets,* and ...*coats,* and ...*trowsers,* and ...*many other things.* Very well, children; and who pays for all this? *His mother.* And who gives his mother the money? *His father, Sir.* Then who gives it to his father? *He works for it.* And who gives his father health and strength to work for the money? *God.* To whom, then, is this little boy really indebted for his jacket, and for a kind father to work for it, and to buy it for him? *To God.* Yes, it is to the kindness of God that this little boy is indebted for a kind father and mother to work for him; and what more, children? *For making the wool to grow on the sheep's back.* Yes, and for providing all the other things for making the... *cloth,* the dye-stuffs to... *dye with,* and wood to make the wheels, and ...*shuttles, Master*—and what else? *The loom-stead.* Yes, and stones and bricks to build the... *mills.* Yes, the factories. What are stones and bricks? *Minerals, Sir.* Yes, and iron too, to make what, children, think you? *The shears.* And what else? I will tell you, children; the wheels of the machinery for spinning the yarn, and for weaving the... *cloth;* and how many other things did God make? *He made every thing.* Ought we not, then, to love such a very kind and good God? how should we feel, children? *Feel grateful.* Now, my little children, what does this boy sit on? *A chair.* Who made the wood? *God made the wood to grow.* Very right. God made the

wood. Then who made the chair? *A wright.*
What is a wright, children? *A man that makes
things out of wood.* Then God made the ... *wood,*
and a man made the ... *chair.* But did not God
make the man too? *Yes.* That will do, my
little boy, for your first lesson. You won't forget
this lesson that the scholars have taught you just
now, will you? *No, no, Sir.*

Master. Now, my little children, Mistress will
take you into the play-ground for a little. I
shall follow directly. First class up—off you
go—now the second sing away :—

> " What is infant education?
> Universal information ;
> Amusement and knowledge well combined."

Granny. Weel, really, I haena met wi' ony
thing this lang time that has sae dumfoundered
me as this—whar did ye find out this way o'
keeping weans quiet, and learning just bits o' babbies sic wonderfu' knowledge. Was it ony thing
about the Mechanics' Ha', in George Street, that
put it in your heads, ken ye?

Master. No, Mistress, it was not the Mechanics' Institution that informed us on the subject;
though that, on many points, is an excellent institution, and ought to have the support of every
man who wishes well to his country.

Granny. Do they ken ony thing about this way
there, then, think ye?

Master. Not much, I believe.

Granny. Do the College gentry ;—they'll ken,
nae doubt?

Master. The Professors of the College, you

know, are great and learned men ; we could not expect them to take much notice of our system, called the Infant system. But, quietly, Mistress, neither the folks in High Street nor George Street would repent adopting a little more of it than they do : I mean more particularly the moral training, Madam.

Granny. Deed, gin ye gang on a' days as I hae seen ye, since I came in the day, I daursay the callants wi' the red gowns would hae a thought better manners than a wheen o' them hae whiles : but ye'll no say I said this, for there's a very decent chiel o' a student bides but-an-ben on our stairhead, he ne'er forgets " the one thing needful." He's just a blessing to a' the neebour-hood, that he is ; he's a bit gude lad atweel.

Master. Now, since the children are at play, I shall be happy to take a few minutes, and walk round the room with you, in order to show our different apparatus. We have lesson-posts—arithmetic ball-frames—brass figures—pictures of the various trades, and an immense variety of Scripture and other picture lesson-boards.

Granny. Now, Sir, about

THE BALL-FRAME.

—Counting wi' balls ; what's the use o' counting wi' balls. Ye say that this school is ane chiefly for Scripture knowledge: what connection has Scripture wi' counting, ken ye, Sir ?

Master. Why, Mistress, I shall give a very short answer. Without the knowledge of figures, we could not find out the chapter or verse in any passage of Scripture. I presume this will satisfy you for the present. You see there are 144 balls, corresponding to the number in the multiplication table; they are placed horizontally on brass wires on the frame—each ball, varying in colour, attracts the child's eye, even at a distance. Thus, when the Master or Monitor says, twice two are four, the understanding of the child perceives that each unit is represented by a something; in fact, that four means four balls. This exercise of the ball-frame in a powerful degree cultivates the understanding, sharpens the perceptive powers, and assists in giving a tone of individuality to the child for life. But, Mistress, take a peep, if you please, at our Scripture and other lessons.

Granny. Scripture—Scripture lessons; a' right —a' right, to be sure; but ye hae rather owre mony monkey and other pictures to learn the weans, I'm thinking.

Master. Well, Mistress, once for all, I shall give for answer, if God made every thing, he also made every thing in wisdom, for the contemplation and happiness of his own animate creation; and although we, short-sighted creatures, like an insect on the fly-wheel of a steam-engine, may not be able to trace the entireness or consistency of that natural and moral machinery which he has thought fit to set a-moving, is it right or proper for us, think you, to withhold from any, even the youngest, those small portions of his works and ways, which are apparent, and from which, limited as they are, we can trace the power, wisdom, and goodness of a God, who is wonderful in counsel, and excellent in working, and of whose superintending care, the planet and the sparrow are alike the objects.——Children, now for the

PENCE TABLE.

Tune—"*In my cottage near a wood.*"

Twenty pence are one and eightpence,
   That we can't afford to lose;
Thirty pence are two and sixpence,
   That will buy a pair of shoes.

Forty pence are three and fourpence,
   That is paid for certain fees;
Fifty pence are four and twopence,
   That will buy five pounds of cheese.

Sixty pence will make five shillings,
   Which, we learn, are just a crown;
Seventy pence are five and tenpence,
   That is known throughout the town.

Eighty pence are six and eightpence,
   We'll always try to think on that;
Ninety pence are seven and sixpence,
   That will buy a beaver hat.

A hundred pence are eight and fourpence,
   Which is taught in th' Infant School;
Eightpence more make just nine shillings,
   So we end this pretty rule.

Granny. That's very right, Sir. But, Maister, I think I maun be awa, for my rheumatics plagued me a gude wee on the causey stanes afore I came in. I haena got my crack half o'er yet.—Let me, howsomever, gie ye a bit o' advice. Ye see ye're a young man, and maybe a thought new-

M

fanglesome eneugh in your ways about perpendiculars and monkey tricks, and nonsense o’ that kind; now, Sir, tak’ an auld wife’s opinion. My opinion is, Sir, that a’ things should be counted naething in comparison wi’ the knowledge of Christ Jesus, my Lord.

Master. In this sentiment we most heartily agree; but you really ought not to be so prejudiced. You know infants, from the moment they can speak, nay, long before that period, are learning something, either good or evil. Now, why should not their minds, from the earliest period, be directed intellectually to know, and rationally to choose, what is right and good? Be assured, if Parents and Teachers neglect to sow good seed, Satan will not omit to sow the tares. Now, our duty is to toss about the weeds so frequently that they may have no time to grow.

Granny. Ye’re really a queer chiel; but next time I come here, I’ll bring my son Sandy wi’ me; he’s weel learned—that he is, and will be upsides with ye, Maister. He’s quicker in the uptak’ than me, and no sae saft o’ the belief. He’s been hearing hale three lectures in the Ha’;—he tells me they’re about Pneumatics and Hydrostatics; —but I’m thinking I must first mak’ out a visit, for twa weeks, to my cousin, auld lucky Paterson, out at Neilston Parish there.

Master. This is a sad season of the year to pay visits.

Granny. Atweel is’t, but my cousin, puir body, we were eildens [equals] at the school thegither, and she sends word to me that she’s gaun aff the stage very soon, and gin I dinna see her e’enow,

that we'll no maybe meet till we see the King
in his beauty, face to face,—what a sight will
that be, Maister!—wi' a' the ransomed friends
that hae stept afore us.——I'll tak' my stick noo,
gin ye please, and aff. Gude day, Sir.

Master. One word, Mistress, before you go: I
have been looking at you ever since you entered
the school, you put me so much in mind of one
of the old wives I used to see when a boy, sitting
on Dr. Balfour's pulpit stair.

Granny. Dr. Ba'four, Dr. Ba'four!—did ye ken
Dr. Balfour, did ye?

Master. I used to hear him preach sometimes.

Granny. Preach, preach; he was a preacher
o' the right sort, that he was, worthy man o' grace;
my vera heart feels warm whan ye speak o' that
faithfu' servant o' Christ;—mony a rap the book-
board got wi' his neeve, that it did. Nae cauld
harangues did he gie,—na, na, the everlasting
Gospel cam' out sae warm, that ne'er ane o' the
frailty e'er fand a puff o' cauld the steevest frost
o' winter. Warm preachers mak' warm hearers,
that's the truth, Sir,—that it is.

Master. He was a worthy man, and very accessible, I believe, to all his people.

Granny. Deed ye ne'er tauld a truer story nor
that. Ay, ay, accessible was he at a' times, in
season and out o' season,—that he was. Nae ill
answer did a body get at his door,—na, na; mony
a spirit has been refreshed wi' his savoury words,
—they cam' just wi' power very aften, that they
did. He had a funny, jocular way o' his ain, to be
sure, for the like whiles we ettled to say a word
or twa; but, as it was a' to the bargain o' the spi-

ritual food, words aye failed us against the honest man. Ay, ay, he's awa' noo, and a' the crowd o' the ripe worthies, right and left o' him, are gathered tae; nane left atweel but ane or twa o' the green hauns like me. May we be soon ripe, Maister, for the barn-yard, and for our Father's house;——but we should wait patiently—that we should.

Master. I fear these subjects must be left to some future opportunity; perhaps, when you bring your son with you, we may arrange matters, so as to spend more time.

Granny. Gude day, then, Maister.——I say, these evergreen bushes will stand a lang time amang sic a flock o' weans, I'm thinking.

Master. Yes, they'll stand—and if we had ripe strawberries or apples here for months together, they would, I assure you, never be touched. Our motto is, "Look at every thing, and touch nothing."

Granny. Maister, ye're telling the truth, are ye.——Leezy, is this you, what's brought ye here, lassie?

Leezy. Ye see, I noticed a drop or twa o' rain fa'ing, and I just daunered this length. Put this cloak on your shouthers, Granny, gin ye like.

Granny. Ay, ye're a' bit thoughtsome lassie, atweel.

[*Grandmother retires with her Daughter-in-law from the Infant School.*]

Leezy. Tak' my arm, Granny, gin ye please. ——Weel, Granny, I'll no say but ye hae seen some fairlies the day——I wouldna wonder.

Granny. Ye're just a haveril, Leezy, to talk about fairlies when the best interests o' your weans are at stake; whatfore did ye no gang into the school yoursel', and see and speer about things?

Leezy. Deed, I wouldna hae muckle to do gin I was to hunt and look after weans a' day, they're weel eneugh there I'll warrand;—and when they're no there they maun just play about like the lave, they'll be nae waur than their neebours, I reckon.

Granny. What! nae waur than their neebours, Leezy, wha swear—say bad words—tell lies—play on the Sabbath-day, and whiles mak' free wi' things that cross their gait!——Ay, ay, Leezy, to be nae waur than them is to be ill eneugh atweel!

Leezy. Now, Granny, ye're very unreasonable to blame me for no looking after my weans; I mind them extraordinary weel, I think, when I mak' their porritch twice a-day; no to speak o' cleeding them, and washing their hands and face sae often as their maister gars me do;—and ye see, Granny, in our wee house, when I hae my turns to put by, I'm glad eneugh to get them out at the door, puir things;——what can wark-folk do, think ye, Granny?

Granny. And our Sandy, puir fallow, has little time either; but he tak's a walk wi' them whiles, I'm thinking.

Leezy. Deed, ye ken baith Sandy and me are working a' day—he's at the loom, and I hae his pirns to wind—but atweel-a-wat, mony a time they sit on Sandy's knee at gloamin, mair parti-cularly since Mary and Geordie gaed to the Infant

School. The bits o' weans tell a' the stories they learn there, and my gudeman speers sae mony questions about the wonderful things they learn there, that I whiles think he'll no syne gang to his wark at a'; and he's sae fond o' singing, that he gars the weans sing ilka hymn they learn, till my head is like to be deaved every night afore THE READING—and up again wi' the laverocks in the morning.

Granny. Ay, ay, Leezy, and should we no pray, that out o' the mouths of babes and sucklings He may perfect praise.

Leezy. Very right, Granny, I wish we were a' as gude as we should be; deed, a heap o' us would thole amends, to be sure: but what a comfort Sandy is to me, Granny! coming straught frae his wark at e'en;—clubs he gangs na to, nor a baubee does he spend in a public-house, like a heap o' them at our gait-end, keeping their wives and families often starving for a mouthfu' o' meat.

Granny. Deed I dinna doubt but ye bulk big eneugh in his een, and deserve a' the attention ye get, lassie, atweel; howsomever, may you and he baith be like the lave that are gaen, for ye ken I hae buried seven in my time, and hae gude hopes o' them a', Leezy—sax bairns, bonny bairns, and the father at the hinderend, honest man! he was just the prince o' men—that he was, worthy man! * * * * * * Gude day, my bonny lassie, I'm muckle obliged for your arm this length——

Leezy. Ye'll no come then, will ye, Granny?

Granny. I'll no say what I may do, gin we're spared in health till the time; but we'll see.

Leezy. Na, that's no like you, Granny, to be sae muckle affected; speak a minute, gin ye please. Ye see Peggy Nesbit, the mantua-maker, and me, are at a new Sabbath-day gown; for Sandy says I maun stay in nae langer frae the kirk now, since wee Tammie's spained, and he's willing to stay in himsel', and haud the babbie ae half the day. That'll please you, I'm sure, Granny. Come your wa's up the night at seven, gin ye please, and tell a' about this grand school ye're sae desperately proud o';—auld folk maun be excused atweel, for they're a wee doitit whiles.

Granny. Deed I dare say I'm doitit eneugh at times, but I hae a gude Guide, that I hae, who will put me on the right road again. I staucher often, Leezy, and am doitit too; but he'll land me safe at last—that he will. He'll "ne'er leave me, nor forsake me;" na, na, Leezy——Gude day, Leezy,—gude day.

CHAPTER V.

GRANDMOTHER'S SECOND VISIT TO THE INFANT SCHOOL.

WEDNESDAY FORENOON.

[GRANNY, *dressed in her new-made cloak, walks to the Infant School, and the outer gate being open, she moves along the play-ground, which she now finds quiet and still as on a Sabbath morn; peeping, however, through the school-room window, she witnesses something very unaccountable—about one hundred and fifty children scrambling on the floor, after something, which her aged vision could not discover.*]

Granny. NAE doubt there's a riot here, and a rebellion too, [said the honest woman to herself,]—whar's the fine discipline, order, and obedience, noo, the Gentleman brags sae muckle about!—but I'll be at him. [So, after two pulls at the bell, the Master presents himself.]

Master. Good day, Mistress.

Granny. Ay, gude day, it's a gude quiet day out-by atweel! but what's this, Maister, what's this?—ye didna expect to be found out at this wark, I'm thinking,—sic a riot ne'er was seen, ane and a' lampin' like a wheen rabbits there, hither and thither. Whatfore do ye no interpose your commands, Maister, and stop this wark? ye'll be for ca'ing this a lesson too, I wouldna wonder!

Master. Well, Mistress, I shall stop the riot, as you call it, immediately; and you will please observe, the moment I strike this bell with the end of my pencil case, every child will be on his feet, straight as a rush and quiet as a lamb, waiting my next order to move to the seats, or to pick up the remainder of the peas still left on the floor. [The bell is touched, all is silent.] To the lesson-posts, children; and you two nearest me will be so good as pick up the scattered peas. Now, children, I hope you who have got most will give some to the very little children who have got few, or perhaps none at all. You see, Mistress, their liberality.

Granny. Weel, that's extraordinary! ye're a witch o' a guesser;——Maister, its just magical, that it is; but I dinna understaun things, I see.

Master. From this frolic and apparent confusion, by simply throwing two or three handful of peas on the floor, as a reward for previous good behaviour, in addition to the bodily exercise it affords, and that generosity you have this moment witnessed, it also teaches mutual forbearance, and that, even in a scramble, children ought to play without quarrelling. No doubt, all lasting moral principle proceeds from the love of God, and the proper fear of God: " Thou God seest me," &c. Still there are many good habits which may be formed in children, both by example and precept, and the conscience of a young unsophisticated child may be kept alive, cultivated and *trained* to a sense of right and wrong, which operates like the hoe, the plough or the harrow, in tossing about the weeds, and preparing the ground for good seed. This therefore is one of the many plans we take to root out the weeds of nature; for quarrelling, fighting, and selfishness, you know, are inherent in us, and it is well that these propensities be early checked; otherwise, they will grow stubborn and luxuriant. Change the heart, of course, no man can profess to do; but while we thus endeavour to " train up children in the way they should go," may we not hope, that, " when old, they will not depart from it."

Granny. Ye speak gay weel to be sure, but you'll maybe be sae obliging as state how ye get Scripture for a' this.

Master. As quarrelling and selfishness are not only natural to all in a greater or less degree, but must be witnessed by all in one shape or other, in real life, we therefore hesitate not to place the children in circumstances in which these feelings will be tried and put to the proof. We shall suppose they have several times before heard such Scripture precepts as these, explained, repeated, and enforced by us: " Love one another;" " Forbearing one another;" " Be courteous, forgiving one another." Then, as already stated, in the case of the peas, their principles are put to the test, and out of any misdemeanor, want of forbearance, or obvious selfishness on the part of any, we are furnished with practical illustrations, whereby to enforce our plain Bible precepts. We shall ask the class at this post, if you please, for one or two proofs that we ought neither to be selfish nor quarrelsome, but that, on the contrary, we ought to forbear and be kind. Now, children, you have heard what I said—Prove that we ought to forbear.... *Forbearing one another in love.* Prove that we ought " to be kind?" ... *Be kindly affectioned one to another....* Prove that we ought to " be courteous." ... *Love as brethren, be dutiful, be courteous.*

Master. Yes, be courteous, that is the proof.

Granny. Now, Sir, ye're no far aff frae the right road noo.

Master. Now, children, for a song.

THE DOG.

I'll never hurt my little dog,
　But stroke and pat his head;
I like to see him wag his tail—
　I like to see him fed.

Poor little thing, how very good,
　And very useful too;
For do you know, that he will mind
　What he is bid to do.

Then I will never hurt my dog,
　Nor ever give him pain;
But I will always treat him kind,
　And he will love again.

A faithful friend he ever is,
　Nor e'er forsakes his trust;
O then, for all the care he takes,
　I'll love my dog—I must!

Master. But, Mistress, I've never got you asked how ye came back so soon; I thought you intended a visit to your friend, Mrs. Paterson. I am happy, however, to see you at any time, or any of our friends.

Granny. Thank ye, Sir; but ye see there's just twa or three questions I want to ask, afore I set off wi' the coach in the morning; for ye maun ken I was at our Leezy's last night, and she had ane or twa o' her cronies there. Maggy Inchbald and twa or three neebour wives sauntered in, and we had a hot dispute about you and your weans. Some will no believe a word I say; others thought a heap o' the school—for mysel', I sleept very little a' night thinking about it; for gin it was all true that ye said, what a wonderfu' change it would mak' amongst us labouring folk, gin a' our bairns were kept aff the street, and trained and educated to a' that's good, frae the time they're babbies.

Master. Your son, Alexander, might have accompanied you, as you promised.

Granny. Weel, ye see, I cam' mysel', for I hadna patience to wait till I cam' back frae Neilston. Sandy's gaun to a burial, and I left the tea-pat masking at the fireside, ready for the four-hours; and I just daunered this length: but, Sir, as I am in a great hurry, ye maun hear a' the objections; and ye'll please answer, gin ye can.

OBJECTIONS.

Master. I cannot promise this instant to answer many objections, for you perceive the different classes are at the lesson-posts, waiting my orders how to proceed; I shall, however, order them to go on so far. Monitors, fix the next set of lesson boards, and go on as you did in the morning.— Well, Mistress, if you please, let me hear what your friends have to say on the subject.

Granny. Na, they're no friends o' mine; but ane says the weans are no taught to read in this school, and that they do naething but play, clap their hands, and the like. Another says it's owre sair confinement for weans like them—o' twa, three, four, or even five, and nane aboon six years o' age. Another didna see the use o' singing sae muckle, and marching athort the place here and there, like a wheen sodgers; and there was ane or twa things I couldna just mysel' answer for. What's the use, Sir, o' flowers and bushes in the play-ground, or cramming the weans thegither in the school on the top o' that seated laft, there?

Master. The Gallery, you mean.

Granny. Ay, ay, it's the Gallery I mean—what's the use o' the gallery?—would forms and desks, like as in my young days, no do as weel, if no better, think ye?

Master. I will explain this by and by; but please to finish the objections.

Granny. Weel, what's the use o' sae mony pictures o' every kind o' thing?—But, I maist forgot ae great objection: it was owre dear, they said, for a mother to pay every quarter three shillings for twa weans, or twa shillings for a single ane, no to speak o' the fash o' cleaning and keeping them decent sae often, as they're obliged to do by your orders, Maister;—but ane and a' say they'll tak' care to hae gude pennyworths o' the school; for now, since they maun pay wages beforehand, no a day will their weans lose frae the school that they can help!

Master. I am exceedingly happy your friends are determined to keep their little ones close at school—this appears more than ever a general feeling; and since wages have been taken in advance, our number has not only increased, but the attendance has been much more regular. Parents, indeed, begin to appreciate this system of Bible training in every point of view. I may

N

state to you, Mistress, that the wages charged, do not, in any case, pay more than one-half or two-thirds of the expense; the remainder must therefore be procured some other way. Private subscription has and will do a little; but, after all, it is but a trifle to the wants of the people. Therefore, unless Government do it, it certainly will not be done. But, Mistress, have you finished your list of grievances?

Granny. Weel, I amaist forgot what ane an' a' insisted on, notwithstanding a' I could unravel —that the weans being sae young, maun forget every thing they learn the moment they leave the School, for I understand ye turn them out when-e'er they grow to six years o' age, just the time they used to begin in my young days to be educated.

Master. To learn to read, I presume you mean, Mistress. Learning to read unquestionably is good—very good; but simply learning to read, we conceive to be a very small portion of a good education. Signs without ideas are utterly useless; we prefer, at their time of life, first giving the idea, before we burden with the sign. The power of reading may be said to be the key of knowledge, but not knowledge itself; and it is important for parents and legislators to keep in view, that this same key which opens the Scriptures to the young mind, also opens up writings of infidelity. How truly important, therefore, to turn this power into a right channel! I assure you, Mistress, I have met with dozens of children, of even ten and twelve years of age, who could read the Bible, but who were ignorant of its con-

tents, and who could not even answer the simple
question, Who was the first man?—ignorant both
of the origin of sin, and the plan of recovery.
But, Mistress, all the objections and difficulties
you have now stated, although common, are, at
the same time, weighty and serious, and I shall
endeavour to answer each in the best way I can:
we must not, however, be so lengthy in our conversation as we were yesterday; for if a Master's
attention is taken much off his ordinary duty, the
scholars are apt to get into disorder, and at this
season of the year, you know, days are short.
Whilst the children are at the *Lesson on Objects*,
I have simply to see that the monitors do their
duty; therefore, if you walk round with me, you
shall see our plan, and, as we proceed, opportunity
may be afforded of answering some of the objections, without at all interfering with our ordinary
course of lessons.

Granny. Weel, Maister, I canna mind a' ye
said e'enow; and, as ye say, I reckon our converse
maun be short after this: but ye ken, Sir, I'm no
sae gleg as I used to be, when a lassie. Ye'll excuse me at a time, I'm thinking.

WILL CHILDREN FORGET ALL THEY LEARN AT AN INFANT SCHOOL?

Master. Before you rise, Mistress, I shall dis-
pose of one of your objections—that children will
forget all they have learned, or been trained to, the
moment they leave the School. Now, Mistress,
is it not a fact, that early impressions are powerful impressions? The character for life is often

early, very early formed. No doubt, children frequently forget what they commit to memory, if not understood; but, as I formerly stated, what is agreeably learned, and clearly understood, is never lost. Whether, Mistress, do you recollect most fondly things of infancy, or those of a later date?

Granny. 'Deed, Sir, that's true; but I forget maist o' the Hymns and Psalms my mother learnt me when very young.

Master. Allow me to ask, Did you understand their meaning?—did you sing them often, as we do, and thus make them the memory of the heart?

Granny. 'Deed I hadna muckle sense then or thought either; I understood naething, atweel, about the meaning.

Master. Very well, then, the whole answer is this: You forgot them because you knew not their meaning; but what is clearly understood is seldom or ever forgot, and easily recalled. I shall notice this again, by and by; but, in the meantime, Mistress, I may say, that I know children who have left our Infant Schools, three, four, and even five years ago, who still retain, and I believe will long retain, a clear remembrance of all they have learned with us. Children, no doubt, who have been withdrawn after *a few weeks'* attendance, may lose the recollection of every thing they learned in school, except the pleasure and delight they experienced with their companions and superintendents; but let a child be trained for two, three, or four years, under our system, and during life, neither the habits formed, the intellectual nor the religious knowledge at-

tained, can ever be effaced. Abstract memory
frequently fails, but the memory of the understanding remains while reason remains. Be assured, Mistress, it was not a well-stocked memory,
nor the knowledge imparted in our parochial
schools alone, which morally elevated Scotland
once above every nation in the universe; but it
was the union of the plain Bible education of her
parochial schools, with the religious, the Christian
homely fireside visits of her parochial clergy, catechising and explaining the Scriptures to both
old and young, from house to house, which rendered Scotland what she was a century or two
ago; and it is the comparative want of this influence now, which has left her to sink below what
she ought to be. Then really was the time,
when, through this united influence, the parent did
fulfil the command originally given to God's ancient people, in regard to teaching and training
their children, " as they walked by the way, as
they sat down, and as they rose up." These,
indeed, were the golden days of old Caledonia,
Mistress, which stamped a moral character upon
her hardy sons, and which, even to this day, make
a Scotchman respected wherever found. Our
large towns, our overgrown parishes, our new and
altered state of society, therefore, render Sabbath
Schools, but more especially the new machine,
Infant Week-day Schools, for moral training, so
absolutely necessary.

Granny. Ye're saying very right, Sir. But
whate'er the days were langsyne, I think they're
no very golden e'enow; for whether our towns
and parishes have grown o'er big, or whether our

labourers have grown o'er few, I'll no say; but I'll say this, Maister, that gin auld ways are no eneugh, of course we must just hae something new.

LESSON-POSTS—FOR FIXING ON THE VARIOUS PICTURES OF OBJECTS.

Master. Now, Mistress, you see five or six children standing and forming half a circle round each Lesson-post, with a little boy or girl, sitting on a stool in the middle, and pointing out the objects on the picture-board to each of the class. Each post has a different board attached to it, of Lessons on Objects, such as Birds, Beasts, Trades, Children's amusements, and Scripture history of Samuel, David, Moses, Eli, Joseph, Timothy, &c.—the miracles of Christ, also of his Parables, the Good Samaritan, the prodigal Son, The Lost Sheep, &c. Each class, having named the objects after the monitors, at the sound of my small bell, or whistle, moves from post to post, until all the lessons are gone over; and as each class finishes at the last post, and which is nearest the door, they move, singing, into the play-ground, not however with fury and confusion, as if breaking loose from a cage, but with suitable propriety. Unquestionably a play-ground to them, as to all children, is acceptable; but the lessons and amusements of the School as well as the play-ground, are so arranged, that it is altogether a moral restraint which is exercised; and therefore emphatically, and with truth, do the children sing, " School is a pleasure." You will excuse this digression, for I had almost forgot my subject. Well then, when the children return from the play-ground, and are seated in the gallery, it is my duty to take up some one or other of these pictures, and endeavour to explain, and draw forth from the children such useful lessons as they are naturally calculated to impart, and it is surprising what a powerful influence the *drawing forth* plan has on the minds of Infants. It fixes an individuality on all that is said or done, keeping in view, to ground them, as much as possible, on Bible History, or Bible illustrations; we also endeavour to trace their simple elements and composition, classifying each article or portion of an article, as belonging to the Animal, Vegetable, or Mineral Kingdoms. These distinctions a child of three or four years of age very quickly understands; and whilst the streams are traced, we do not forget the Fountain, the Grand Source and centre of all Nature, and of all her springs.

Granny. Weel, let me see what the bits o' weans are learning, bonny things!—A Tinsmith —A Smiddy—ay——Horse-Shoeing——Clock-face——Goosy Ganders—nae doubt——Owls ——Turkeys——Grasshoppers——Locusts—terrible beasts, to be sure——Frogs—Puddocks, I suppose ye mean, Sir?—ye're no nice in your company here, I think.——What's next us?—let me see what my glasses say, for the print on some o' thae boards is small eneugh atweel. A Sow— nae better yet, Maister!——a Collie Dog—yelping thing——a Leopard—bonny beast! what a bonny skin it has, Maister!

Master. We must not, I suspect, judge either beasts or men always by their appearance, Madam.

Granny. Very right, Sir; I stand corrected—but still it's bonny on the outside, whate'er the in may be. I see there's *ae* gude thing I didna notice before—that's a gae decent-sized Bible, on that stand, Maister.

Master. Yes, Mistress, that's a quarto Bible, from which I read the lesson of each day to the children.

Granny. What does the next picture say, Maister?—Jesus walking on the sea—Blessing little children——The good Samaritan—ay, ay, that's gude for ance——Names o' kings—big folk here now, I think——Crowned heads—ay, ay, a crown o' glory, that's the warst wish I hae—— A Joiner's Shop—'deed laddie, I fear ye're trying to join the world and religion: na, na, Sir, that'll no do.

Master. We wish not to join the world and religion, but simply to teach what things in the world, are lawful and right, and what are sinful, of the world, and therefore wrong. " Be diligent in business," you know, Madam.

Granny. Ay; but, Maister, ye hae forgot the hinder-end, " Be fervent in spirit." Dinna split the Bible that way—ye're no the worse o' being looked after, I see.

Master. Now, Mistress, we shall proceed, if you please.

Granny. I'm amaist wearied wi' standing sae lang, for ye ken I'm aulder now than I was ance, ——What's this I see—-weans playing at the ball—cawin' girrs—spinning tops—and, if my een serve me right, twa laddies fighting—twa bairns knocking ane anither down—I reckon I mauna say that's wrang, for a's right that ye hae, nae doubt.

Master. You know, Madam, as children are apt to quarrel, and even fight, we make such pictures a distinct subject of lesson, by exhibiting to the whole children, when seated in the Gallery, the picture of two boys quarrelling, and drawing forth (with the solemnity of a petty jury) their opinion of the practice; and this we find all boys in their cool moments uniformly condemn. Thus, through the medium of such pictures as this, and any accidental quarrel which a new or old scholar may pick with his play-mate, we are furnished with an opportunity, not simply of *teaching*, but *training* the children, and their attention being so frequently turned to the evil practice of fighting, it rarely occurs amongst them; and, when it does, the boys not engaged instantly stop it.

TEACHING TO READ.

Granny. Ay, ye learn the weans to read, I see, as I go alang.

Master. No, Madam, we do not profess to teach the children to read, nor does it form any *necessary* part of our system. If, however, they are taught the form of the letters, which we do by means of brass figures, even were we willing, it is not possible to prevent them going on as far as words of one or two syllables, or proper names. For example, they are taught that the capital letter D, is composed of a perpendicular line and a curve—that O, is simply a circle—that G, is half a circle, with a club foot, and so on. Now, when the picture of a Dog is presented to the eye of a child from day to day, with its name printed in large characters at the bottom, how is it possible to prevent them knowing that D, O, G, means the animal on the picture, namely, a Dog. Farther than words of one or two syllables, or proper names, however, we do not go, nor would we recommend the practice in Infant Schools. The training of Infants to good habits, Physical, Intellectual, Religious and Moral, is of such importance in the early stage of their existence, that little enough time is afforded for such important cultivation. Why then burden them at their age with so uninteresting a subject as learning the A B C, which is too generally knocked into their memories without explanation? Imagine with what relish and interest the Infant scholar of six years of age, in a School for Juvenile Training, would embark in acquiring the knowledge of reading, (to him then almost intuitive,) that he might for himself read about those natural productions, and important moral and religious duties, to which his attention has been so frequently turned, and to the practice of which, perhaps, for fully three years, he has been so happily trained. Teaching to read is not the difficulty; but we have reason to fear, that a smattering of reading received here, would satisfy some parents in regard to the education of their children: and besides, we desire our schools to be additional and preparatory, never to supersede, or prove in any case an interference.

Granny. The light's nae doubt opening up a

wee as ye proceed, Maister, but my een have just
glanced on that inexplicable hen-scart thing;——
but I'm amaist frightit to speak noo, ye hae sae
muckle to say for yoursel'——

Master. Mistress, I presume you mean

GEOMETRICAL FIGURES :—SQUARES, ANGLES, CIRCLES, TRIANGLES, &c.

Granny. Ay, ay, Triangles—triangles, sic a
noise they mak', sometimes, at our gait-en'!—
What's the use o' a' these kickmaleerie strokes,
like L's and C's? Ye'll maybe be sae obliging
as tell me about this, Sir; I think I cast my een
on that board ance before.

Master. Why, after the explanation of the
D, o, G, I thought this would have been unnecessary; however, I shall shortly show you the use
of these figures—lines, or hen-scarts, as you call
them. If you look at this chair, you will find
the legs, seat, back, all form lines. Look at any
article of furniture—a building—a cart, its wheels,
spokes, &c.; one and all of these present lines or
figures, namely, horizontal, perpendicular, curved,
square, circled, angled; all articles of daily use,
every piece of mechanism presents one or more
of these figures on the lesson-board; and, although
it served no higher purpose than amusement, this
practice of affording clear and distinct perception
of things would not be lost. You know, children,
if they are to be taught and trained, must be
amused, and if amusement is rendered improving, so much the better. You know, Madam,
the Bible, which I believe you highly value, is

composed of single letters, and every letter is
formed of single lines. Parents do not object to
having their children at the task of the compound
lines A B C,—would it not, think you, be much
wiser first to learn children the simple lines, and
afterwards the compound, as I have just explained
in the case of the D, o, G; such a plan would render learning the letters at once agreeable and intelligent. This mode of simplification ought to
be carried through every branch of education,
and if the idea cannot always precede the sign,
it ought ever to accompany it.

Granny. Ye're clean ayont me now; all I ken
is, I learned reading before I learned lines: but,
atweel-a-wat, it was a dreigh eneuch job, till I
got the Testament, and could understand what
I was about.

Master. Is that not precisely what I say?
Learning to read is a sad task until the meaning,
and the reason why, is understood.——The last
class I observe is now on the Play-ground; if you
please, therefore, we shall follow, for I or my wife,
or both of us, must always be there to superintend, and take a part in their amusements; keeping the children from quarrelling, and directing,
but not unnecessarily curbing them. From experience, I hesitate not to state my conviction,
that every school, from the Infant, up to those for
the more advanced branches of education, ought
to have an enclosed play-ground—that every
teacher ought to superintend and train his pupils
there, while engaged at their sports; and that a
seminary without enclosed play-ground and superintendent, is destitute, not simply of a good,

but, perhaps, the only practical means of suitably training youth to good and proper habits.

PLAY-GROUND.

Granny. This is really a bonny place, and the weans seem unco pleased-like and happy, Sir. Do they no fall, swinging and running sae fast round these twa big poles?

Master. Very seldom, Mistress; and when they happen to do so from carelessness or inattention, the fall is easy, and very convenient. This kind of amusement is planned so as to afford full and free exercise without danger.

The Gymnastic Pole you allude to, or perpendicular post, you perceive, has four or six ropes attached to a circular iron plate at the top, which moves round in a socket. This plate, is at the height of fifteen or sixteen feet from the ground; the children grasp the rope with both hands, as you see them doing, and their arms being necessarily extended, has the effect of opening the chest, and allowing the lungs freely to play; and as their feet reach the ground, the whole four or six children run as fast as possible round the circle, and the centrifugal accelerated force gradually throws them off their feet, until one and all find themselves whirling in the air to their inexpressible delight; and the motion is continued, by occasionally extending their feet to the ground, and running a few steps. Arms, limbs, and indeed the whole body, are thus exercised and strengthened. This exercise, or swing, is greatly superior to what is commonly termed a swing, which consists of a rope suspended between two trees or poles, with a seat in the middle; the former, or gymnastic pole, is more healthful, less dangerous, and possesses this advantage, that each, in a great measure, regulates his own movements, and, independent of the others, may leave off or continue at pleasure; also, when the art is properly acquired, the exercise affords a greater variety, equal delight, and engages a larger number of children in the same space of ground. Compare such amusements, Mistress, with what are to be met with in streets, lanes, and filthy closses.

Granny. 'Deed and it's better too than obliging puir wee creatures like them to sit at the chimney lug, whiles for an hour or twa thegither, and no speaking ae word, for they daurna. Ye ken, folks have their wark to mind; and what can they do, but gar a wee thing, no muckle bigger than the bairns themsel's, haud them a wee-bit.

Master. You see these children building arches and pillars with wooden bricks—four or five are building, and twenty or thirty appear quite content to be barrowmen, and carry the bricks; the best builders soon show themselves, and the rest acknowledge the superiority.——What's this, child, you have got? *A penny, Sir. I found it among the gravel.* Very well, I shall find an owner by and by. Mistress, provided you have got over your serious objections to a Master's playing with his pupils, I shall take a swing now, for unless I occasionally do so with the children, I cannot possibly know the real disposition of some of our boys and girls.

Granny. Off again!—weel that's strange——

round he goes! I'll say nae mair, that I winna.
——Now, Sir, since ye hae got your legs stretched,
ye maun excuse me ance mair speering a question,
What's the use o' bushes round the play-ground,
just to get them torn down and spoiled? Ye'll
hae flowers in summer too, I'm thinking; for I
see some o' the roots and bits o' leaves aboon the
ground?

Master. I would give for answer, that we have
evergreens, flowers, and bushes, not simply to
embellish the play-ground, but in order that the
children may be trained to " look at every thing
and touch nothing,"——to smell the flowers without
handling them, and to play, even unguarded,
amidst ripe strawberries, cherries, and gooseber-
ries, without pulling one, though within their
reach. I assure you, during a whole summer,
one hundred and fifty children have amused
themselves here without touching one, with the
exception of a single case or two, in regard to
new scholars; but social sympathy and good example, accompanied by the sentiment, " Thou
God seest me," soon moulded them into better
manners. What I have now stated, is the professed purpose of flowers and fruit; sometimes,
however, they lead us to Scripture stories and
metaphors. You know, Mistress, we may think
of the " rose of Sharon," " the lily of the valley,"
" the grass that withereth," " the flower that
fadeth."

Granny. Ay, but ye tak' the plainest. What
mak' ye o' the trees, Sir, the saugh-whauns [wil-
lows] and plane-trees?

Master. Why, Mistress, it was a plane or syca-

more tree that Zaccheus mounted, when he wished
to see Jesus; and, as to the willow, think of cap-
tive Judah's plaintive song, " By Babel's streams
we sat and wept,"—" and hung our harps the
willow-trees upon." You see that boy and girl
with hands behind their backs, smelling, or endeavouring to smell, a Christmas rose, Mistress,
do you?

Granny. Weel-a-weel, Sir, I reckon I maun
just say as our Sandy says, " quietness is best;"
that it is—just so;—but, Maister, Maister! what's
that, what's that? look at that boy stealing that
plaything frae that other ane; why don't ye run
and give him a right good skelpin'? Maister,
have ye nae indignation against that mean laddie
walking behind the other sae slyly, and picking it
up, when he thought naebody saw him?

Master. That certainly is very shocking, and I
am sorry to see it; but, you know, human nature
is human nature—our duty is to instil good moral
and religious principles into these young children, and you see very young children in their
own way do many bad things. I shall endeavour
to show you by and by how we make conscience
speak.

Granny. I could amaist whip him mysel'; for
if you don't stop sin in the very bud, ay, the very
minute it's committed, the heart will get hardened
in sin—that it will, Sir—be assured of that.

Master. There is some truth in what you say,
but we ought not to be rash: cautious inquiry
and investigation have a very powerful influence
on the guilty; besides, I wish to hold up this and
such like bad actions to the detestation of the

whole children, which could not be rendered so obvious, were the boy punished on the spot. I may repeat to you, Mistress, the sentiments of an intimate friend of mine respecting the play-ground :—

An infant play-ground is a little world, where each man, in miniature, acts his part; where every variety of disposition is fully developed, either amiable in itself, or, on the contrary, hurtful to others. Fury and revenge, on the one hand, or mildness and gentleness, on the other—generosity or selfishness—compassion or hard-heartedness—are all fully exhibited—*here a child is known by his doings.* He is trained—not simply instructed; and while the juvenile pickpocket is elsewhere trained to *his* art, children here are taught to exercise and apply the valuable lessons received at home or in school, which in a great measure affect the character in after-life. Here also the conscience—that faithful monitor—is kept alive to a sense of the evil of sin in general, and strengthened in all the natural graces.

The power of right sentiments is put to the proof where all, on a level as to years and pursuits, and being influenced by a perfect sympathy, the dispositions to forbearance or quarrelsomeness are openly and fairly exhibited.

The play-ground, in its effects upon moral character, and in promoting habits of order, obedience, and cleanliness, forms full one-half of the value of what is peculiar to the infant system ;—other schools may, as here, teach Christianity, and cultivate the understanding; but it is the peculiar province of what is termed the Infant

System, with its superintendence, out-doors as well as in-doors, to *train* physically and morally. And this may be applied to children above six as well as below it; always, however, keeping this in view, that the earlier the better, and that *prevention is at all times better than cure.*

Granny. Weel, I'll no oppose ye ony mair; but, afore we gang into the school,—for I'm sair forfoughen, standing sae lang amang this crowd; and they're sae happy, puir things, I amaist forgot my ain weakness,——ye aye speak, Maister, about training; what do you mean by

TRAINING?

Master. By training, we mean not simply instruction addressed to the understanding of a child, but an endeavour to reduce the instruction or right principle into practice, and in circumstances where such principles are called into exercise—in other words, practical wisdom.

For example, a child may be told by his parent or teacher, that in play it is wrong to be overbearing or quarrelsome with his playfellows; but unless he is overlooked by such guardianship when actually at play—suitably checked, and right moral principles enforced and gradually formed into a habit, the child may be said to have been instructed, but certainly not trained. Parents or masters may teach or train children in-doors, and this, under continued restraint, may accomplish, very completely, an eye-obedience; but the same child, when out of sight and among his playfellows, not having been suitably trained, will generally manifest a disposition to be overbearing and quarrelsome, invidious or deceitful, as inclination naturally disposes him.

The development of good or bad propensities in children being more apparent at play than anywhere else, the advocates of early moral training, therefore, choose the time and place of healthful physical exercise and play, as the best and principal arena, both for discovering each LITTLE MAN to himself, as he is, and for endeavouring to train him to what he ought to be. *Let us ever recollect, that while sympathy and example are powerful means in training to good, we see every day among our unrestrained youth its sad effects in training to evil.* Take that boy, who is just five years of age, as an example. Several times in school, even during the few weeks he has been here, has he heard stealing, lying, and deceit, represented as dreadful and detestable sins. Yet, still forgetting that God saw him, and thinking nobody else did, his covetous disposition was such, that he very slyly picked up one of the other boys' playthings, and in a moment stuffed it into his pocket, looking round as if nothing had happened. I trust, however, his simple conviction, by and by, in the face of the whole scholars, may prove to him a salutary check, and a warning to others. You now perceive, I trust, Mistress, what is meant by training ——moral training——and for nearly half an hour you have witnessed one part of our plan for physical or bodily training. Intellectual training you also have seen a little of, in the gallery, in our usual course of instruction, or development, as we term it;—and religion—the religion of the Bible—we make the foundation and cope-stone of the whole system; for although the eye of the Master may train to habit, his superintendence cannot affect or influence the heart, and out of it, you know, Mistress, " are the issues of life." Prov. iv. 23.

Granny. Ay, ay, training! weel-a-weel, gang on wi' training—train them up " in the way they should go," and, gin ye hit the right way o't, the promise, the faithful promise, will be fulfilled, that when old, they will " not depart from it."

Master. You are very right. Mistress, for not only does the Bible say, teach, but train—" train up;" the public, however, are content with, and say *teach*, simply teach, and that too when the children are half grown; and, at the same time, wonder most marvellously that the promise is not fulfilled. Who would expect, for example, that a wall-tree could be so beautifully trained were it permitted to grow for five or six years unattended to? So is it with children. It is a clear principle, founded on experience, and of considerable practical value, that half-a-dozen children of different ages, cannot be so easily nor so well trained, as if the ages of the whole were equal; and the reason is obvious:—in the one case, the power of sympathy is in full operation, in the other it is awanting. It is now time to return to the gallery. I shall ring the bell, and within sixty seconds, you will see nearly every one, except the brick gatherers, within the school-doors. Instant obedience is, or ought to be, the first lesson taught in an infant school; next to that, order; and, therefore, those who bring out the wooden bricks, and enjoy the amusement, must, of course, replace them on the proper shelves.

I may conclude, Mistress, respecting the Playground, by remarking, that while, at the gymnastic pole you see some swinging, there are others looking on and counting to the number forty, when they in their turn get swinging. In another place, some, with wooden bricks, are building arches, pillars, or squares, others forming figures with gravel-stones amidst the sand, each according to his taste or natural propensity; while three or four others, you perceive, are sitting on the school-door steps in abstract reverie, if not in utter thoughtlessness. The whole of these parties described, may be influenced comparatively easily; but many—many, indeed, do we find, who are sadly too gross in all their propensities, and, regarding the hoped-for effect, upon whose habits it may almost be said, teaching is nothing, while training is every thing.——Children, come, sing away, if you please.

INFANT SCHOOL SONG.

TUNE—" *The boatie rows,*" &c.

O may our Infant School
Be greatly blest indeed;
In number may we still be full,
In learning fast proceed!
We dearly love, we dearly love,
We dearly love the place,
Where health and cheerfulness appear
In every little face.

Here may the Infant thought
   Be trained to shoot aright;
Here, also, may our hearts be brought,
   In goodness to delight.
We highly prize, we highly prize,
   We highly prize the scheme,
Which all we hear, and all we see,
   Makes an instructive theme.

Master. Now, children, before walking into the gallery, see that your hats and caps are all neatly hung up, each in their proper place.

Granny. What a regiment o' bonnets, cloaks, and caps, Sir! How do ye get them a' in sic grand order? the bits o' bairns are hanging them up just as quiet as if they were gaun into the kirk. The laddies in my young days, used to buff ane another sweetly wi' their bonnets when they were gaun in or coming out o' the school; that they did——

Master. And in mine too. You know, order is a good habit, and training in that respect, is nearly every thing; but, Mistress, I must *see* that order is kept, as well as tell them to do it. Amidst my answers to the various queries, Mistress, I completely forgot your serious objections to the

GALLERY.

And although you may guess the important use to which it is made subservient, from having witnessed the children in it, and the mental develop-ment we attain by our elliptical and interrogatory system—yet in order to furnish you with an answer to your friends, the disputants, at their next meeting of council, I shall simply state the importance of the Gallery, by showing why we could not do without it.

The Master could not catch or arrest the eyes of the whole children on presenting a Picture or Object, or gain, to an equal degree, the assistance of the eye as well as the ear in informing the understanding, neither could he be so distinctly heard, if the children were seated on forms, or on a level surface like the floor, as infant school children were placed, on the first introduction of the system, a dozen or fourteen years ago. You know, Mistress, a good story or lecture is best heard when every eye can be easily fixed upon the speaker; and this is best attained, we think, by the auditory being closely seated in a gallery: in one word, when I tell a story the child gives but half his ear if the eyes wander, but if the eye is fixed by a picture representing the subject, or object spoken about, I have not simply the attention of half an ear, but the eye, and with it the whole ear, at one and the same moment, informing the understanding; you need not wonder, therefore, at the powerful influence of a gallery, and picture-lessons, too, in a school for training.

Now, children, as you are all seated, we shall sing a hymn. Who will be monitor?——Well, we shall have four leaders this time, if you please, two boys and two girls; see that you all be very attentive, and sing prettily. What should you do, children, when you are singing a hymn? *We should think about the meaning of what we sing.*

Very right, children.　We shall sing three verses of the Hymn,

HOLY SAVIOUR ! NOW BEFORE THEE.

TUNE—*Helmsley.*

Holy Saviour! now before Thee,
　We an infant race appear;
Teach us how we should adore Thee,
　Fill our hearts with godly fear.
　　Friend of infants,
　Bless our exercises here.

Have us in thy holy keeping,
　Out and in our goings guide;
Guard us in the hours of sleeping,
　Let no evil e'er betide.
　　Friend of infants,
　Always in thy bosom hide.

Granny. Maister, I think ye're aye singing hymns or sangs—ae kind o' lesson or another—would it no be just as weel to repeat them *by heart,* as we used to do in my young days? What's the use o' sae muckle singing, Maister?

WHY SING SO MANY LESSONS?

Master. I formerly gave you my opinion. I think, Mistress, that what was committed to memory, without being understood, was frequently forgot, at all events, that it was of no practical value; but I may farther state, that when a lesson, which is committed to rhyme, is first understood, as is uniformly our plan here, then committed to memory, and afterwards sung, we have, as a security for its being permanently remembered, not simply the memory and understanding, but the memory of all those feelings of harmony which are brought into play by the powers of music; in fact, what is understood and frequently sung in youth is never forgot. The number of days in a particular month frequently escapes our memory; but we never forget the simple rhyme, so generally referred to, " Thirty days hath September, April, June, and November," &c.

Granny. Weel, Sir, I'll no say,—ye're far eneugh ben for me, I think, noo.

Master. Now then, children, for a little exercise. Suppose we have the saw-mill—saw away, children—very well—go on—stop now—silence.

LESSON FOR THE DAY—(WEDNESDAY.)

Master. Now, little children, for to-day's particular... *lesson,*—but I must first state, that I shall postpone the examination of yesterday's lesson upon Natural History of animals. The lesson for to-day was upon... *the Bear.* Well, I must postpone this and last Wednesday's... *lesson,* upon moral duties, till the afternoon. You recollect, I read to you on that day a nice story about a little obedient... *boy,*—who was that, children? *It was little Samuel, Master, and he was a good boy, and ran and did whatever he was bid*—to... *do.* Very right: then the revisal of both these lessons, the ...*Bear,* and about...*little Samuel,* we shall leave till the... *afternoon.*——Well then, children, this being—what day, children? *Wednesday, Sir*—

P

this being Wednesday, the lesson for this day is also upon ... *moral duties;* and we shall take another example from the ... *Bible.* Do any of you recollect what the story was to be?—Perhaps some of you did what I asked you to do;—what was that, children? *To ask our mother or father to read it to us at home.* Now, have any done this? *Yes, my father read it to me, for I asked him; it was about a man that was knocked down on the road, and robbed.* Very well, I hope every one of you will make a point of telling your parents, whenever you go ... *home,* what the next lesson is to ... *be,* and ask them if they will be so good as read to you the story out of the ... *Bible,* and also to explain it to ... *us;* and then you will know a great many things that poor, ignorant children don't know any thing at all ... *about.* The passage, children, which I shall read to you, very slowly and distinctly, is in Luke, that is, the Gospel according to ... *Luke,* in the tenth chapter.———— Be very attentive, and keep your hands resting upon your ... *knees.*

————Now, children, I hope you have heard all I read, I shall see if you remember it;* and I shall also assist your memory, by a picture of the various objects in this beautiful ... *story;* yes, or parable. Children, what is this I hold in my hand? *A picture.* You see a number of figures on this picture? *Yes, Sir.*

This picture, children, represents that very nice

---

* The master reads sentence by sentence; and, as he goes along, develops the children's ideas upon the particular sentence, elliptically and interrogatively, and afterwards, also, upon the whole passage. See Chap. VI.

Scripture... *story*, or ... *parable*, which our Saviour Jesus Christ, when on earth, told his ... *disciples*, and which I have now read to you.——What is a parable, children? *An instructive story.* Well, this is an instructive ... *story*, which our Saviour ... *told*, when he was in this ... *world*, that you and I, and every one, on ... *reading it*, or hearing about it, might know how we should act in similar circumstances. You will please listen, my little children, very ... *attentively*, whilst I repeat to you the ... *story*, and keep looking at the ... *picture*, to see if you understand it.——What sense do I now ask you to use, children? *The sense of seeing.* And when I am telling the story, what other sense should you use at the same time? *The sense of hearing.* Very well—then listen very attentively to me with your ... *ears*, and keep looking at the picture with your ... *eyes*.

A certain man went from Jerusalem to ... *Jericho*. You know Jerusalem was the capital city of ... *Judea?* and you remember something about Jericho? *Yes, Sir, the walls of Jericho fell after the Priests had blown the trumpets seven days.*

Well then, this man, as he was going from Jerusalem to ... *Jericho*, fell amongst ... *thieves*,— you know what thieves are? *Yes, stealing folk.* And they stripped him of his ... *clothes*. Yes, raiment, the Bible says, or clothes—and wounded him ... *very sore*, and left him half ... *dead ;* and by chance there came a ... *Priest*—yes, a Jewish Priest, that way, and the moment that he saw him, he ... *passed by* on the ... *other side of the road. That was very cruel, Master.* Very cruel, indeed, children. Well, a little after this, a ... *Levite came*, and when he saw him, he also passed by on *...the other side.* You know who the Levites were? *Not very well.* You know how many tribes there were in Israel? *Yes, twelve. Oh, we know now, Master, the Levites were one of the twelve tribes.*

Well, then, both the Priest and the Levite were neighbours, or brothers, to the *...poor man*, who had been going down from *...Jerusalem* to *...Jericho? Yes, Sir.*

And what ought brothers and neighbours to do to one another? *They ought to be very kind to one another.*

Now, you see what they did. What did they both do? *They passed by on the other side* without... *helping him.*

Well, the kind person that came up to the place where the poor wounded... *man* lay, was a... *Samaritan*—and when he saw him he had... *compassion on him.* What is compassion, children? *Liking to do him good.*

And this good man bound up his... *wounds*, and poured in... *oil*, and... *wine*, and set him on his own beast. *Was it a horse, Master?* The Bible does not say, children, whether it was an ass or a horse that the Samaritan had; however, whatever animal it was, this kind, good man, set the... *wounded man* on it, and took him to an... *inn*, and took care of him; and on the morrow, that is... *next day*, when the good Samaritan was ...*going away from the inn*, he took out... *two pence*, that is, Roman pence, much more valuable than the copper pence we have; well, he took out two of these valuable silver pence, and gave

them to the host, that is, the landlord that keeps
...*the inn*, and said to him, take care of this...
man, and when I come back this...*way*, whatever
more you spend than the...*two pence*, I will...*pay
you back.* Was not that very kind, children?
Yes, very kind.

But I must tell you, children, that the Jews
and Samaritans were enemies, and had no deal-
ings together; and yet this good...*Samaritan*,
instead of passing by the...*Jew* on the other...
side, like the...*Priest and Levite*, did all these
kind things to the poor wounded...*Jew.* Now
then, children, see if you can point out the various
figures in the picture. Whom does this represent,
with his head tied up with a white handkerchief?
*The robbed man, and his arm is all streaming
with blood; Master—look at it!*

And who is this? *The good Samaritan.*
And what is this in his hand? *The oil-bottle,
Sir, pouring it into his sore arm.* And whom does
this represent, think you? *The Priest.* And
this? *The Levite.*

Why did you say that was the Priest, and not
the Levite? *Because he is farthest away on the
road.* Why farthest away on the road? *Because
he came up first to the poor man,* and therefore
must be...*farthest off.* Very right.

And what are these, children? *Trees growing
on the side of the road.* Of what road? *On the
road from Jerusalem to Jericho.*

Now, children, I have shown you the outline
of this beautiful moral picture; the filling up we
shall proceed with some other day; but I shall
ask you just a single question or two. What does

this parable teach you and me, children? *It teaches us not to be cruel, but kind.*

Who were cruel? *The Priest and Levite.*

Who was kind? *The Samaritan;* and therefore this parable-lesson is called the... *Good Samaritan.*

What would you do, children, if you saw a person hurt on the street, or on the road-side? *We would help him up, and take care o' him.*

And if you saw a poor person very hungry, I mean a poor neighbour's child, perhaps,... *starving,* and you had a slice of... *bread* in your hand, what would you do? *I would give him the half o't. I would give the whole o't, Master;—my mother would give me another bit.*

Who is it, children, that can heal diseases, and cure wounds, and bless the means used to make you better? *God.*

Yes, God is very kind, and very compassionate. Whether do you think, children, the Samaritan, or the Priest and Levite, most resembled God? *The Samaritan. The Samaritan was like Jesus, too, for he was very kind,* and went about... *doing good.*

Very right, children. Jesus, you know, was God as well as... *man,* and in all that he did, he showed the love that God had to... *us.*

Now, my little children, I will, as usual, tell you the lesson for next week. Next week's lesson, on moral duties, children, will be the love which Jonathan showed to David; and perhaps you will ask your parents to read over that beautiful story to you at home: from where, children? *From the Bible.*

Now we shall sing the pretty hymn, "*We should do as we should be done by.*" Peter, you will lead the tune.

TUNE—*Devizes.*

To do to others as I would
   That they should do to me,
Will make me honest, kind, and good,
   As every child should be.

Whether I am at home, at school,
   Or walking out abroad,
I never should forget this rule,
   Of Jesus Christ the Lord.

Now, children, a little girl brought me this, saying, she found it among the gravel in the playground. What sort of a little girl must this be, children? *An honest girl.* Why? *Because she brought it to you, and did not keep it to hersel'.*

When the penny was not hers, if she had said to herself—nobody will know, for nobody saw that I found the penny, and I will keep it to myself, what would you have called her then? *A thief.*

Yes, a thief. That would have been shocking, would it not? *Yes.* Well, but she brought it to master, and therefore she is an ... *honest lassie.* Yes, she is an honest girl; and I hope every one of you, when you find any thing here, or elsewhere, will always return it to the ... *owner.* If you found some money, or clothes, such as a shawl, or any thing on the street, and did not know to whom it belonged, what would you do, children? *We would cry it—we would send the bell-man through the town—*and try to find the... *owner.*

Now, suppose no man, woman, or child, saw you find it, would any one else have seen you? *Yes, God always sees us, and is very angry with people that steal,* or keep what is not their...*own.* And what would you call this? *A sin, Master.* A sin against whom, children? *Against God.* And would it not be hurting your neighbour also, to keep what is his? *Yes.* And that also is a...*sin.*

Well, then, what is this in my hand? *A penny.*

How many farthings are there in a penny? *Four.* How many halfpence? *Two.*

Well, then, are there two farthings and two halfpence in a penny? *No, Sir, there are four farthings, and two halfpennies, in a penny;—that would make six farthings.*

Six farthings, do you say, children? Are four farthings and two halfpence equal to six farthings? Think for a moment. *Oh, eight farthings, Master.*

And two pennies would make...*eight farthings,* or...*two pennies? Yes.*

Very right, my little children, always look sharp when at your lessons, lest any mistakes be made. Whose penny is this? *Mine, Sir.*

It is yours, little Betsy, is it? Well, I believe it must be yours, for no one else claims it, and certainly it is not mine. *Yes, I lost it, for there's a hole in my pocket, and it slipped out when I was swinging——Betsy, Master, got it last Saturday from her grandfather.*

Oh, how these grandmothers and grandfathers will spoil children, and lead them into temptation, by giving pence to little children, before they are trained to know how to use them!

Now, suppose you had seen this little girl with a penny belonging to you, would you have snatched it from her, or what would you have done? Come, answer little children,—would you have given her a ... *cuff*,—would giving her a cuff have been right, children? *No, that would have been wrong.* It would have been more than this, too, children: it would have been a ... *sin.* Yes, it would have been a sin. Why a sin, children? *Because we should not render evil for evil.* Then, although any one gives you a ... *thump on the face.* Yes, or on the ... *back.* You are not to ... *give another one back again,* but to ... *forgive him.* Very right, children; it is a bad thing to ... *quarrel,* or to render evil for ... *evil,* because it is forbidden by ... *God* in the ... *Bible,* and it also leads children oftentimes to ... *fight,* which is a very bad ... *thing.*

Now then, Betsy, there is your penny; but first let me see what each of the scholars would like to buy, if they had a penny;—now, my dears, what do you say? *I know what I would like. I would buy parlies. I would buy sweeties.* Well, go on. *Gibraltar rock, Master—a doll—a whip—two tops—we get two for a penny, Master.——* Well, are you done? *I would like a book. I would like sugarally—it would be fine.*

Now, then, children, I think you have chosen variety enough. You have told me what you would like to buy; but what ought you to buy, children? Whether would you have some sweet-meats, which are eaten in a...*moment,* or should you like something that would last? *I would like a book, Master.*

Well, I approve of that little girl's choice of a book; although dolls and whips are very good in their way, still a book oftentimes has beautiful...*pictures in it,* and tells pretty...*stories. Yes, they tell about heaven, and a great many other nice things.*

Very right, children. Do you know, that in the bookseller's...*shop,* they sell some pretty... *books,* two for a penny, and sometimes four for a penny? What good do sweetmeats do to you, children? *Nothing but spoil our teeth.*

Well, children, I hope you wont forget the use of a penny—there take it. Now, Betsy, suppose you saw a very poor person that had no bread, or money to buy...*bread,* and you had a penny, what would you do? *I would give the half o't, —take it now, if you please, Master.* No, my dear, take the penny, and give it yourself; perhaps you may get an opportunity soon.

Children, what does the Bible say about those that shut up their bowels of compassion from their poor brethren? Can none in the gallery answer? What say you oldest boys on the top seat? *It says, in the Bible, " Whoso seeth his brother in want of food, and hath no compassion upon him"*——Go on, child, I will assist you—how dwelleth the...*love of God in him?* Then, because God loveth us, and giveth us every thing that ...*we have,* we ought, therefore—to do what, children?... *to love one another*, and to be very kind to...*each other.* Very right, children.

Master. Now, since the revisal of both last Wednesday and yesterday's lessons are put off till the afternoon, suppose we anticipate the afternoon's exercise, and have a trial at

RESPONSES.

—I know you are extremely fond of this exercise.——This is done, Mistress, by two boys or girls being brought out in front of the gallery, in sight of all the scholars, and questioning each other on some particular lesson or story. We also, sometimes, give the children a choice of subjects.——We shall begin with the girls, if you please; it is their turn, for the boys had it last.

Master. Now, girls, what subject will you choose? allow me to recommend Biography to-day. What shall we have, then?

Girls. The Shunamite's son—Little Samuel—Joseph in the pit—Jesus in the Temple with the Doctors—Three good boys in the fiery furnace.

Master. Stop now, children; I am happy that these interesting stories present themselves to you, but as we have had all of them now mentioned lately, more than once, suppose you take an older lesson.

Girls. Will Jonah do, Sir?

Master. Yes. The prophet Jonah will do; we have not had his history for a considerable time: which of you eldest girls will try the Responses?
——Plenty of hands stretched out, I see.——
Come out, Margaret and Jane, in front of the

gallery here——you appear the youngest——Now ask the questions clearly and distinctly; don't roar; but, at the same time, speak fully out, so that all the scholars may hear what is said. You know the subject is ... *Jonah.* Remember to commence at the beginning of the story, for you are apt to begin at the end, or the middle, or any part of the story most interesting to you. Now begin, Margaret.

Margaret. Was Jonah cast out into the sea, Jane?

Master. Now, Margaret, remember what I said; think of the beginning of the story; some of the other scholars will recollect what Jonah was sent to do. Jonah was a prophet of the...*Lord,* and he was sent to a large...*city.* Oh, yes; I know now.

Margaret. What city was Jonah sent to preach to, Jane?

Jane. Nineveh. Was it a large city, Margaret?

Margaret. Yes, almost as big as London. Were they good people, Jane?

Jane. No; they were bad people.

Master. Go on——ask Margaret another question.

Jane. Did Jonah go to Nineveh to preach?

Margaret. No; he ran away in a ship. Where did he sail to, Jane?——

Master. As Jane cannot answer, you must do so yourself, Margaret. *He went away down to a sea-side place, where there was a boat going to Tarshish, and he paid the money for the passage, and tried to run away from the Lord.*

Now, Margaret, since you have answered the question, you may ask Jane another.

Margaret. When Jonah ran away in the ship, did God see him?

Jane. Yes, God saw him all the time, and he sees every body. He sees you and me just now.——Did Jonah think God saw him in the ship, Margaret?

Margaret. No, for he fell asleep.——Was Jonah a bad man?

Jane. He was doing a bad thing just now; but he was a good man, and he repented, and became good after again. You know he was a prophet of the Lord.

Master. Children, all be very attentive—up hands—down—up again—fold arms. Now, answer me this question:—What is the reason why we so often sin against God? Is it because we remember God, or is it that we forget him, or try to forget him, like... *Jonah?*

Children. Because we forget.

Master. Then you do what is wrong, because you forget... *God,* and don't think that he sees ... *us.* Can any of you give me a proof that we cannot flee from the presence of the Lord? *Adam and Eve tried to hide themselves,* but they could ... *not.*

Margaret. God sent a great storm into the sea, and the sailors thought they would all be drowned. Were they drowned, Jane?

Jane. No; Jonah was cast into the sea, and there was a large, big fish swallowed him up.

Master. Something happened before he was thrown into the sea—but we must, I fear, leave the rest of this... *nice story* till another day; all of you, however, will recollect that God always

... *sees us*, whether it is dark or ... *light*, and that it is impossible to flee from the presence of ... *the Lord.*——You may take your seats.

Now, children, answer me this question; you proved to me just a little ago that stealing was a sin. From where are thieves excluded, does the Bible say? *From heaven.*

And where do they go to when they die? *To the bad place*, where all the ... *wicked people go.* Now I once heard of a man that was hanged for robbing a dwelling-house, and he said that when he was young he commenced stealing things from his playfellows, then he took larger things as he grew older, stole apples from people's ... *gardens*, their eggs and chickens, and then from one thing to another, till at last he grew so hardened that he and his bad companions (for bad companions, you know, are a very bad thing) agreed to rob a dwelling-house, and he was caught, put in jail, and tried, and condemned to be executed. *And was he hanged, Master?*

Yes, he was hanged. Now, my little children, I hope none of you will ever come to such an awful ... *end*, and in order to prevent that, you must pray to God to keep you from doing ... *what that thief did*, and especially from beginning to steal, or taking playthings from ... *one another*, as you call it.

Now, children, I have a sad story to tell you about a little boy who stole a plaything, which another little boy had dropped, and he was seen doing this bad ... *action* this forenoon; will you try to find out who did this; look about and see who it may be. The little boy, children, saw other five or six boys playing very ... *nicely* and quietly, and a little boy, whom this old lady saw walk slyly behind the boys playing, and when the boys were not ... *looking*, he snatched up the little ... *toy ;* yes, the little toy, and put it ... *into his pocket*, and never spoke or said a word. Now this little boy thought that nobody saw him, and I fear, from the way he did it, that it was not the first time that he had done the like ... *bad thing.* Did any one else see him, children? *Yes, Sir, God saw him ; and He sees every thing.*

Who, do you think, could do such a thing, children?——*Master, it's Willy Waterston that did it, for his face is red, and he's beginning to greet.*

Willy, Willy, what have you to say for yourself?——answer me, boy.

Master, I have—I have—I—I did—didn't—haven't it—I haven't it, Master.——Master, when you were speaking he threw it behind him ; here it's.

Well, I really am sorry to witness such conduct. What shall we do to him? *Beat him—cuff him. No, Master, tell him what the Bible says.*

Well, girls, what shall we do? *Forgive him, Sir, for once, if you please.*

Is this the first time, think you, children, that Willy Waterston was guilty of such a thing? *Yes ; for Willy's greeting and crying, Master.*

Well, girls, I do believe this is the first time that he has been found out doing any thing so bad, and no doubt a difference ought to be made between a first and second offence; at the same time, there has been so much duplicity and deceit, both in stealing the boy's ... *plaything,* and in trying to hide it, that I must think what punishment should be awarded him ; it cannot be easily passed over. In the meantime, Willy, you must sit in that window-seat alone, and not be allowed to repeat any lesson with the other children this afternoon ; and, before you leave the school, if you acknowledge your fault in a proper manner, we shall determine whether we take the advice of the girls, or what should be done. Now, children, when you pray this evening, before going to bed, what should you do ? *Pray for him.*

And for yourselves, too, I think, that you may be kept from such ... *a thing.* Give me an example of one who prayed ? *Daniel prayed three times a day.* Another, if you please. *The publican went up into the temple to pray ; and Peter prayed too.*

Which commandment forbids stealing, children ? *The eighth.*

And which forbids deceiving or lying ? *The ninth.*

You see, Mistress, we must leave him to himself a little. Firmness is absolutely necessary, but severity with boys has one of two effects : it either breaks the spirit, or it hardens. We prefer training to a right sense and a right understanding of the evil, by every possible mean rather than corporeal punishment.

Granny. Now, Sir, I may be wrang, I wadna say, but I would not have had sae muckle patience wi' the wee scoundrel. A right gude skelpin' first and last, afore them a', would hae matched him better, I think.

Master. I believe, Mistress, we have both the same object in view, but we desire to soften, to convince, and, if possible, make conscience speak. For the principle, "Thou God seest me," "The eyes of the Lord are in every place," is infinitely more powerful than any human superintendence ever can be. The Bible says we must not spare the rod; that is, we must make the child suitably feel, by proper restraint and correction. A mere animal can be made to feel correction only by the presence or remembrance of the literal rod; a child, however, ought to be made to feel correction, *if possible*, from a higher principle.——Well, children, answer me this: When you play games any where, is it right to play for money? *No, Sir.* Do you play for winning? *No, we play for fun, just for amusement.* Very right, children; playing for amusement ought to be quite sufficient, without playing for... *winning.* Playing for winning oftentimes leads boys to do very ...*bad things.* Yes, very bad things. Ought boys to play at pitch-and-toss? *No, Sir; that is a game of chance.*

Now, children, we shall sing a Hymn.

I'M NOT TOO YOUNG FOR GOD TO SEE.

I'm not too young for God to see;
He knows my name and nature too;
And all day long he looks at me,
And sees my actions through and through.

He listens to the words I say,
And knows the thoughts I have within;

And whether I'm at work or play,
He's sure to see me if I sin.

O ! how could children tell a lie,
Or cheat in play, or steal, or fight,
If they remembered God was by,
And had them always in His sight!

Then when I wish to do amiss,
However pleasant it may be,
I'll always try to think of this—
I'm not too young for God to see.

Granny. Weel, Sir, ye'll maybe be sae obliging as let me see what the children will say on this picture—The Brazen Serpent in the Wilderness.

Master. I will, with much pleasure; but as our time is nearly exhausted, and the boys partly expect a turn at the *Responses,* I cannot enter into all the particulars which it is proper the children should know. The children, however, having several times before had lessons upon it, I shall simply draw from them what your favourite Minister would call, I suppose, the practical conclusion.

Children, you see this? *Yes; the picture of the Brazen Serpent.*

Did you ever see a serpent? *No, Sir.*

Does the Bible speak about serpents? *Yes; the devil appeared to Adam and Eve in the shape of a serpent,—and Moses placed that brazen serpent on the pole, Master.*

You see the pole? *Yes; it is perpendicular.*

And the serpent? *Yes; it forms a waved line on the top of the pole.*

What do you call the person who made the Brazen Serpent? *A brazier, or...brass-smith.*

What is brass? *It's a metal—It's a mineral.— Master, my mother's new candlestick is made of brass.*

Does the Bible speak about brass-smiths or braziers? *Yes, Hiram was a brass-smith to king Solomon.* Another. *Goliath had a helmet of brass on his head.* Another. *Tubal-Cain was a smith too, Master.*

Very well, children, now look at the picture; you see the Israelites and their tents? *Yes.*

Do these people appear in good health? *No. They were bit with fiery serpents.*

Why so? *Because the Israelites were very discontented, and murmured against Moses,—and so God sent...fiery serpents among them, and they died.*

Did they all die? *No; those that looked at the Brazen Serpent on the pole lived,—and those that would not look...died.*

Were they commanded to do this? *Yes.*

And how could they be healed by simply looking at the Brazen Serpent? *Because God promised that they would be healed by doing so.* And whatever God promises is sure to be... *done.*

Very right, children. What did the people ask Moses to do for them? *To pray that the serpents might be chased away.*

Now tell me, children, what this teaches you and me? What does the Bible say about it? *In the third chapter of John,* Jesus said to Nicodemus, " *As Moses lifted up the Serpent* in the wilderness, even so must the Son of... *Man be lifted up.*"

And for what purpose was he lifted up on the

cross? *To save sinners—to make us good.* Yes, and to wash us in the... *blood of the Lamb*——to suffer punishment instead of... *us.*

Very well, children, I shall tell you what reason Christ himself gave to Nicodemus, and which is in the following verse in the chapter: " The Son of Man was lifted up, that whosoever believeth in him should not... *perish,* but have eternal life;" that is, whosoever looks to Christ, believing on him, and depending on him, shall be healed of... *their sins.*

Now, children, what is a miracle? *Something done contrary to the natural order of things,* which ... *man* cannot... *do;* like healing the... *folk that were bitten* with the... *fiery serpents.* Healing the folk who were bitten with the fiery serpents, then, was a... *miracle.*

Then who can perform a miracle? *None but God.*

Name one or two miracles, besides the one we are now speaking about. *Turning water into wine—Raising the widow's son.* Any other, children? *Raising Lazarus from the grave.*

Well, children, would any one come from his grave though you or I said, Come forth? *No, Sir.*

Why? *Because none but God could do that.*

Did Jesus raise Lazarus from the grave after he had been dead? *Yes.*

Then what does that prove? *It proves that Jesus must be God.*

Was Jesus more than God? *Yes. He was both God and man,* for the Jews saw... *him,* and he... *lived amongst them.*

—— I fear you may be tired, children. I shall therefore close immediately after a short lesson on Objects, or perhaps on the Ball Frame.

Children. We're not tired, Master. If you please, may we (boys) have our turn at the Responses.

Master. You may, if you particularly wish it; but we must be very short.——Now then, boys, for the

RESPONSES.

What shall be the subject? *The Goat, if you please. We have not had it for some time.*

Well then upon the Goat. Mistress will be so good as reach the picture of the Goat.——Which of you boys are disposed to try?——Several are willing, I see.——Come out my two little fellows, Donald and John; but, first, let me see that all hands are out of mischief——Clap hands——hands forward—stand up—down again.——Now then, silence, children.

You see, Mistress, what interest this exercise excites; all eyes glisten with expectation at this youthful intellectual combat. Boys, you will ask a few general questions first about the Goat itself, and then about what use is made in the Bible of it, in the way of illustration or story. *Who shall begin, Master?*

Donald shall begin. I think he is the youngest.

Donald. Of what size is the Goat, John?

John. About the size of a sheep. What sort of horns has it?

Donald. Long upright horns. Are the horns of any use, John?

John. Yes, to make handles for knives, spoons, and other things, and combs for combing our hair. Is the Goat a quiet beast?

Donald. Only sometimes. Has the Goat hair or wool on its back?

John. Hair, long shaggy hair. Where do the Goats live?

Donald. There's plenty of them in the Highlands, and in Wales, and in Ireland too. Did you ever see a Goat, Johnny?

John. No; but we have a picture of one in this school. Did you ever see one?

Donald. Yes, many a time, at my uncle Hector's, at Glenorchy, in the Highlands. Does the Goat eat flesh or corn?

John. It eats neither. What does it eat? Donald, ye can tell, I suppose?

Master. Come now, boys, keep to the point, as to the questions about the distinct qualities of the Goat.

Donald. It eats what it can find on the high mountains and steep rocks; bits of young trees, and things of that kind. What is made of its skin?

John. Leather for gloves. What's the use of its milk?

Donald. For cheese and butter in the Highlands, and for weak, sick folk in the town. Sometimes they are funny beasts, when they jump from one side of the glen to the other, and up the steepest rocks. How many feet has a Goat?

John. Four. What is an animal with four feet called?

Donald. A quadruped. Can the Goat look backwards as easily as the hare?

John. No ; it looks forward, in case it should tumble on the rocks.

Master. Now, boys, I think you seem nearly done ; give me a single passage in which Goats are noticed in the Bible. Do you know, boys ? ——Come, answer quickly, if you can. One of the monitor class will perhaps tell you.——*In Matthew, 25th chapter, Master, Goats are compared to the bad people at the last day, and Sheep to the good people.* Very right, my little fellow. Now, my little boys, you hear what is said. Can you go on with one or two questions ? It is your turn, Donald.

Donald. What will Jesus say to the Sheep on his right hand, John ?

John. " Come, ye blessed of my Father." What will he say to the Goats on the left hand, on that wonderful day ?

Donald. " Depart from me, ye cursed, into everlasting fire."

Master. Will not that be a solemn day, my dear children ? *Yes.*

It will be what to the wicked ? *An awful day, Master.* But to the righteous, those that love Christ, it will be what ? *A happy, happy day.* Yes, it will be a happy day, children.

Donald. Whether would you like to be a Sheep or a Goat, John ?

John. I would like to be a Sheep, if I was big.

Master. But little children are compared to... *lambs.*——Go on, John.

John. Who carries the lambs in his arms, Donald ?

Donald. Jesus took the lambs in his arms. Who do you mean by lambs ?

John. Little children like us, Donald.

Master. You will recollect, Mistress, that we have a great many Bible stories about the Goat, but this is enough for one lesson.———Now, children, what shall we sing?

Children. The Goat, if you please.

Master. Well, we shall sing about the Goat. Who shall be monitors?———Come out, Mary, you and Thomas will lead. Let me hear how sweetly and softly you will sing

THE GOAT.

The Goat in size is like a Sheep;
He climbs up mountains very steep;
He has no wool, but shaggy hair,
That makes stout cloth for men to wear.

You will observe, Mistress, that too much form, in regard to lessons, wont do in training Infants. When this is the plan, it uniformly tends to destroy the happiness, cheerfulness, and activity, of the children. Every incident, as it occurs, ought to be laid hold of and applied to the understanding and conscience of the little ones, in the simplest method possible; always, however, keeping in view some one point which you mean to impress, which ought to flow from the subject naturally; and which the children, on reflection, will perceive to be plain and obvious. While, however, it is wrong to have too much formality, yet some arrangement of Bible lessons is necessary. The following we attend to, as the prominent lesson for each day in the week:

Monday.—Bible Biography.

Tuesday.—Illustrations and Bible History of Animate Nature.

Wednesday.—Moral Duties, from Bible Examples and Precepts.

Thursday.—Miracles, from the Old and New Testaments; and the Parables of our Lord.

Friday.—Illustrations and Bible History of Inanimate Nature.

Saturday.—Prophecies concerning Christ, Bible Geography, Promises, &c.

You see, Mistress, there is scarcely any limit to these subjects. Whilst, however, we thus far recommend one particular and distinct lesson for each of the six days in the week, which ought to be read audibly and slowly, sentence by sentence, by the Master, from the Bible, and afterwards analyzed very minutely, (I mean more minutely than any old lesson,) yet he may, and, to keep the children in activity, he must recur to several other lessons, taking advantage of any incident that presents itself: thus sucking honey from every flower.

Granny. Ye told me, gin I mind right, that out o' the Scripture ye tak' bad characters to show the weans. Is that just as it should be, Maister, think ye.

Master. Why, we shall hear what the children say on the subject; we shall take the first criminal after Adam, if you please, and then judge whether a good lesson even may not be drawn, by holding up such bad characters as a beacon to avoid. But, Mistress, I must be extremely short;

our time is quite exhausted, although the children declare they are not tired.——Children, answer me this question, Who was the first murderer? *Cain.*——We must, however, in the first instance, Mistress, sing a verse or two of

THE INFANT SCHOOL.

TUNE—*Sweet Home.*

Though our home be so sweet, and our parents so dear,
There's a place from whose doors we wish not to rove,
Where Teachers, affectionate, kind, and sincere,
Awaken our feelings to goodness and love.
   School, school, sweet Infant School,
 We like well our School, we like well our School.

Then while our dear parents are tender and kind,
And our Teachers still point us to wisdom's abode,
Our home and our School round our hearts closely twined,
Shall point us to virtue, and lead us to God.
   School, &c. &c.

——The whole class may answer, as usual, although the oldest I address particularly. Now, be attentive. Was Cain a good or a bad man? *A very bad, cruel man, Master. He killed his brother.*

What was the first commandment we are told he broke, children? *The tenth.*

Why? *Because he envied his brother.*

And which is the next? *The sixth.*

Why? *Because he killed Abel,* his...*brother.*

Did Cain break any other? *Yes, the ninth, for he told a lie.*

What did he say? *" I know not. Am I my... brother's keeper?"*

The first part of Cain's answer, children, was...
" *I know not.*"

Was that a lie ? *Yes.*

And the last part of the answer was..."*Am I my brother's keeper ?*

Was that a lie, children? *No, Sir; but he meant to deceive.*

Is it always necessary to say untrue words before you tell a lie ? *No, Sir; meaning to deceive is a lie,* even though the words spoken ... *be true.*

The class at the top may now sit down. Clap hands once more—hands on...*knees.*——We might take twenty such bad characters, Mistress, which are noticed in the Scriptures. Absalom, for example. I might first read or tell the story, afterwards question them upon it, and then draw forth from the children that Absalom broke the fifth commandment by disobeying his father—the tenth, by coveting the throne of Israel—and the eighth, by attempting to steal, by war, the throne of his father David. Of course, did our time permit, I would endeavour to cause the children, by a slow, yet sure process, to draw the application for themselves.

Granny. Weel, Sir, I see it's very true that " all Scripture is profitable;" but I ne'er thought afore that gude could come out o' bad men, or that beasts and fowls, and a' kind o' things ye bring out o' the Bible, were amaist in't at a' ; but atweel its very true, what's no in canna come out. Sae lang, therefore, as ye stick to Scripture, my best wishes gang wi' ye, and my prayers too. But the weans, Sir, the bits o' babbies, sic knowledge sae dumfounders me ; and the way o' keeping them sae quiet, that's surely new. Gin I hadna read somewhere at hame, in my Bible, that there was naething new under the sun, I would hae amaist thought this way o't, and this place a' thegither, was surely new. What think ye, Maister?

Master. Nothing new. Infant training, which includes teaching, is not new; it is as old as God's command by Solomon, " Train up a child in the way he should go." *Nothing new.* That is, the principles and elements of all things under the sun are the same at all times. The principles of man as a sinner, and the plan of recovery, are, and have been, at all times, the same; and the elements of nature—fire, air, earth, and water— and the grand divisions of the animal, vegetable, and mineral kingdoms, also remain the same. But we may apply them to new purposes; we may give them a new shape, and suit them to the present altered, and ever-altering state of society, and we may have new or improved methods of analyzing their properties: still, however, it holds true, that no material things are new. " There is nothing new under the sun."

CHAPTER VI.

DAILY BIBLE TRAINING FOR INFANT AND JUVENILE SCHOOLS.

THE Quotations in this chapter are intended to show the daily plan, which may be adhered to in training children to scriptural knowledge, and are merely a small selection from that inexhaustible store which is to be found in the Sacred Record.

The plan of varying the subject each day, has been found to work well both in Schools for Infant and Juvenile training. Each line contains generally enough for the Bible exercise of one day, which, in the Juvenile School, is revised on the corresponding day of the following week, and in the Infant School on the following day, and also on the corresponding day of the succeeding week;—each lesson, therefore, passes under review twice in the Juvenile, and thrice in the Infant School. In both circumstances the subject is reviewed in the simplest manner possible. A great error in the ordinary plan of communicating Bible knowledge is, that the application of the subject is usually given *first*, both by Parents and Teachers, before the premises are understood, and, therefore, the application, which otherwise might have been self-evident, is literally lost.

Children ought first to be exercised on the meaning of every word or term in the particular passage—next on the leading points—and, afterwards, the lesson afforded, which is naturally deducible. In some passages, each of these divisions are found sufficient for a separate day's lesson.

The general plan pursued is not to tell or inform the pupils any thing, which, by analysis, comparison, or illustration, they can find out for themselves; in other words, they are trained, rather than taught to think.

The mode of development, as may be seen from the foregoing chapters, is by a mixture of the elliptical and interrogatory plan—say, forming one ellipsis after every one or two questions, or reversed, as the children may be found more or less acquainted with the subject under consideration.

No system of simple question and answer is so powerful, or can possibly keep up the attention of young children equally with this mixed plan, which is now pursued in the Model Schools.

Simple reading of the Scriptures by children, without being accompanied by an exercise of the understanding and heart upon the subject-matter of what is read, is found of much less value than many are apt to imagine. In most cases, the pupils leave the school sadly ignorant, and generally continue so, unless they are privileged with intelligent, pious parents, who can perform this duty at home. We need not wonder, then, that the preaching of the Gospel should be nearly lost upon such young persons alluded to, when even the narratives and common illustrations of Scripture are a dead letter, and almost unknown. Had they received, however, such a daily training in school, how vividly would much appear which now seems dark and unmeaning.—Each lesson for the day is read from the Bible itself, which, as noticed, (see page 75,) is placed in the middle of the floor, on a stand, in front of the gallery.

Although these quotations may be exhausted in somewhat less than a couple of years, yet the Master or Parent can very easily afterwards select for himself; and we are convinced that the thorough understanding of even these few selections, on such varied and interesting subjects, will prove to the mind like so many finger-posts, from which the Bible student may more easily find his way to the filling up of those higher and more minute points in the revealed will of God.

Although the plan of development may be gathered from Chapters IV. and V. yet we have added one or two short examples, in order to show how the Teacher or Parent may proceed. The difficulty which is usually felt in the first instance, diminishes at every trial, until it produces, both in master and pupil, a warm attachment to the system.

The training system has been found to work well in Sabbath Schools, as also in regard to the children of a family, and takes up but a very few minutes, perhaps not longer than otherwise would be occupied in the ordinary reading of a larger portion of Scripture. So powerfully does it interest children, that they will sometimes urge their parents not to proceed with the ordinary morning lesson, lest they should miss it on being called away perhaps somewhat earlier than usual to school.

As to the examples, we must be understood as having left much to be filled up by the Parent or Teacher; formality in question and answer, or by regular plan of ellipsis in each sentence, will be found not to suit; these must be varied and mixed. As the children acquire the power, by practice, of answering every question, or of rapidly filling up an ellipsis, so does the Teacher gradually acquire the habit of more rapidly propounding them. Even among advanced scholars, the meaning of terms, and the outline of the subject, ought uniformly to be drawn in the first instance; for to those who already are acquainted, the exercise amounts to a revisal, and to those who are ignorant, it is of course a necessary instruction. If the premises are well laid, the children generally will give the inference.

It is, perhaps, unnecessary to remind our readers, that this exercise is done when the children are sitting in a body in the gallery, and every eye upon the Master—for in this position alone can there be mutual development and strict attention. The children answer simultaneously; and although one-half, or one-third only, answer at any one time, yet it must not be supposed that the silent pupils are not learning, for these have frequently been found really to know the most. The great point in the Master to attend to in all mental training is, to keep the eyes of the children fixed upon himself, and the attention fully awake, and then he need not fear but that his pupils are gathering in all that their powers of mind are capable of.

In the Infant School the master reads the passage to the children. In the Juvenile School, those who can read do so audibly, in the hearing of all; those who do not read sit in the gallery, and listen. Whether able to read, therefore, or not, all receive the benefit of the lesson. In both cases it is read from the Bible itself, as being found decidedly more authoritative and influential than from a book of extracts. In all cases, previous to every lesson, the children of course being in the gallery, the preliminary physical or *manual* exercise of moving the hands, or rising and sitting down simultaneously, ought to be followed out. The superior attention thus acquired needs only to be tried, in order to be appreciated. In particular circumstances, or when desirable, these rapid movements may be made in perfect silence; and the more frequently they are repeated, the more fixed will be the attention throughout the whole exercise.

MASTER AND SCHOLARS.

Now, children, I shall read to you a passage out of the...*Bible*. What do you mean by the Bible? *The Word of God.* Give me another meaning. *The will of God.* Give me the literal meaning of the word Bible. *The Book*, or which is usually termed the Holy...*Book*, or...*Scriptures*, because it contains the will of...God, who is...*holy*. Very well.

Now, children, let there be perfect silence; let me see if all your hands are out of...*mischief.* Hold up both hands as I do; cross them as I do,—rest them upon your knees. Very well.

Now keep your eyes fixed on me while I read, verse by verse, of the first Psalm; and afterwards I shall hear what you think about the meaning of it. [In the *Juvenile* School, of course, the children read by turns.]

Psalm i. 1.—"Blessed is the man that walketh not in the counsel of the ungodly, nor standeth in the way of sinners, nor sitteth in the seat of the scornful: 2. But his delight is in the law of the Lord; and in his law doth he meditate day and night."

We have already said, that the first point is to see that the children understand the MEANING AND ANALYSIS of every word in the passage. The words requiring attention may be supposed to be—blessed—counsel—ungodly—sinners—scornful—delight—law—meditate.

Tell me, children, what is meant by ' blessed.' You can't tell, I see. Tell me then what is the opposite of blessed. *Cursed.* Very well. Tell me what is meant by cursed. Is it a person who is praised by every one, and honoured and happy; or is it one who is disgraced and miserable? *Disgraced.* Then a person who is disgraced and unhappy is...*cursed.* You told me that cursed was the opposite of...*blessed,* and that a person who is cursed is...*unhappy.* Now, then, tell me what is blessed. *Happy.* A man who is blessed is...*happy.* Who can make us most happy? *God.* Then those whom God makes happy are...*blessed.* Now, then, tell me what ' counsel' means. *Advice.* Well, counsel in one sense supposes advice; but when people are counselling together, must there be more persons than one? *Yes.* More than

...one, perhaps*...several.* Well, then, what do you mean when you say that two people, or several people, are counselling together? *It means that they are speaking together.* Yes, consulting *...together* about what they intend to*...do,* at some future*...time,* whether it be about doing some good thing, or some*...bad thing.* Then counselling means talking together, and consulting together about something. *Yes.* Now we shall take another word—what is meant by ' ungodly ?' Do you mean good people or bad people? *Bad people.* How do you think so ? *Because*—— Go on, children. *Because they're not good.* Not being good means not being*...godly.* Because God is*...good.* Then those who are not good are un*...godly.* Those that disobey God, and don't wish to do what God wishes them to do, are *...ungodly.*

The other words are proceeded with in a similar manner, more or less minute, and with less or more illustration or analysis, to suit the degree of information the children may possess. Every step, let it be borne in mind, in the Training system, strengthens the habit of attention and judgment, as also the capability for future exertion. The Master should then take THE LEADING POINTS OF THE PASSAGE, or second part of the plan, before he draws out, or causes the children to give, the inference or application, just as he would do in regard to a picture or natural landscape, namely, the trees—hills—house—birds—water—cattle— all these before the hue of the sky, or tint of the trees, are descanted upon.

Master. Now then, children, tell me what is

meant by a man not walking in the counsel of the ungodly. It would be walking in the way of whom? *Of the counsel*——I shall help you to understand this question a little better by illustration. You know what illustration means? *Yes, it means*——Well, then, suppose you met on the street with some bad...*boys* or...*girls*, who were talking together about some mischief which they intended doing, such as that they would go and steal some peas out of a...*field* in the country, or apples from a...*garden*, or from a fruit-stand on the...*street*, and instead of running away from these bad boys, when they were going to do such...*mischief*, that when they asked you to go with them, you went away with...*them*,—do you think that, if you did this, you would be walking in the counsel of the un...*godly?* *Yes.* You recollect what walking in the counsel means? *Doing what they bid us.* Doing what bad...*boys* or...*girls* bid, you would be walking in the counsel of the un...*godly.* Now, children, is it proper for any of you to walk with, and listen to, or engage in, the counsel and conversation of bad boys? *No, Sir.* It is not right to walk with bad...*boys;* and those who walk and consult with bad...*boys*, are walking in the counsel of...*the ungodly.* What does the Bible say about sinners enticing you? If sinners entice you,...*consent thou not.*

Now then, children, we shall take the next point—look at your books. *Ver.* 1. "Nor standeth in the way of sinners."

It would be quite superfluous to multiply words, by narrating the conversation which must take place ere children can thoroughly be made to understand the progress in sin, from meeting with and " walking in the counsel of the ungodly ;"— then waiting on to meet these sinners in the way of folly, even at the very corners of the streets; and, lastly, to that highest and most hopeless of all states of wickedness—" Sitting in the seat of the scornful." The next points are, " delighting in the law of the Lord "—" meditating on it day and night ;" not indeed every moment, but frequently, confining our exercises not exclusively to a particular time, but, as it were, " day and night," morning and evening at the least, " instant in prayer."——" A tree planted by the rivers of water." Of course, the difference between a tree planted in a hot climate, where there is little rain or moisture, beside or close to a river, and one at a distance from a river, must all be fully explained. " Fruit in his season,"—" leaf shall not wither." Here again we have the difference between warm and cold climates in regard to vegetation. " Chaff which the wind driveth,"—" standing in the judgment, in the congregation of the righteous." What is meant by " the Lord *knowing* the way of the righteous," &c.? This would finish the second division, or leading points, in the narrative, picture, or passage. The third would be very naturally given by, or drawn out from, the children. As—The righteous, who delight in the law of the Lord, and meditate, &c. and walk not with—stand not in the way of sinners—nor sit in the seat of the scornful —shall continue to flourish like trees by... *a river* in a warm ... *climate,* whose leaves never ... *wither ;* and that not only shall they ... *prosper,* but that the

Lord shall...*know* and acknowledge them. Whereas, those who do the reverse, and walk in the opposite course of life, shall be...*destroyed*, like the chaff which the...*wind driveth away*, and, in the impressive words at the close of the Psalm, "shall perish." It is evident that a Psalm such as this will be enough for at least two days' Bible lesson.

Were we to take the 144th Psalm, 1st and 2d verses, which would be sufficient ground for the lesson of one day.

Ver. 1. " Blessed be the Lord my strength, which teacheth my hands to war, and my fingers to fight. 2. My goodness, and my fortress; my high tower, and my deliverer; my shield, and he in whom I trust; who subdueth my people under me."

Of course, the meaning of every word would be the first object,—war—fight—goodness—fortress—high tower—deliverer—shield—subdueth. The scholars must, of course, be made to understand the literal meaning of all these words, not by telling or teaching, as we said before, so much as by development. In the second process, namely, THE LEADING POINTS, it will naturally strike every boy as a strange thing, that David the king gave thanks to God for teaching his hands to war, and his fingers to fight, when every expression of parents at home, and master in school, and every rhyme, and every sentiment, from, " Let dogs delight to bark and bite," to such Scripture commands—" Be not overcome of evil; but overcome evil with good,"—all go to prove the evil and folly of quarrelling and fighting; but when, agreeably to the plan partially exhibited in regard to the first point of Psalm i. 1. the children find, that while they are forbidden to fight, King David was actually commanded to fight with God's enemies, and to root them out of the land of Canaan, for their... *great wickedness*, the name of all the nations being mentioned, and perhaps pointed out on the map, the children then see clearly and intelligibly how that what is a sin in the one case is a virtue in the other; obedience or disobedience to the command of God being alone the principle and test of duty. Again, a " high tower:" why a high tower, and not a low tower? It is the better to see the... *enemy*. God, therefore, is our... *high tower*, and looks out for the enemy. Of course, what a tower is must be fully explained. And in the third process, we would get the children to say... *delivers us*, or delivered... *David the king* of... *Israel*, the anointed servant of ... *God*. God is also the "shield" of his... *people;* but the shape, &c. of the shield will, of course, have been gone over fully in the first process; its use in former times, when swords and arrows were the opposing instruments of battle, and its uselessness now, when bullets would so readily pierce it; as well as why it was placed on the left arm, and not the right—to protect the... *heart, &c.* and to give liberty to the right... *arm*, to wield the... *sword*, or draw the... *bow*. Some persons may say, Why explain so minutely that which is so worldly and secular in its character? does not this amount to an unnecessary lowering, or prostituting of Scripture to ordinary history? We answer, Till this is done, the word " shield" might as well be printed in Hebrew or Greek, as in English, for, of course, it is not understood; and we add, it never ought to be felt beneath us, or in the least degree improper, to explain that which God has thought fit to reveal, or to use in illustration. The third and last lesson on every passage, or from every illustration, ought just to be the obvious lesson which the Spirit of God intended by writing that passage. Thus, whether in biography, as in the case of Josiah, the good... *little boy* and ... *king*, walking in the way of David his... *father*, or Timothy knowing the Scriptures from ... *a child*, or the Peacock with his gaudy, splendid... *feathers*, or ... *plumage*, *without*, but his hideous... *cry*, and otherwise revolting flesh and disposition, ... *within*,—the master, under this system, is furnished with that which, independent of its moral results under the Divine blessing, will afford a variety, at once pleasing, improving, and intellectual.

MONDAY.—*Bible Biography.*

Genesis iii.		Adam and Eve.
...	v. 5.	Adam's death.
...	iv. 2—15.	Cain and Abel.
...	v. 21—24.	Enoch translated.
...	v. 25—27.	Methuselah, the longest lived.
...	vi. vii. viii.	Noah, the ark, and the flood.
...	xii. 1—9.	Abraham called.
...	xxii. 1—19.	Abraham offereth Isaac.
...	xiii.	Abraham and Lot.
...	xxiii.	Sarah's death.
...	xxv. 7—11.	Abraham's death.
...	xxiv. 63.	Isaac's character.
...	xxvii.	Jacob's deceit.
...	xxxii.	Jacob's name changed.
...	xxxvii.	Joseph sold by his brethren.
...	xli.	Joseph advanced in Egypt.
...	xliv.	Joseph made known to his brethren.
...	xlviii.	Joseph visiteth his sick father.
...	xlix. 28—33. l.	Jacob's death, and Joseph's death.
Exodus ii. 3—10.		Finding of Moses.
Numb. xvi.		Korah, Dathan, & Abiram's rebellion.
...	xxi. 4—9.	Moses lifting up the brazen serpent.
...	xxii.	Balaam and the Angel.
Deut. xxxiv.		Moses' death.
Joshua x. 6—14.		Joshua commands the sun to stand still.
1 Sam. iii.		Samuel and Eli.
...	iv. 10—18.	Eli's death, and his two sons.
...	xvii.	David and Goliath.
...	xviii. 1—4. xx.	Jonathan's love for David.
...	xviii. 5—16.	Saul's hatred of David.
1 Kings x.		Queen of Sheba visits Solomon.
...	xvii.	Elijah and the widow.
2 Kings ii. 15.		Elijah is taken up into heaven.
...	v.	Naaman and Gehazi.
...	xxi. 18.	Manasseh's wicked reign.
...	xxii. 1—3.	Josiah, the good king.

2 Chron. i. ii. iii. iv. v. vi. Solomon's temple.
Esther ii. 5—8. 15—20. Esther made queen.
  ... —following chapters—Haman and Mordecai.
Job   i. ii.   Job's trial of patience.
Psalm cxliv. 1—4. David's experience.
Eccles. xii. Solomon's sermon.
Isaiah xxxviii. Hezekiah's sickness.
  ... vi. 1—4. Isaiah's vision.
Daniel i. Daniel and the three children.
Jonah i. 1—3.
    i. 4—10. } Jonah.
    i. 11—17.
  ... ii. Prayer and deliverance of Jonah.
  ... iii. Jonah preacheth to the Ninevites.
  ... iv. Jonah and the gourd.
Luke i. Christ's birth.
  ... ii. 1—20. Shepherds of Bethlehem.
Matth. ii. 1—10. Wise men of the east.
  ... ii. 11—23. Joseph fleeth into Egypt.
Luke ii. 40—52. Christ with the Doctors.
  ... xix. 1—10. Zaccheus.
John x. 11—18. The good Shepherd.
Matth. iii. John preaching in the wilderness.
  ... iv. 1—11. Jesus tempted in the wilderness.
Mark x. 13—16. Jesus blesseth little children.
Matth. xxvi. 17–56. Judas betraying Christ.
  ... xxvi. 57–75. Peter's denial of Christ.
  ... xxvii. Jesus crowned with thorns.
John xix. Christ crucified.
Matth. xxviii. Christ's resurrection.
Acts i. 1—14. Christ's ascension.
  ... v. 1—11. Ananias and Sapphira.
  ... vii. Stephen stoned to death.
  ... vi. 8—15. viii. 26—40. Philip and the eunuch.
  ... ix. Saul on the way to Damascus.
  ... xii. Peter delivered from prison.
  ... xvi. 25—34. Paul and Silas in prison.
2 Tim. iii. 14—17. Timothy knew the Scriptures early.

TUESDAY.—*Illustrations and Bible History of Animate Nature.*

1 Kings xiii. 20—26.	The disobedient prophet slain by a lion.
1 Sam. xvii. 32–37.	David killeth a lion and bear.
Daniel vi. 10—28.	Daniel cast into the lion's den.
2 Kings ii. 23—25.	Naughty children destroyed by two bears.
Prov. xxx. 17.	" The eye that mocketh his father."
Mark xi. 1—10.	Christ rideth into Jerusalem on an ass.
Isaiah i. 3.	" The ox knoweth his owner, and the ass," &c.
Numb. xxii. 4.	" As the ox licketh up," &c.
Deut. xxv. 4.	Ox treading out the corn.
Judges xv. 14—20.	Samson killeth a thousand Philistines. with the jawbone of an ass.
Psalm xxxii. 9.	" Be ye not as the horse or the mule," &c.
... cxix. 176.	1 Pet. ii. 25. " Like sheep going astray."
Acts viii. 32.	" He was led as a lamb," &c.
Matth. xxv. 31—33.	The goats.
Genesis iii. 1—6.	Serpent deceiveth Eve.
Matth. x. 16.	" Be wise as serpents," &c.
Isaiah xi. 6.	" The wolf," &c.
Exodus viii.	Plagues of frogs, flies, &c.
Numb. xxi. 4—9.	Israelites plagued with fiery serpents.
1 Kings xvii. 1—7.	Elijah fed by ravens.
Jonah i. 11—17.	Jonah swallowed by a fish.
Genesis viii. 6—12.	Dove sent out of the ark.
Acts xxviii. 1—6.	Paul and the viper.
Matth. xxiii. 37.	" Even as a hen," &c.
... xxvi. 34.	Mark xiii. 35—37. Cock-crowing.
2 Chron. ix. 21.	Job xxxix. 13—18. Peacock and ostrich.
Levit. xi. 29, 30.	Tortoise, ferret, mole, &c.
1 Chron. xii. 8.	Swift as the roes.
Zeph. ii. 11—15.	The bittern and the cormorant.
Luke x. 3.	Isaiah xl. 11. Like lambs.
Heb. x. 4.	The bull.

Matth.   xix. 24.   The Camel.

Jer.   viii. 7. Isa. xxxviii. 14. The Swallow and Dove.

Psalm   lxxxiv. 3. Matth. x. 29. The Sparrow, &c.

Luke   xii. 22—24. The Ravens sow not.

Levit.   xi. 13—19. The Vulture, &c.

Prov.   xxvi. 11. Luke xvi. 21. The Dog.

Esther   viii. 10. Jer. ii. 23. The Dromedary.

Exodus xv. 19—22. Psalm xx. 7. The Horse.

Genesis xlix. 17.   The Adder.

James   iii. 3—10.   The Tongue.

Psalm   cii. 6.   The Pelican and Owl.

Job   xxxix. 9—12. The Unicorn.

Isaiah   xiii. 19—22. ⎫

Jer.   l. 39, 40.   ⎬ " Owls shall dwell in Babylon.

2 Sam. i. 23.   Swifter than Eagles.

Jer.   xvii. 11.   The Partridge.

2 Peter ii. 22.   " The sow to her wallowing," &c.

Job   xvii. 14. xxi. 12—26. " Worms shall," &c.

Psalm   xlii. 1.   " As the Hart panteth," &c.

Lam.   v. 16—19. Matth. viii. 20. " The Foxes," &c.

Jer.   xiii. 23.   " Can the Ethiopian," &c. " or Leopard," &c.

Isaiah   xl. 28—31. Wings as Eagles.

Psalm   xxxiii. 17.   " A Horse is a vain," &c.

Isaiah   xi. 8.   Child—hole of the Asp.

Psalm   xvii. 8.   As the apple of the eye.

WEDNESDAY.—*Moral Duties, from Bible Examples and Precepts.*

EXAMPLES.

Genesis xxxvii.	Envy:—Joseph's brethren.
Joshua vii.	Covetousness and theft:—Achan.
Numb. xv. 32—36.	Sabbath-breaking:—The man stoned by the Israelites.
Matth. vii. 12.	*The golden rule :* " Whatsoever," &c.
2 Sam. xviii.	Disobedience to parents:—Absalom.
... xvi. 1—14.	Cursing:—Shimei.
Acts v. 1—11.	Lying:—Ananias and Sapphira.
2 Kings ii. 23—25.	Mocking:— Children destroyed by the bears.
Daniel iii.	Pride:—Nebuchadnezzar.
1 Kings xx. 1—21.	Drunkenness:—Benhadad.
Daniel v.	Impiety:—Belshazzar.
Matth. xxv. 1—13.	Idleness:—Foolish virgins.
Genesis xl.	Ingratitude:—Chief butler.
... xxii. 1—19.	Faith:—Abraham.
... xix. 12—29.	Unbelief:—Lot's wife.
... iv. 2—15.	Murder:—Cain.
... xxxix. 1—6.	Trustiness:—Joseph.
Luke ii. 46—52.	Subjection to Parents:—Jesus in Nazareth.
Numb. xii.	Meekness:—Moses.
James v. 7—11.	Patience:—Job.
Jer. xxxv.	Obedience to Parents:—The Rechabites.
2 Tim. iii.	Early Piety:—Timothy.
Acts x. 1, 2.	Fear of God:—Cornelius.
Mark xii. 41—44.	Almsgiving:—The widow's mite.
Daniel ix.	Prayer:—Daniel.
Psalm v. 3. cxix. 164.	Do. David.
Matth. vi. 5—15.	Do. "Be not as the hypocrites."
Luke vi. 12.	Do. Jesus prayeth.
Acts xvi. 13—34.	Praising God in affliction:—Paul and Silas.
... vii. 54—60.	A forgiving spirit:—Stephen.
Luke xxiii. 32—34.	Do. Jesus on the cross.
Acts xvii. 1—15.	Searching the Scriptures:—Bereans.

PRECEPTS.

Exod.   xx. 12. Col. iii. 20.   Obedience to Parents.
John   v. 39. " Search the Scriptures."
Colos.   iii. 9. Prov. 12—22.   Lying.
Matth.   v. 34—37. Levit. xix. 12.   Swearing.
Exod.   xx. 15.   Stealing.
Matth.   vi. 1—4.   Almsgiving.
Exodus xx. 17. 1 Cor. xii. 31.   Coveting.
Prov.   xxx. 17. Prov. xiv. 9.   Mocking.
Matth.   vi. 5—15.   Praying.
Prov.   x. 18. Psalm ci. 5.   Slandering.
...   xi. 1. Hosea xii. 7.   Cheating.
Ephes.   v. 4. Matth. xii. 36.   Foolish and idle talking.
Prov.   xix. 15. vi. 6—11.   Slothfulness.
John   xv. 12—20.   Loving one another.
Prov.   iii. 31. Gen. xxxvii. 11.   Envy.
Matth.   xxii. 37. Psalm xcvii. 10.   Loving God.
Prov.   viii. 17.   Seeking God early.
...   xii. 10. Deut. xxv. 4.   Cruelty.
...   xx. 19. xxix. 5.   Flattering.
Eccles.   x. 18. Prov. xxxi. 27.   Idleness.
Rom.   xii. 10. Prov. xxv. 21.   Being kind to all.
John   xiv. 15. xv. 10—14.   Obeying God.
Jer.   xiii. 15. 1 Peter v. 5.   Pride.
Rom.   xiii. 13. 1 Cor. vi. 10.   Drunkenness.
Ephes.   iv. 25. Zech. viii. 16.   Speaking the truth.
Prov.   xxiii. 20—22.   Gluttony.
Exodus xx. 13. Matth. v. 21, 22.   Murder.
Jer.   xlix. 11.   Trusting in God.
Eccles.   xii. 13. Psalm cxi. 10.   Fearing God.
Titus   ii. 9, 10. 1 Peter ii. 18—20. ⎰ Duty of Servants to
Colos.   iii. 22—24.   ⎱   Masters.
1 Peter ii. 17.   Duty to Superiors.
Rom.   xiii. 1—7. Matth. xxii. 15—22.   Duty to Magistrates and Kings.
Colos.   iv. 1. Eph. vi. 9.   Duty of Masters.
Rom.   xii. 19—21. " Be not overcome of evil."

THURSDAY.—*Miracles, from the Old and New Testament; and the Parables of our Lord.*

MIRACLES.

1 Kings	xvii. 17–24.	Elijah raiseth the widow's son.
2 Kings	iv. 1—7.	Elisha multiplies the widow's oil.
...	iv. 18—37.	Elisha raiseth the Shunamite's son.
...	v. 1—19.	Naaman's leprosy cured.
Exod.	xiv. 19—31.	Moses divideth the Red Sea.
1 Kings	xvii. 8—16.	Elijah multiplieth the widow's oil and meal.
Joshua	x. 12—14.	The sun standing still.
John	vi. 1—14.	Feeding five thousand.
Mark	vii. 31—37.	Making the deaf to hear.
Luke	v. 1—11.	Miraculous draught of fishes.
John	ii. 1—11.	Turning water into wine.
...	v. 1—16.	Healing the impotent man.
Luke	vii. 11—18.	Raising the widow's son.
John	xxi. 1—14.	Draught of fishes.
Matth.	xiv. 22–33.	Jesus walking on the sea.
...	viii. 23–27.	Stilling the tempest.
Mark	x. 46—52.	Bartimeus restored to sight.
Luke	ix. 28—36.	Christ transfigured.
...	viii. 26–30.	The man among the tombs.
...	viii. 49–56.	Raising the ruler's daughter.
...	viii. 2.	Seven devils cast out of Mary Magdalene.
John	ix.	Restoring sight to the man born blind.
Luke	xvii. 11–19.	Cleansing ten lepers.
...	xiv. 1—6.	Man cured of the dropsy.
Matth.	viii. 5—13.	Healing the centurion's servant.
...	ix. 1—8.	Paralytic healed.
...	viii. 14–17.	Peter's wife's mother cured of a fever.
...	viii. 1—4.	Leper cleansed.
...	xvii. 24—27.	The tribute-money.
Luke	ix. 37—42.	Child healed of an unclean spirit.
Acts	iii. 1—18.	Peter healeth a lame man.
...	ix. 32—35.	Peter healeth Eneas.
...	ix. 36—43.	Dorcas brought to life.

Acts	xii. 1—19.	Peter delivered by an angel.
...	xiv. 8—18.	Paul healeth a cripple at Lystra.
...	xvi. 13—26.	Paul casteth out a spirit of divination.
...	xx. 7—12.	Eutychus restored to life.
...	xxviii. 1—11.	Paul healeth the father of Publius.
Matth.	ix. 27—31.	Two blind men cured.
...	ix. 32—38.	Dumb healed.
Mark	iii. 1—12.	Healeth the withered hand.
Luke	xiii. 11—17.	Heals a woman who had a spirit of infirmity eighteen years.
John	ix.	Restores to sight a man born blind.
...	xi. 1—19.	Lazarus' death.
...	xi. 19—46.	Lazarus raised from the dead.
Luke	xviii. 35—43.	A blind man restored to sight.
...	xxii. 50—53.	Heals the ear of Malchus.

PARABLES.

Matth.	xiii. 1—9.	The sower and the seed.
Mark	iv. 26—29.	The springing of the seed.
Matth.	xiii. 24—30.	The tares and the wheat.
...	xxi. 33—46.	The rebellious husbandmen.
...	xxv. 14—30.	The talents.
...	xiii. 44.	The hid treasure.
...	xx. 1—16.	The labourers in the vineyard.
...	xiii. 45, 46.	The pearl of great price.
...	xiii. 47—58.	The net cast into the sea.
...	xxv. 1—13.	The ten virgins.
...	xxii. 1—14.	The wedding-garment.
...	xxi. 28—32.	The obedient and disobedient sons.
Luke	xii. 15—21.	The rich fool.
...	x. 25—37.	The good Samaritan.
...	xiii. 6—9.	The barren fig-tree.
...	xv. 1—7.	The lost sheep.
...	xv. 8—10.	The lost piece of money.
...	xv. 11—32.	The prodigal son.
...	xviii. 1—7.	The unjust judge.
...	xvi. 1—15.	The unjust steward.
...	xvi. 19—31.	The rich man and Lazarus.
...	xviii. 9—14.	The publican and Pharisee.

FRIDAY.—*Illustrations and Bible History of Inanimate Nature.*

Prov.	xxvii. 17.	" As iron sharpeneth iron," &c.
1 Cor.	xiii. 12.	Glass darkly.
Prov.	xxvii. 19.	Water.
Song	ii. 1. Matth. vi. 28—30.	Rose and lily.
John	viii. 12. Matth. v. 14—16.	Lights of the world.
Matth.	xvii. 1—8.	Shine as the sun.
...	v. 13.	Salt of the earth.
Rev.	xxii. 16.	Jesus the Morning Star.
Psalm	ii. 9. 1 Tim. iv. 2.	Iron.
John	vi. 31—35.	Christ the bread of life.
Eph.	ii. 20—22. 1 Pet. ii. 6, 7.	The chief Corner-stone.
John	x. 9.	Christ the door.
Rev.	iii. 20. James v. 9.	Standing at the door.
Exod.	xvii. 4—7.	Smiting the rock.
Psalm	xviii. 46. xxxi. Matth. xvi. 18.	Christ a Rock.
...	lxxxiv. 11. cxliv. 2. Prov. xxx. v.	God a Shield.
Ephes.	vi. 16.	Shield of faith.
Psalm	xxxii. 7—9.	A hiding-place.
Jer.	ii. 21, 22.	A vine.
John	xv. 1—6.	Christ the true vine.
Job	xxi. 17, 18. Nahum i. 10.	The wicked as stubble.
1 Cor.	iii. 11, 12.	Wood, hay, stubble, &c.
Prov.	i. 27. Psalm xi. 6.	Whirlwind and tempest.
Isaiah	xlii. 3.	A bruised reed.
Genesis	vi. 14.	Ark of gopher-wood.
...	xix. 22—26.	Pillar of salt.
Jer.	viii. 22.	Balm in Gilead.
Exodus	iii. 1—6.	Burning bush.
Genesis	xi. 1—9.	Tower of Babel—making bricks.
Exodus	ix. 22—26.	Plague of hail.
Deut.	x. 1—5.	Ark of shittim-wood.
Exodus	xvi. 11—15.	Manna sent.
Psalm	xix. 10.	" Sweeter than honey."
Mark	xiv. 3—9.	Alabaster-box.
1 Sam.	xvii. 5. Eph. 6—17.	Helmet of salvation.

T

John   iii. 8.   " The wind bloweth," &c.
Psalm   cxxi. 6.   " The sun shall not smite," &c.
...   xcii. 10. cxlviii. 14. Luke i. 69. Horn of salvation.

TREES.

Psalm   cxxxvii.   Willows on Babel's streams.
Isaiah   lxi. 3. Psalm i. 3. Trees of righteousness.
Matth.   iii. 10. Jude 12. Axe laid to the root of the trees.
Genesis ii. 15—17. Tree of knowledge, &c.

STONE.

Gen. xxviii. 10—22. Jacob's pillow.
Exodus xxxi. 18.   Ten Commandments.
Numb. xv. 32—36. The Sabbath-breaker stoned.

GOLD.

Genesis xli. 41—44. Joseph's chain.
Exodus xxxii. 1—4. Aaron's golden calf.
Daniel   iii.   Nebuchadnezzar's image.
...   v. 29.   Daniel's chain.
Matth.   ii. 11.   Wise men's offering.

SILVER.

Genesis xliv. 1—13. Joseph's cup.
2 Kings v. 20—27.   Gehazi's deceit.
Matth. xxvi. 14–16. Jesus sold.
Acts   xix. 24—28. Shrines for Diana.

SEAS.

Exodus xiv. 26—31. Egyptians drowned in the Red Sea.
Matth. xiv. 22—33. Jesus walketh on the sea.

MOUNTAINS.

Genesis viii. 4.   Ararat—Noah's ark rested.
Deut.   iii. 25. 2 Chron. ii. 8, 9. Lebanon—Cedars.
Luke   xxiii. 33.   Calvary—Jesus was crucified.
Acts   i. 9—11.   Olivet—Jesus ascended up to heaven.
Exodus xix. 16–20. Sinai—God gave the ten command-
                       ments.

SATURDAY.—*Prophecies concerning Christ—*
Bible Geography—Promises, &c.

PROPHECY.	FULFILMENT.
Genesis iii. 15.	{ Luke ii. 10, 11. / 1 John iii. 8.
Isaiah xl. 3.	Matth. iii. 1—3.
Numb. xxiv. 17.	Rev. xxii. 16.
Isaiah ix. 6.	Luke ii. 10.
... lxi. 1, 2.	... iv. 16—21.
Micah v. 2.	Matth. ii. 4—6.
Haggai ii. 7—9.	Luke ii. 27, 32.
Zech. ix. 9.	Matth. xxi. 1—9.
... xiii. 7.	{ John x. 30. / Matth. xxvi. 30, 31, 56.
Psalm xxii. 7.	... xxvii. 29, 39.
... xxxiv. 20.	John xix. 33—36.
... cxviii. 26.	Matth. xxi. 9.
... xxii. 1.	... xxvii. 46.
... xxii. 16—18.	{ Mark xv. 25. / John xix. 34—37.
... xvi. 10.	Acts ii. 31, 32.
Isaiah liii. 4.	Matth. viii. 16, 17.
... liii. 7.	... xxvii. 12, 16.
... liii. 12, 5.	{ Mark xv. 27, 28. / Luke xxiii. 33, 34.
Luke ix. 44.	... xxiii. 1.
Isaiah liii. 9.	Matth. xxvii. 38, 57—60.
Luke ix. 22.	... xxviii. 1—6.

BIBLE GEOGRAPHY.

Journey of the Israelites from Egypt to the Promised Land.
—This may commence from Pharaoh's giving Jacob's
family the land of Goshen to dwell in: see Genesis, chapter xlvii. and carried forward through Exodus, &c. The
judicious Teacher, whether he reads a passage from the
Bible to the children, as in Infant Schools, or allows the

children to read to him, and in hearing of all the scholars, as in the Juvenile School, will of course select for each successive day such passages as their minds can be exercised upon with propriety, and as bear in some measure upon the progress of the Journey—causing the children to point out, on the map, the various positions of the Israelites, as the history proceeds—giving also familiar illustrations, to elucidate the different points and particulars of the narrative.

Paul's Journey to Rome.—Commencing from Acts xix. 21. when Paul, in the Spirit, purposed to go to Jerusalem, and afterwards to see Rome.

THE CREATION,

As contained in Genesis, 1st and 2d chapters. These two chapters, if suitably and familiarly illustrated, are quite sufficient for five or six days' exercises in succession.

PROMISES.

Temptation.—Isaiah xli. 10. Psalm i. 1—3. Exodus xiv. 13. Isaiah xliii. 1—4. 2 Corinthians xii. 9. James i. 12. Hebrews ii. 16—18. Revelation iii. 12.

To Backsliders.—Jeremiah iii. 12. Deuteronomy iv. 25—40. Jeremiah xxxi. 20. Hosea vi. 1—3. Hosea xi. 8—11. Hosea xiii. 9. Hosea xiv. 1. Luke xv. 20. Ezekiel xviii. 30—32. 1 Samuel vii. 3—8.

Affliction.—Proverbs iii. 11, 12. Psalm xxxiv. 19. Psalm l. 14, 15. Isaiah lvii. 15. Psalm xlvi. 1—5. Lamentations iii. 31—33. Hebrews xii. 5—8. Revelation iii. 19. Isaiah xliii. 2. Psalm xxxii. 7.

Death.—Psalm xxiii. 4. Psalm cxvi. 15. John iii. 14—17. 1 Corinthians xv. 51—58. Revelation xiv. 13. 2 Corinthians v. 1. Revelation xxi. 4.

CHAPTER VII.

JUVENILE TRAINING.

Parochial Model School, St. John's, Annfield.

Moral training the same in Infant and Juvenile Schools—Juvenile training a cultivation of the whole man—it embraces the monitorial system of Bell—the intellectual system of Wood—and the moral training of the Infant School—Play-ground—Gallery—Objects, and pictures of objects—Bible stand—Demonstration-board—Box of objects—Dr. Mayo's lessons—Examples—Transposition lesson—Mental arithmetic—Game on natural history for play-ground—Responses—Plan of Model Juvenile School, St. John's parish—Plan of Infant and Juvenile School, Chalmers Street—List of branches taught—Endowments for the masters—Wages—Weekly course of education—Memorandums.

THE Scottish Parochial School system, and the schoolmasters, as a whole, are indeed worthy of high commendation. The masters of some of these seminaries, as well as many respectable private teachers, especially in towns, have, or are now introducing most of the late improvements in this art; still, however, as we have already shown, the system pursued is *teaching*, not *moral training*. We make no apology, therefore, for proposing the universal adoption of juvenile training into our existing schools, which, as under the system of infant training, provides for the cultivation of the whole man, as a physical, intellectual, religious, and moral being. We are happy, however, that the adaptation of this system to children above six years of age, is now no longer pro-

T 2

blematical, having the actual fact in the Parochial School of St. John's, Annfield, which, as an exhibition of the system of juvenile training, may be considered an excellent model.

The system of moral training, or of training the whole man, is one and the same, whether in an Infant or Juvenile School; and, as we have already shown, in Chapters I. and II., does not depend so much upon the amount, as upon the quality, of the knowledge which may be imparted; and is dependent, not simply upon the intellectual perception, but also upon the practical habit. Moral training, in its proper and highest sense, therefore, embraces an intellectual cultivation of the head and the heart upon the truths of revelation, and the practical habit of its duties and requirements in real life; and, in regard to children, their real life is, of course, at play; and nowhere can they be properly superintended at play, but in an enclosed play-ground. It refers not to the age, but to the principle, and is applicable to any and every age of boyhood. There is no science, from the most common to the most sublime, which it may not adorn; and there is none which may not be made subservient to it.

There may exist a very high morality in a country, where little more is known but what the Bible contains; but there cannot be, and the world does not, at this moment, exhibit, one community with such a character, where its simple truths are unknown.

Let there be superadded in our schools, a knowledge of as many sciences and arts, as the most ardent admirer of intellectual cultivation may be pleased to demand, so long as these are conjoined with a daily Bible training (not simple reading) and moral superintendence. We fear not, but rather rejoice to know, that " knowledge is power." If, however, on the contrary, the power of reading is granted to children, without their being trained to what they ought to read, and if any thing and every thing is read and studied but the word of life, let us not wonder at the fact, that worthless political publications, immoral songs, and blasphemous publications, all of which are so consonant with nature, should be so eagerly and extensively read. In this case, also, " knowledge is power;" but it is a power to do mischief.

The child, having arrived at six years of age, should now be transferred to the Juvenile School, where the moral training, begun in the Infant School, may be carried forward up to the age of twelve or fourteen—where the elements of reading, writing, &c. may be acquired, and where other branches of knowledge may be carried forward; the simple, yet grand outlines of which, they had, in the Infant School, been made acquainted with.

Juvenile training, now under consideration, may be stated as a combination of the excellencies of the several most approved systems of education, which are conducted under different names, but may be best explained as follows :—The monitorial system of Bell, with the intellectual system of Wood, and the moral training and plan of development peculiar to the Infant School.

Without the partial adoption of monitors, the master cannot fully employ every child, every moment of the day; nor can he feel himself at liberty, rapidly, and by turns, to superintend in the play-ground or school-room, or see that the monitors and children are each attentive to their duty; nor could he find the opportunity of examining each class, separately, in the adjoining class-room. The peculiar excellence of the system pursued in this school, is, that it has all the advantages of the monitorial system, without any of its disadvantages; for while the pupils are all employed under well-trained monitors, they are generally twice a-day examined by the superintendent, in a separate class-room.

Three things absolutely requisite in infant training, are also indispensable in juvenile training. 1. AN ENCLOSED PLAY-GROUND. 2. A GALLERY. 3. OBJECTS, AND PICTURES OF OBJECTS. The gallery for mental development and sympathy—the picture lessons and objects, to arrest the eye, in regard to the subject under consideration, and to render present and visible, that which otherwise might be conceived mysterious and inexplicable.

To these a BIBLE STAND is added, in the middle of the floor, in front of the gallery, on which is placed a quarto Bible, from which the daily lessons are taken: (see Chapter VI.) The same stand serves for fixing the DEMONSTRATION, or large BLACK BOARD,—the use of which shall be noticed hereafter; small slates, also, are required for the children, which they ought to be trained to use from the time they enter the school, in forming lines, or figures, or maps, of various kinds.

A Box of Objects ought to be had, with three drawers, or trays; one for each of the kingdoms in nature—animal, vegetable, and mineral. These, with Geographical Maps, Scriptural and otherwise, and Gymnastic Poles, Flowers, Shrubs, Wooden Bricks, &c. in the play-ground, form the peculiar machinery requisite in every school for juvenile training.

To prevent mistakes in regard to juvenile training, we remark, that the infant system has certainly made a considerable stir, and even some improvement in every branch of elementary education; and, as one mean, is, no doubt, destined to render every other system more in accordance with nature than they have hitherto been. Masters are extremely slow, however, in embracing it, although we never met with an individual, who, after due investigation, did not acknowledge its power.

Bits and portions of this system have, of late, been adopted in various public and private seminaries. One adopts one division, without any of the others, taking objects for examples; another pictures of objects; a third adopts the elliptical plan; another mixes the elliptical and interrogatory: each stating that they have adopted the infant system; but unless all the peculiarities are combined, including, of course, the play-ground, success cannot be looked for.

Dr. Mayo's "Lessons on Objects" form a distinct exercise twice a week: we shall give two examples, which are found in his excellently arranged publication.

QUALITIES OF WATER.—It is liquid, reflective, glassy, colourless, inodorous,* tasteless, transparent, heavy, bright, wholesome, purifying.

Uses.—To cleanse; to fertilize; to drink; for culinary purposes.

* In order to direct the attention of the class to the force of the syllables *less* and *in,* the teacher would ask: What is meant by tasteless?—Having no taste. What is meant by inodorous?—Having no odour. In what are these words alike?—They both tell us what the substance is not. They mark then the absence of a quality. What syllables of the words mark the absence of the quality?— *Less* and *in.* Give examples of words in which *less* and *in* are so used.

QUALITIES OF SPONGE.—Ideas to be developed by this lesson—*porous, absorbent.*

It is porous, absorbent,* soft, tough, opaque, elastic.

* The quality of absorbing will be made obvious to the class, by showing that the sponge sucks up any liquid. It possesses this quality in consequence of its being full of pores. The use to which an object is applied, often leads to the observation of the quality upon which the use is dependent.

Pictures of Objects, whether of nature or art, are in use in the Model School, and may be carried still farther forward, more particularly in natural history, mineralogy, and botany. The importance and necessity of pictures of objects, when the object itself cannot be presented, require no comment. This department is extremely pleasing to the child, as well as improving. The exercise is gone through, when the children are seated in the gallery. The Demonstration, or large Black Board, affords an opportunity of forming figures of various kinds, from the form of a letter in the alphabet, to the map of a kingdom ; any and all of which the children may copy on their small slates.

Another plan may be pursued in regard to using the Demonstration-board, and form an unlimited variety of words.

TRANSPOSITION LESSON.—The master writes in characters, large enough to be seen by all in the gallery, a word at the top, such as, Salvation, N o t w i t h s t a n d i n g, or

T r a n s p o s i t i o n,

from which let the children, in turn, make as many words as they can, *reading forward* only, of course, and only using such letters as are contained in the above word, as trap, an, ant, ran, post, it, ton, tin, in. As discovered, print them on the board or slate, below, and by turning their attention to each word, they form a subject of conversation.

MENTAL ARITHMETIC is introduced in relation to objects and things, and may be commenced from the time a child enters the Juvenile School. This, in conjunction with, or as a successor to, the Infant School Ball-frame, will be found an excellent preparative to the severer study of practical arithmetic. We may give one example. Add 5 nuts, 7 plums, and 10 apples —divide by 2—multiply by 4—subtract 7: product, 37. This may be proposed in a variety of ways.

Game on Natural History in the Play-Ground, in regard to *birds, beasts, fish, or insects*, which may be taken up by the children occasionally as a variety.

Divide the whole, or a portion of the number of children, into two parts; or, to use a play-ground phrase, " choose sides :" suppose the following to represent the play-ground :—

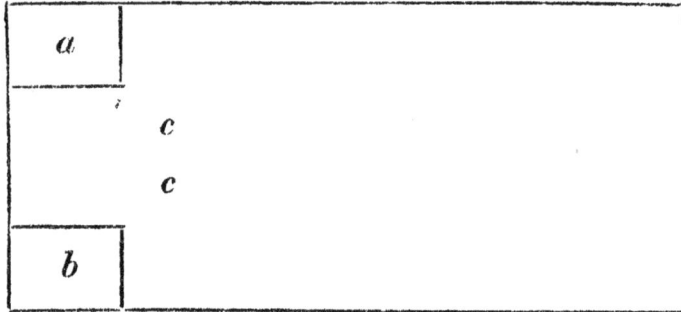

Place one party at *a*, and the other at *b*, after which, one from either side—say one from *a*, as directed by an appointed leader, goes out to *c*, and puts some such question to those at *b* as this: Tell me the name of a fine singing-bird, or a web-footed bird, or an amphibious quadruped, or a bird of prey, &c. &c. Each boy of the opposite side, in turn, endeavours to find out what bird, quadruped, or insect, is alluded to, each naming but one; if it is discovered, the boy is won over to that side; if not, he returns to his own side, and the opposite side put a question, &c. &c.

This is merely a hint to the superintendent, which he may carry out, or simplify, according to his own judgment. The letters of the alphabet, for example, may form a starting point in regard to any animal.

Responses.—This is found a very interesting and improving exercise. The master asks who are willing to try the Responses: those who are so, hold up their right hand. The master then selects two boys, or girls, and, after mentioning, or allowing them to choose, whether the subject is to be on Bible history, moral duties, or natural history, &c. they are called upon to stand up, either in their seats, or on the floor in front of the gallery, so as to be seen and heard by all the scholars: (for examples, see pages 188, 197.) Biography or simple history is more generally the foundation; but we shall give a short example on moral duties, and shall suppose that two girls, Margaret and Jane, are selected, and that it is carried on in some such method as follows:—

Margaret. Prove that we should not tell lies, Jane.

Jane. Ephesians 4th chapter, " Putting away lying, speak every man truth to his neighbour."—Prove that we should not steal, Margaret.

Margaret. Eighth Commandment, " Thou shalt not steal."—Prove that we should obey our parents.

Jane. Fifth Commandment, " Honour thy father and thy mother."—Prove that we should not play on the Sabbath-day.——

Master. Since Margaret cannot answer, you must do so yourself; and, of course, you are entitled to put another question. What is the answer, Jane? Fourth Commandment, Sir, " Remember the Sabbath day to keep it holy."

Jane. Prove that we should love our brothers and sisters.

Margaret. Epistle by John, " If God so loved us, we ought also to love one another."—Prove that we should do to others as we wish to be done to.

Jane. "All things, whatsoever ye would that men should do unto you, do ye even so to them."—Prove that it is a sin to speak evil of our neighbour.

Margaret. Ephesians 4th chapter, " Let all evil speaking be put away from you."—Prove that God sees every thing we do——

Master. Remember, children, that although that is a most important proof, yet it is moral duties we are on at present—duties to God, and duties to man.

Margaret. Will this do, Sir, That we should not return evil for evil?—Prove that, Jane.

Jane. 1 Peter 3d chapter, " Not rendering evil for evil."

Master. We shall stop there, if you please, girls.

PUNISHMENTS.—The rod, or taws, has not been in use for nine or ten months past in the Juvenile School, ever since the training system was introduced: for the reasons why, see pages 82—84, 193. A variety may be introduced, by causing a monitor, or assistant teacher, to write the name of any delinquent, or delinquents, on a large slate, placing it in view of the scholars. We may here mention, that in every parochial school in Scotland, boys and girls are taught together; the balance of good and evil being found uniformly in favour of the practice. In this school, they sit on parallel forms, and form distinct classes while under the monitors; and it is only when under the eye of the superintendent, that they are examined together; but even then, they stand or sit by themselves, on the right hand of the superintendent, but form a condensed mass in the gallery. We are aware how shocked some of our southern friends feel at this practice; notwithstanding which, our experience compels us to give it our decided support, as really tending to a great moral good. There is a humanizing influence in boys and girls being brought up together. In certain circumstances there may be some danger, if they are simply taught together; but there cannot be, if they are properly trained.

We do not give the annexed sketch of the Juvenile School-room, (page 250,) as a model to be followed; but merely to show how a teaching school may be turned into one for training.

The whole area in front was a common spot to the children of both departments, without any division—was used chiefly as an entrance to the school, and, frequently, as a scene of quarreling among themselves, and oppression, the older against the younger children. Now, however, since a division has been made, and the master superintends the children at play, the most perfect order and obedience are established. Narrow footpaths are formed, and flower-borders, with box-edgings, along; and about which, 180 boys and girls are trained to move, walk, march along, and chant their lessons, without treading on the border. The Model English School play-ground is to the back, which is an addition made by the kirk-session of St. John's, and is in size, 42 by 65 feet, where they have gymnastic exercises at the poles, are at perfect liberty, and yet the flower-borders remain untouched.

The small play-ground, for the Commercial Department, is in front of the building.

The class-room for the English School is an addition; as also the enlargement and proper division of the out-door conveniencies. The doors of each are fixed, half open, with an iron rod, hooked at the top, so that from the school-room window, the master has a control over the children in this, as in every department.

The school-room being still decidedly too small for training more than 90 or 100 children, it has been found impossible to have a fixed gallery, as in the Infant Schools. Small seats, with backs, each capable of seating three or four children, and which are easily moved by the monitors or older children, from the form or line of a gallery, to squares for the different classes, and from this again into the form of a gallery.

The proper size and arrangement for a Juvenile School, ought precisely to be a counterpart of Chalmers Street Infant School, now subjoined: (see Plate II. page 250.) A master may teach in a confined room, but he cannot train.

The following are the branches of education in the MODEL ENGLISH SCHOOL, for children above six years of age.——Mr. Auld, Superintendent :—

Reading.

Root, construction, and meaning, of English words.

English Grammar.

Geography.

Objects, and Pictures of Objects.

Practical Sacred Music.

Mental Arithmetic.

Daily Bible training, (see Chapter VI.) which includes illustrations of animate and inanimate objects.

Moral Superintendence.

COMMERCIAL DEPARTMENT.—Children from about ten to fourteen.—Mr. Bannatyne, Master.

Writing.

Arithmetic.

Mathematics.

Daily Bible training.

The Moral training in the English School, may be stated as in full operation. It is found that about one-fourth of the 180 children, now in attendance, have been trained in the two parochial Infant Schools of St. John's; so that those who fear that the exemplary habits formed in these Infant seminaries, may be lost on entering an ordinary teaching school, will now find, that such habits, in this school, are not only continued, but confirmed. The improving influence of this one-fourth upon the other three-fourths, is very apparent.

The peculiarities of the system are now being introduced into the Commercial Department, and in so far as untrained children of ten, twelve, and fourteen, with previous deep-rooted, oftentimes improper habits, are capable of being trained, the attempt has succeeded; and we have no doubt, that, after a few months' perseverance, the system will be as complete as it can be. We may notice, that a child at two has improper tendencies, but no habits—at six he has the same tendencies, with the addition of habits to overcome and subdue—at ten, however, while the tendencies generally remain undiminished, the habits of improper thoughts, feelings, and actions, whether to a greater or more limited extent, are still more difficult to be overcome.

Let all be attempted which is possible for the old in the way of improvement; but with the young, ere bad habits are formed, we cannot begin too early in the way of training.

The whole of these branches, no doubt, may be taught, and a proportionate, increased number of scholars trained, by one master and assistants, provided the one school consisted of two rooms, each a third larger than those of the model school, and with class-rooms to each. But we prefer the present plan, of two distinct departments, each with an independent master over his own scholars, and under his eye, in their own enclosed play-ground; for, under the training system, it is preferable that, as in the Infant School, those of two to six years of age play together, so in the Juvenile, those of six to ten should be in a separate playground from those of ten to fourteen—their plays, physical strength, and mental energies, are different at each of the three stages.

Each of the masters has a salary of £25 a-year, (which in large towns is too small an endowment—see Chapter II.) also free school-room, and dwelling-house above the school. Provided each school-room was one half larger, and each with a good-sized class-room and play-ground, we would consider this an excellent model for every parochial school in the United Kingdom.

The wages, per quarter, in the English department, is 2s., which includes the outlines of grammar and geography ; but when a regular course is gone through, in private classes, it is then 4s. Foundling and destitute children, left under the care of the parish, are paid for by the kirk-session, and in these parochial schools receive an excellent education. In the commercial department it is 3s.; and in both cases the master of course receives the wages. Under this plan we have the beauty and perfection of the Scottish Parochial School system—a partial endowment, and partial dependence upon the scholars. We have also all that can comfort the master, and yet stimulate his energies. We do not say that some slight improvements might not be made, especially as regards decayed, and imperfect or defective teachers, but, taken as a whole, Prussian, French, Irish, or English systems, are not to be compared with this simple, yet wise arrangement, of our illustrious forefathers. This school, like all the parochial schools of Scotland, is open to and embraced by the children of various ranks, and of every religious denomination. Wages ought never to be taken weekly, but always quarterly or half-quarterly, *in advance.* See page 153.

We shall close, by a very cursory sketch of the daily course pursued, and a few memorandums, which may be useful to Teachers at a distance, desirous of adopting the Training System, but who have not the opportunity of witnessing its operation.

Weekly course of Education in the Parochial Juvenile Model School.—Mr. Auld, Superintendent.

School opens at ten o'clock, precisely. Ten to eleven o'clock, each day—Bible training, &c. in the gallery : see Chapter VI. Eleven to half-past twelve, formed into classes for reading—occasionally in the play-ground, &c. &c. Half-past twelve to one, at play, with the master as companion and superintendent, or the children may go home for a refreshment. One to two o'clock, intellectual development and training in the gallery. Two to half-past three, play-ground, and again formed into classes.

Every morning,—Ten o'clock, four verses of a psalm or hymn sung—Prayer by the master, the children standing with folded hands and eyes shut—A short prayer repeated by the children, then all are seated—The Bible lesson of the corresponding day of the previous week, is revised elliptically and interrogatory—Manual exercise ; next, the lesson for the day—Manual exercises— Hymn or moral song—Marching tune, when the whole children, in perfect order, form themselves into classes under monitors—Then each class, in rotation, marches into the class-room, to be examined by the superintendent—and should they repeat, read, and explain their lessons accurately, and conduct themselves with propriety, they are allowed to march into the play-ground, headed by their monitor, and, if the weather permit, each of the sexes engage in their own particular sports and gymnastic exercises. When the bell is rung, within a few seconds every child must be within the school-room, and by a particular signal, so many strokes of a bell or blasts of a whistle, any individual class may be called in. Every movement in school is accompanied with singing generally some moral, improving song or rhyme, and set to some well-known, enlivening tune. Afternoon, one to two o'clock, hymn sung—children in gallery. At this hour, the exercises vary, as follows :—

Pictures of objects, thrice a-week—Mayo's objects, from the animal, vegetable, and mineral kingdoms, twice a-week—The Assembly's Shorter Catechism, with Proofs ; also N. Leitch's Shorter Catechism analyzed, thrice a-week—Responses, thrice a-week—Transposition lessons, twice or thrice—Geography, twice a-week—The outlines of English Grammar occasionally in the course of training—Root, construction, and meaning of words—Sacred Geography, once a-week—Practical music at intervals, during the lessons.

Of course, the whole is conducted upon the principle of development, and the great object is, to give every lesson a moral, practical tendency, to give the children frequent cheering exercise in and out doors, to keep every thing in life and activity, and to allow none to be idle.—The school is open for parents and visitors, Monday, Wednesday, and Friday, from one to two o'clock. Teachers desirous of learning the system, by proper application, may remain the whole day, or for days successively, and engage in the exercises of the school, so as to be trained to the practice. A transient visit can exhibit, of course, only part of the system.

The system of training teachers must ever be defective, until Government grant a few hundreds a-year for the partial support of young men, while under training as teachers; and for endowments for the different superintendents of the Normal, or Model Schools, for training such teachers.

MEMORANDUMS.

The books used are those of Mr. Campbell of Dundee; Alphabet Analyzed; Economic Instructor, Parts I. II. and III.; Junior and Senior Collection. Mr. Auld, who has exercised much judgment in promoting this system, prefers these books for their arrangement, without desiring to throw the slightest disparagement on the very many excellent books of other Compilers.

Those children who bring their dinner, are required to meet in the class-room or play-ground; and, previous to eating, one of the number asks a blessing. This gives an opportunity for the exercise of generosity and disinterestedness, and, we may add, self-control—dinners, during school hours, remaining untouched. We have here, and in the play-ground, the combined influence on the children's minds of companions, conscience, and the Eye of God; and in **regard** to the plan of infusing these principles, see previous chapters.

Give short lessons to commit to memory; and whatever is given to learn, exact it most rigidly.

Nothing ought to be said or sung, until first understood; keeping always in view, as much as possible, to cultivate the conscience and heart.

For the mode of training, see Chapters I. and VI.

When a question is at any time put by the children, which ought not to be answered, the master, without hesitation, says that is an improper question; or if a question is put by the children to the master, which he cannot answer, but which, by consulting some book, he may easily find out, the master ought instantly to acknowledge the fact, and may promise to inform them to-morrow, or some other time. This has an excellent effect upon the children, and when openly and candidly done, never detracts from the master's dignity.

Cruelty to animals may be prevented in a great measure, by a suitable course of training, and by lessons frequently and judiciously given by the teacher, reprobating the practice. Thus, if the master sees a child torturing a fly, telling him not to be so cruel, or scolding him for it, has not half so powerful an effect as asking the boy, Do you think that insect feels? How would you like to have your leg or arm pulled about so? Or, elliptically, this little animal feels ... *pain*, when little boys take their ... *legs*, and pull them ... *about* so. The question and ellipsis divert the attention, and leave the boys time to reflect on the subject. Torturing insects is often practised by children from mere thoughtlessness, nay, absolute ignorance of the pain they inflict. Children ought to be trained to treat every animal kindly: a tame pigeon, or other bird, hopping about the school-room, affords a practical opportunity for the exercise.

In regard to the mode of checking improper conduct, which may have occurred in the play-ground—see Chapter IV.

Five short rules—see page 84.

Masters located near each other, ought frequently to have conferences in regard to improvements of the art.

In training, the master ought always to prefer asking a question, rather than telling; asking in such a way, as to awaken the understanding and the affections of the child.

It is perhaps a good rule to give children ten minutes for play each hour, say five minutes before, and five minutes after, in addition to the stated play-times at mid-day. This deduction from the hour's lesson is a gain, even in an intellectual point of view, from the sympathy which health and vigour of body has with that of the mind.

In a Juvenile Training School, as in one for Infants, a female assistant is of great importance, in regard to the habits both of girls and boys. A first charge, however, is quite beyond their physical strength—but there is this distinction, that while in the Juvenile it would be a decided advantage, in the Infant School a female assistant is indispensable.

Mildness and gentleness of manner ought to be cultivated, both in repeating lessons, answering questions, and in moving in and out of the school. It is quite evident that noise and bustle has no connection with cleverness, as is sometimes imagined.

Manual exercises, varied according to circumstances, ought frequently to be repeated, as they are found to quicken the attention, prevent languor, and afford amusement.

Bell's monitorial system ought to be introduced into every school; which, independent of every other advantage, enables a master to superintend and train a much larger number of pupils.

Every superintendent of a Training School ought to make himself acquainted with the names, customs, and products, of Eastern countries, so that he may be enabled to elucidate to his pupils the immense and beauteous variety of Bible illustrations.

DESCRIPTION OF PLATE I.

a a a Flower-borders.
  b Play-Ground.
  c c Gymnastic Poles.
  d Teacher's Water-closet.
  e Retiring place for Boys.
  f Boys' Water-closet.
  g Girls'   do.
  h Ash-pit.
  i Class-room for Model School, 13 feet square.
  k School-room.
 l l l Flower-borders, fronting airing-ground.
  m Marching-ground for English scholars.
  n Entrance-gate to Model School.
  x Bible Stand.
  y Gallery.

The Picture lessons and Maps are hung in double rows round the walls.

  o Stair to Dwelling-house.
  p For Boys.
  q Boys' Water-closet.
  r Girls'   do.
  s Ash-pit.
  T School for Commercial department.
u u u Flower-borders.
  v Play-ground for Commercial department.
  w Entrance to Commercial department.
  x Bible Stand.

DESCRIPTION OF PLATE II.

a a a Flower-borders round Play-ground.
  b b Gymnastic Poles.
  c Play-ground for Infant School, 66 feet by 45.
  d Infant School, 46 feet by 26. Ceiling 13 feet high.
    With Class-room, 12 feet by 12.* The ten small
    circles are formed by brass nails in the floor, in

* The class-room ought to be at least 13 by 15.

PLATE I.

PAROCHIAL JUVENILE SCHOOL
Annfield St Johns

250 ft

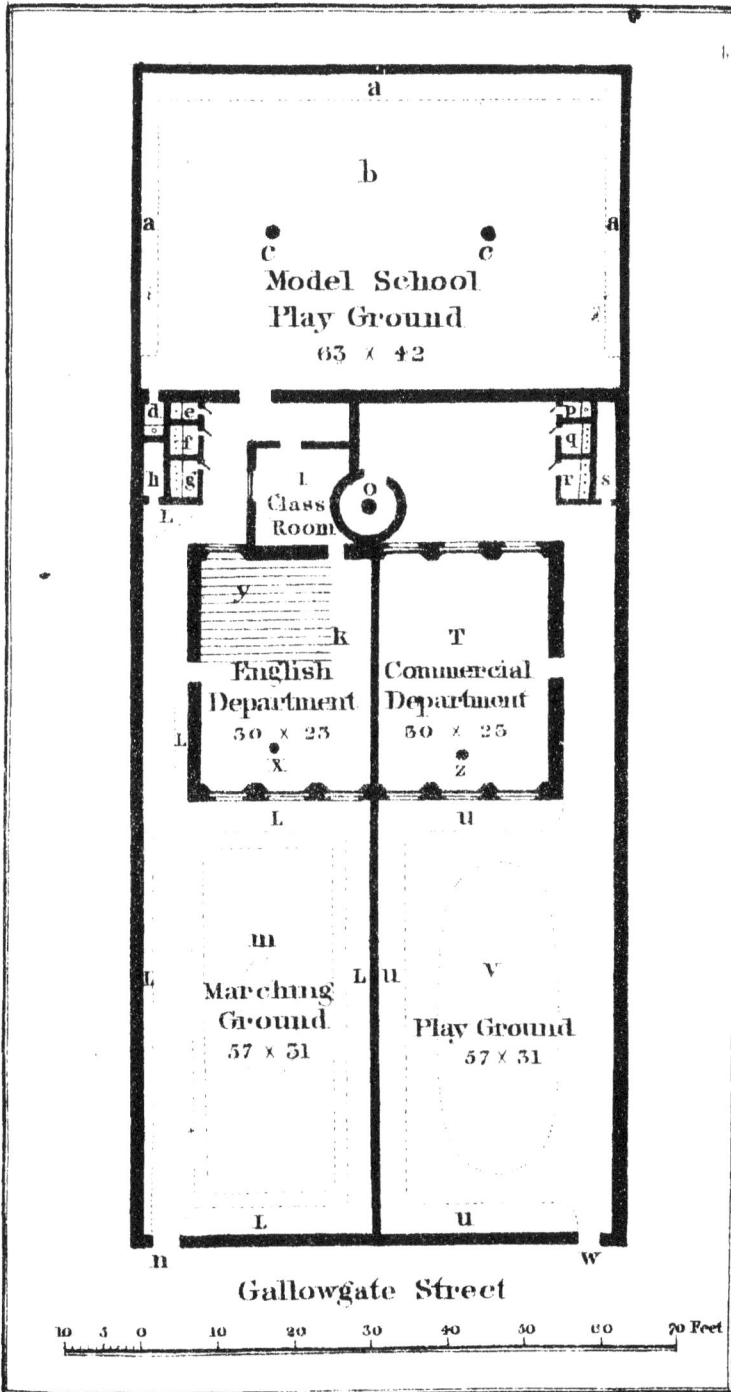

a

b

a   a

c   c

**Model School
Play Ground**
63 × 42

d e   p q

f   r s

h g

L

Class
Room   o

y

k

**English
Department**
30 × 23

**T
Commercial
Department**
30 × 25

X   z

L   u

m

L u

v

**Marching
Ground**
57 × 31

Play Ground
57 × 31

L   u

n   w

Gallowgate Street

10 5 0   10   20   30   40   50   60   70 Feet

PLATE II

PAROCHIAL INFANT SCHOOL
Chalmers Street

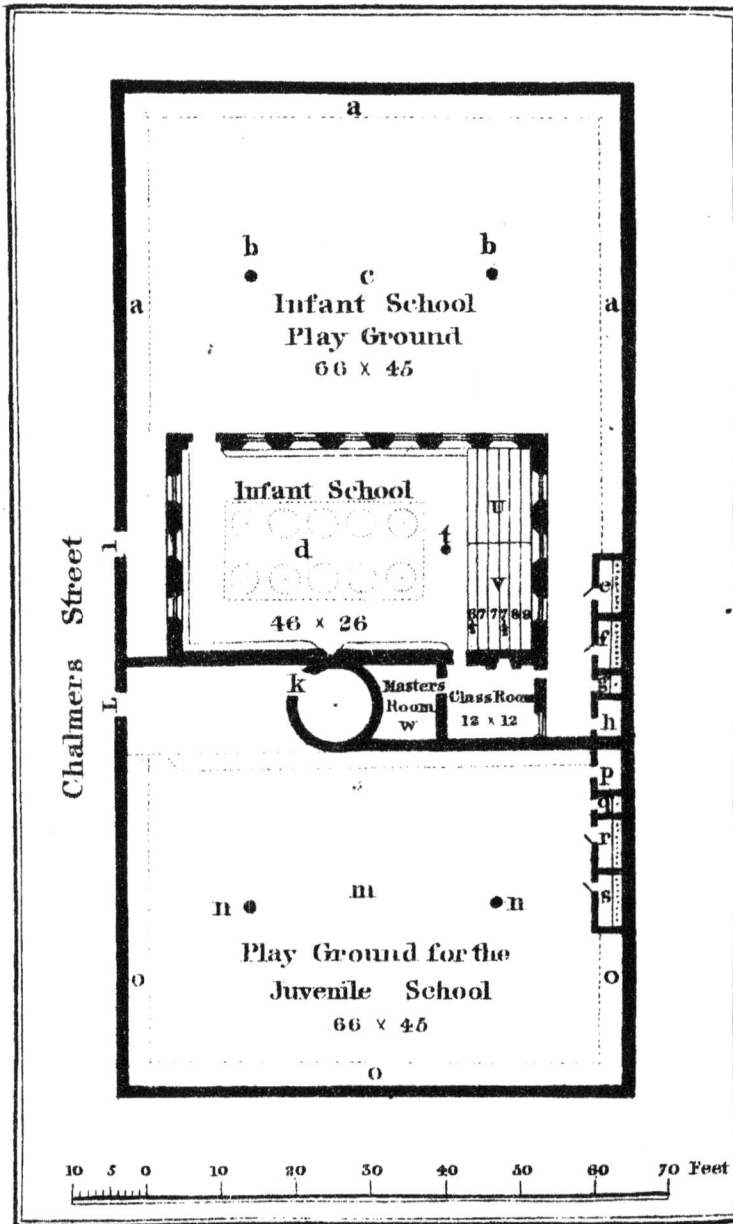

a

b · b ·
c
Infant School
Play Ground
66 × 45

a | | a

Chalmers Street

Infant School
d
46 × 26

U
t ·
V
87 77 88

e
f
g
h
p
q
r
s

k
Masters
Room
w
Class Room
12 × 12

n · m n ·

Play Ground for the
Juvenile School
66 × 45

o | | o

o

10 5 0 10 20 30 40 50 60 70 Feet

the centre of each of which is placed a lesson-post for Objects. *N.B.* Every Juvenile School ought to be the same in size and arrangement.

e Boys' Water-closet.
f Girls'   do.
g Master's   do.
h Ash-pit.
i Entrance to Infant School.

The Picture lessons are hung in double rows round the school-room. Hats and cloaks are placed in double rows round the class-room, or in single rows round the school-room; but the former is preferable.

k Stair to Juvenile School, which is immediately over the Infant School, and of the same size.
l Entrance to Juvenile School.
m Play-ground for the Juvenile School, 66 feet by 45.
n Gymnastic Poles.
o o o Flower-borders.
p Ash-pit.
q Master's Water-closet.
r Girls'   do.
s Boys'   do.
t Bible Stand.
u Boys' Gallery.
v Girls'   do.
w Master's Room; one story, and lighted from the roof.
x Place for one of Professor Nott's Patent Stoves.

The bottom of windows fronting the Play-ground are 3 feet from the floor; and in size, 4 feet by 8.

The end windows rise above the top-seat of the Gallery, say 4 feet 9 inches from the level of the floor. The other window-soles are 3 feet above the floor.

The Gallery rises each step as follow:—$16\frac{1}{2}$, 27, 37, $47\frac{1}{2}$, 58, inches; and top-seat lined at back 9 inches: the front of each step is rounded, and projects half an inch. Each step in the Gallery, which is perfectly level, is 18 inches broad; except the top, which is only 12 inches.

The whole walls must be lined with wood, to the height of 4 feet 6 inches above the floor.

The floor ought to be well deafened, so as to deaden the sound of the children's feet.

CHAPTER VIII.

SURVEY OF THE MORAL MACHINERY OF LARGE TOWNS, ESPECIALLY IN REFERENCE TO GLASGOW.

Scotland, as it was and is—Why fallen—Large towns at present nurseries for vice, not of necessity such, but for want of early moral training—Parents do not, and in many circumstances cannot, train their children; no machine has been put forth to afford assistance—Different grades of the population—Facts regarding the Roman Catholic portion of it—Ancient and successful means applied for the intellectual and moral elevation of Scotland—City or Home Missionary Society, extent of influence—Sabbath Schools—Parish with a considerable parochial agency, and one extremely limited—The contrast—List of Training Schools, Infant and Juvenile, and how supported—Scottish schoolmaster, how appointed—Introduction and adaptation of the country parochial system to large towns, by Dr. Chalmers—What is doing in some factories for the moral improvement of the workers—The power of sympathy and example, in regard to congregated numbers in towns, may, by proper training, as in the Infant School, be turned to a power for increased good—Plate, No. 3. Parochial machinery for large towns—Proofs of its necessity, and especially for the addition of Schools for early moral training.

THE welfare and stability of a state depends, not on the amount of its wealth, but on the degree of the moral worth of its inhabitants. With all wise legislators, therefore, the most important consideration is, how can the greatest amount of moral worth be attained and maintained; for, in proportion as the mass of the people are moral and virtuous, so, in exact proportion, will they prove themselves good subjects and sound patriots.

Whatever influence a naked sense of honour may have on the habits and courtesies of men in the upper walks of life, such sentiments are perfectly nugatory and inefficient in forming good characters among the great body of inhabitants in every community.

On close inspection it will be found, that religion alone introduces good morals among the working classes; and that, in proportion as the religion of Christ is diffused, so, in exact proportion, will the people be virtuous and happy.

Apart from moral feeling, it is really wonderful how little a man's happiness depends on mere outward circumstances; it is not gradation in rank, but degrees in moral virtue, which form the difference.

The wealth of an empire may increase—political privileges may be bestowed—the means of intellectual knowledge may be afforded, and the understandings of the whole mass of the people in consequence may be cultivated and improved—but unless the heart is impressed, so as to prove a regulator within, and to form the man into virtuous habits, such political privileges, and this mighty power of improved intellect, will fail in giving security or happiness to any country; on the contrary, insubordination, insecurity, and national profligacy, must inevitably follow; and, in accordance with the experience of all past ages, national vice is uniformly followed by a nation's ruin.

What is true in regard to kingdoms and states, is true also of particular towns and cities; and must be so, of course, in regard to families and individuals: for the largest empire is composed simply of individuals and families; and if families and individuals are moral and happy, so must the kingdom or empire be, of which they form a part.

Scotland, as a nation, during the last century, has been pointed to by almost every enlightened statesman in Europe, as a pattern of moral virtue. A very important question may now be proposed—Is Scotland so at this moment? We answer, *No.* Was she ever so? We answer, Yes. When, then, was that blissful time? It was at that period of her history, when the parent trained his child from infancy to fear God—to avoid sin—to pray for a new heart—to love the Saviour; and this spirit, on the part of parents, was attained and maintained, through the instrumentality of, and at the time when parish pastor and parish schoolmaster were enabled to fulfil the Christian duties assigned to them. When pastor and teacher had under their charge, parishes not exceeding 1000 souls—when the intelligent parochial schoolmaster, for a trifling charge, could overtake the education of every child, poor and rich, within the bounds of the parish; and the parochial minister could, besides visiting the sick, afford at least, within a year, one visit, and a pastoral address to, or examination of the household of each family separately; which, in unison with the occasional visits of the eldership, and sometimes a catechist, under the blessing of God, were the means of raising Scotland to a height of moral culture never before equalled by any nation upon earth. The parochial schoolmaster then taught the children in school to read the Bible, and the parents trained them morally at home. This was practicable, when parents generally were employed in rural pursuits; the boy following his father at the plough, or his mother at the dairy, and, of course, in these circumstances, was comparatively free from the influence of evil example.

Scotland, however, has sadly fallen from this high eminence: and why is it so? Is the nature of her sons changed? or are the instruments of her moral cultivation less efficient than formerly? Let us examine the facts—let us look into society as at present constituted, and observe the working and amount of that moral machinery, which has been applied to the altered state of her circumstances.

During the last century, the population of Scotland has more than doubled, without a proportionate increase of such means of improvement as we have described; and the inhabitants, from being almost exclusively agricultural, are now generally a manufacturing population: at all events, almost the entire increase of population are thus employed. It is true, that in very many small country parishes, where the inhabitants have not unmanageably increased, the parochial minister, elders, and schoolmaster, are as influential as ever; but great masses of people have formed themselves into towns—nurseries for vice, many say—not necessarily so, we reply— not necessarily so, but from ignorance of the plan how, or inattention in not *early* enough, or extensively enough, applying the moral machinery which has worked so well in rural districts, and accommodating its movements to the new and more condensed population of city parishes.

It is to large cities, now, that British legislators must look for the maintenance or destruction of the empire's power, for there union is strength; how important, therefore, then, that it should be a union of enlightened moral principle, not a condensation of profligacy and vice!

Sad lamentations are frequently made, regarding the attendant evils of overgrown cities and large factories; but instead of spending our time, or wasting our energies, in making complaints which will neither prevent the increase of the one, nor establishment of the others, let us see rather what can be done with towns as they really are; and a patient investigation may possibly prove, that while condensed masses of human beings afford peculiar facilities and encouragement to open vice, such contiguity may, by proper cultivation, prove the very means of an increased degree of moral virtue. In fact, the present supposed bane of our country, namely, large cities and factories, may possibly be turned morally, and consequently politically, into great national blessings. We must not expect, however, that such moral results will be accomplished by feeble efforts or sentimental wishes. *A great national good cannot be brought about without a great national expenditure.*

This subject, however, if fully followed out, would lead us far beyond the limits or direct object of the present publication; and, therefore, we shall give a very short summary of the principal means employed, in comparison to the necessities of the inhabitants, more especially in reference to Glasgow; after which, we shall propose what we conceive to be a suitable and proportionate remedy.

We have already stated, that the principal increase of inhabitants in Scotland, has been of those engaged in manufactures; and which, for the convenience of business, have formed themselves into towns. This is acknowledged by all, to be a comparatively new state of society; and, we may add, that this new state of society has not had applied to it any new moral agency suited to its altered circumstances, nor has the increase of population been met by a corresponding increase of that moral influence, which had been applied in olden times, which worked so well, and has been so efficient in rural districts. Unquestionably, in this matter, much has been done by the parties themselves; yet, notwithstanding this, it is a melancholy fact, that in Glasgow, and, we have reason to believe, in every large town in the United Kingdom, full one-third of the working population in each, are, at this moment, without the means either of intellectual or moral improvement,—such have not been provided for them— they have little or no concern about the matter, and generally are so sunk in ignorance, as to be alive to few wants, except those of a physical kind. No engine, fitted to accomplish a moral purpose, is applied, and therefore no moral influence is effected.

Such a state of things is not at all wonderful, for it seems a matter of history, as well as observation, that neither in the old nor new world has any nation ever fully provided for themselves the means of intellectual or moral improvement. The truth is, our physical, intellectual, and moral wants, are not active in an equal degree. Man feels hunger, and, therefore, seeks for bread to satisfy the cravings of nature; but he has no such strong desire for intellectual food, and still less for moral or spiritual instruction. Our great object, therefore, is, to see how this class—this most important, numerous, and neglected class of our fellow-subjects—can be got at, and raised to the rank of moral and happy citizens; and certain we are, that the coercive measures of prisons or bridewells, or even a house of refuge, will not accomplish it. Such institutions are all useful in their way, but they go not to the root of the evil. We must begin earlier—we must begin at the beginning—we must labour to prevent, rather than to cure—we must have education, not merely intellectual, but moral—we must have moral training; and if parents, from the particular circumstances in which they are now placed, or from inability, cannot accomplish this in regard to their own children, we think such ought to be done by accomplished, pious teachers in schools; not, indeed, to supersede the exertions of parents, but to assist. When children however, unfortunately, have profligate parents, the less, of course, they are with them the better.

It may, perhaps, assist our conclusions on this subject, if we, in the first instance, take a glance at the comparative numbers in the various ranks of society in this city.

According to Dr. Cleland's Statistical Tables
for 1831, the city of Glasgow, including suburbs,
contains 202,000 inhabitants, of which number
about 27,000 are Irish Roman Catholics; and these
are inaccessible to any religious or moral influence
at present in operation.

Some proof may naturally be asked why we
hold this opinion. We may, in the first instance,
state, that it has not been formed hastily or incau-
tiously, but has been forced upon us by an observation of nearly twenty years. The facts are
numerous; but we shall content ourselves with
two, which have taken place on a large scale.

Particular circumstances led us and others frequently into the houses of Roman Catholics
throughout the city, in common with other portions
of the population, and we found that previous to
1817–18, we could not learn that any of the Roman
Catholic poor families were visited by the priests,
except in extreme cases. At this period the parents, generally, especially the poorest and most ignorant, seemed willing, and did send their children
to the Sabbath schools which had been formed,
or which were then forming by Protestants; no
sooner, however, was the Catholic School Society
formed, which, with the reading of the Protestant
Bible as a school-book, we hailed as an omen for
good to this interesting, but degraded portion of
the population, than the priests became extremely
active in visiting; and during one short week,
from the Saltmarket and Bridgegate Sabbath
schools alone, it was calculated that the whole of
the Roman Catholic children, 105 in number,
were withdrawn—none of which returned, with

the exception of one or two occasionally, as it were by stealth.

We do not blame, but rather extol and admire, the *great activity displayed* by the Roman Catholic priesthood; a *zeal well worthy of imitation* by our Protestant clergy.

These week-day schools for teaching Catholic children to read, were supported jointly by Roman Catholics and Protestants—the Committee of Management also was formed equally of both parties. The schools, therefore, of course, on Sabbaths, ought to have remained shut to both creeds, in order that a strict neutrality might be kept. The Catholics, however, really are in possession of them on Sabbaths, so that the Roman Catholic teachers, who teach the children to read on week-days, take these children into the same school-room on Sabbaths, and teach and train the children to the peculiar dogmas of Popery. In this respect, also, we must hold up their superior management, address, and zeal, to the imitation of Protestants.

The next fact to which we mean to allude, occurred fourteen years after; namely, in the spring of 1832.

An Infant School was established in the neighbourhood of a dense mass of Roman Catholic families. Out of 150 children, whose names were enrolled, about 60 were of Roman Catholic parents, chiefly of the more respectable class, who paid for their children each 2s. as wages in advance. They expressed considerable anxiety to have their children trained under this system—especially that they should be instructed in "*so many nice Bible stories.*" An order, however, was issued one Sunday from *head-quarters*, and on the following day every child was withdrawn.

These two facts, with many more which might be mentioned, we think sufficiently prove that Roman Catholic parents, however highly they, as individuals, may desire the Bible training of their offspring, are yet inaccessible to any religious or moral influence in operation apart from priestly domination, with the single exception of the elementary branch of reading.

After deducting, therefore, these 27,000, or say 30,000, of our Roman Catholic population, there remains 172,000 souls, nominally Protestant, which, for the sake of classification, we shall take the liberty of dividing into three portions :—

The first, or No. 1, containing 43,000, or one-fourth of 172,000, we understand to comprehend the richer classes—the master tradesmen, and all employed in the rank of clerks and managers. These we may suppose to be in such circumstances as to render unnecessary, in as far as wealth is concerned, any endowment either for their intellectual, moral, or religious education.

The second class, or No. 2, we may state as double the number of the former, or 86,000, and we suppose contains such of the working classes as, from moral culture, are disposed, were they able to pay for the education and improvement of themselves and of their children, and who do pay something for the support of the Gospel ministry, and to the schoolmaster, in behalf of their offspring. For the working classes, in such circumstances, partial endowments are very necessary, and have proved eminently beneficial—complete endowments, however, would be quite uncalled for, at least in towns.

The third, or lowest class, we state as half the number of the former, say 43,000, and which, we are quite sure, from extensive surveys made in very many districts, and on several occasions in Glasgow, is greatly under the truth; and while it is of little importance whether the first or second classes contain 3000 or 4000, less or more, it is highly important to know pretty nearly the amount of the third or lowest class; for the interests of which we more particularly pen these sentences; and which ought to be the special objects of our attention; for they are, to a man, *unable*, at least *unwilling*, to pay for or provide means of instruction for themselves. *Complete* endowments for *them*, or pretty nearly so, in the first instance, are absolutely requisite, or they will continue, as heretofore, in ignorance—lost to the empire and to themselves.

Although some families among the third class are really poor, (and the poor we shall always have with us,) yet the mass are not necessarily poorer than those of No. 2. Immorality, dissipation, and improvidence, chiefly, have caused the distinction. In this class the greater proportion are labourers and artizans; and from the careless, and often half-infidel and turbulent, we descend to the very lowest class of a city population—to ballad-singers, sand and match sellers, thieves, and pickpockets; all of whom, from the low tippling-house keeper downward, form a much larger number than any who have not surveyed the kernels of the city lanes and closses, could possibly imagine.

From every survey which has been made, and from proofs which might be subjoined, not fewer than 40,000 or 50,000 are without the pastoral care of any Christian minister, and do not attend any place of worship; fully one-fourth also of the whole juvenile population are growing up in ignorance, and are under no moral restraint whatever. We believe, from what we have witnessed elsewhere, that this is a fair statement of the actual condition of every city and large town in the United Kingdom; some of which, if properly surveyed, would be found decidedly worse than Glasgow.

The important question then is, How can these 43,000 persons, or one-third of the whole working (Protestant) population be morally elevated? If present means have not, and cannot accomplish it, what can? and how can such be applied?

In regard to the means used in towns for the improvement of the population, we beg to premise, that the success has been quite an equivalent to the quality and extent of the means used —we have sown little, and therefore we have reaped little. From the late improvements in trade and wages, whereby the temptations arising from want are, of course, less urgent, public crime, extensive even as it is at this moment, is no doubt less apparent than it otherwise would have been; but let a depressed state of commerce follow, and from what we know of the fermentation and present reckless state of society, fearful may be the results. It is an important, we might almost say, it is a solemn question, Have the mass of the working population in this country received sufficient religious or moral training to regulate them in the event of a famine, or extreme stagnation of trade? Let the legislature solemnly look to this, and answer the question.

The ancient and successful means applied for the intellectual and moral elevation of Scotland, were, a parochial minister, elders, deacons to take charge of the poor, and parochial schoolmaster, to every 1000 souls. Calculating that 2000 in towns are as easily managed as 1000 in the country, what then is the comparative amount of this influence in Glasgow? We have had for some time twelve parish churches, with twelve parish pastors, and about as many parochial schools, partially endowed, for a population of 202,000, or about one-eighth of the proportionate amount of the moral machinery, for the improvement of the people, which our forefathers had. For, by the ecclesiastical records of the city, it appears that in the year 1701, with only a population of 12,788 souls, Glasgow had provided for the instruction of the people six parishes; with a minister to each, and an elder to every nineteen families, besides parochial schools; that is, half the number we now have.

But it will be immediately said, Have not the twelve Chapels of Ease, and the many churches and other places of worship, belonging to various Christian denominations, not fully made up this want of endowed parochial churches? and have not our charity schools, and other private schools, supplied instruction for the young?

We answer, No! and that for two reasons. First, because vast numbers in almost every district of the city and suburbs are found unable to read: and, secondly, because we find, from actual enumeration, that were all the places of worship, of every name, actually filled, still there would be a population left out who could not find accommodation, equal to *above* 20,000 adults, or 40,000 of the whole population. High seat rents have elbowed out, and tend to keep out, the poor and often well-disposed labourer from almost every one of our places of worship: hence the value of partial endowments for the minister, in order to afford cheap sittings for the poor. Chapels of Ease, and other churches and places of worship not parochial, while they, in common with the parochial minister, keep alive and extend the spirit of Christianity among classes, Nos. 1 and 2, who, being in better worldly circumstances, and already somewhat impressed with the importance of such things, do willingly, and of their own accord, attend places of worship, and pay more or less for the support of the ministry; but these not being parochial, do not embrace or influence that class, No. 3, on whose behalf we more especially plead; and as none of this class belong to any Christian communion, they are consequently left to parochial provision. It is not the profession, neither is it the practice, except in rare cases, for ministers, who are not parochial, to visit the poor, unless such are attached to their own communion. It is the duty of the parochial pastor and his agency to visit from house to house, thus making sure that none are overlooked or neglected. The pastor of a parish may be said to be the captain or leader of every aggressive enterprise of benevolence in regard to his parishioners, especially to the poor, the ignorant, and *the heathen at home.*

One of the greatest evils under which Glasgow now groans, is, that the prodigious extent of some, we may almost say of all the parishes, renders it nearly impossible for the minister to get through the families, except at extremely distant periods of time, so that our poorest and lowest class are but slightly impressed with parochial influence, especially in such parishes as the Gorbals and Barony; the former containing 36,000, and the latter, 78,000, souls. The destitution of these parishes, the Barony in particular, is truly awful.

A City, or Home Missionary Society, intended to supply the deficiency in the number of parochial pastors, was established about the year 1826–7. We say, to supply the deficiency; for it is the duty of the parochial minister to visit, more especially, that class who may be stated as in the "highways and hedges," but which it is impossible to accomplish, except in a very limited degree, there being, as we have shown, only twelve men to do this work, instead of eighty, the requisite number. We therefore say, this Society was intended, in some degree, to supply the lack of pastoral parochial superintendence. The agents have risen from seven or eight, during the first year, to the maximum, or stationary number, which their funds, during the last five years, could afford, of twenty-one missionaries. The Society has been supported by Christians of all denominations. The missionaries have been spread over about two-thirds of the city and suburbs. They visit from house to house; and thus, so far as their numbers extend, meet with that destitute class, No. 3, which ought to be the peculiar and primary object of all Christian philanthropy.

These Christian labourers have done much good in individual cases, especially to the sick, and have accomplished all which men, placed in their circumstances, possibly could do; at the same time, in comparison with the wants of the people, their greatest efforts have been as nothing. This may sound strange to those whose information is derived solely from attending public meetings, or reading annual statements; for when many scattered cases are condensed into the focus of a report, we are exceedingly apt to be deceived as to the real amount of good accomplished. Good has unquestionably been done, but we must not expect twenty-one men to do the work of two hundred; besides, the position of a city missionary is this—he may request, and even urge, the poor to go to church, and to send their children to school, but he has neither church nor school provided for them; the poor man must provide for himself: besides, the personal influence of a missionary seldom commands the attendance of any at his evening addresses, except a very few pious persons, who stand least in need of instruction; and his forenoon addresses are only to such as he may find at home; and these generally are simply the wife and youngest child, the older are on the street, and the father and elder branches, male and female, are out at work; at all events, few, very few, of the third class are influenced by this department of Christian philanthropy.

The visits of the minister of a congregation, or the pastor of a parish, are decidedly more influential than those of any missionary; there is much in the station and authority of the party which gives weight to the sentiments delivered. This may be objected to as an unsound proposition, but we ask such to imagine, how much more honoured he would feel by the visit of a king to his fireside, than by any of his ministers: the feeling exists in every station of life, and is not affected so much by the real worth, as by the rank of the individual.

Having stated these facts regarding the City Mission, we may say that, although various other minor Societies, under different names, or individual visitors, from various Christian denominations, have done good to very many individual cases, yet, in comparison to the wants of our overgrown and overgrowing population, such efforts have really been as a drop in the bucket. Ignorance, immorality, and crime, go on increasing in a fearful ratio, and, if we wont rouse ourselves, to propose a thorough cure, such may soon summon us into a fearful activity.

Sabbath Schools have unquestionably done more good than any other moral influence, upon the children of those who do not attend public ordinances. The local system of establishing these, has alone influenced, to any extent, class No. 3. For want of previous training, however, even this system has failed in thoroughly bringing out neglected children. See page 36.

We are therefore brought to this conclusion, that not only is the present amount and influence of all our institutions insufficient, but that some new or additional moral power must be applied, not merely for the adult, but as an antidote to the unprotected circumstances of our infant and juvenile population,—something must be added, for the intellectual and moral elevation of that neglected and degraded class, No. 3, which form one-third of the Protestant working classes.

From extensive surveys which have been made by many individuals, it appears, that while vast numbers of this class are to be found in every district of the city and suburbs, they are congregated in large masses, where the fewest parochial exertions have been put forth for their improvement. The following is the result of a late survey, which shows this in a striking light. The respective parishes contain about 12,000 and 78,000—are each inhabited by the same ranks of the working classes—and are divided by merely an ideal line—say the breadth of a thirty feet street. The smaller parish, containing 12,000, has only *one* parish church, but it has four Juvenile and two Infant Parochial Schools, and also a limited number of parochial labourers, consisting of elders, deacons, and teachers. In the other, or largest parish, on the opposite side of the street, there are few elders, comparatively, and only one parochial school, for 32,000 inhabitants, and, of necessity, scarcely any pastoral superintendence. The people are thus left to their own free will: and their will, we are sorry to say, has been, that vast numbers neither attend divine ordinances themselves, nor do they, in general, give their children a suitable education.

We have said, that a thirty feet street divides the one parish from the other. On one side of the street, out of 123 families, 66 children above eight years of age could not read; while, on the other side, or smaller parish, out of 232 families, there were found only two above the age of seven who could not read.

Out of the parish, containing 12,000, it was found, that five families on the average, out of every twelve, attended no place of worship. This is a sad state of things, and a loud call for increased parochial exertion, and farther subdivision of parishes. But what shall we say of those families on the opposite side of the street, where it was found, by their own candid confession, that instead of five-twelfths, as in the one case, which was a melancholy result, that nearly ten families out of every twelve attended no place of worship! nay, that in one Sabbath School district, out of fifty-eight families, four of which were Roman Catholic, only two individuals attended any church, and one of those persons attended only occasionally! Thus we see, that whether the people are able or not, they are certainly not willing, either to provide education for their children, or religious instruction for themselves. Their highest idea of education, is simply the knowledge of letters. Indeed, some of them are so sunk, as to have said, We need and want no such things; we would not attend a church, though you built it, and gave us sittings free. And is this really in Scotland, the sentimentalist will inquire?

Yes, in Scotland, we answer, and in our boasted commercial city too, does all this ignorance, and vice, and heathenism prevail; and in that very city, whose motto was wont to be, "*Let Glasgow flourish by the preaching of the word.*" The latter clause, however, has been torn from her banners, why and when we know not: but certain it is, that while the upper and middle classes are in general attentive to the preaching of the word, the poorer, if they *do flourish* at all, do not so certainly by this gracious influence.

Schools for Infant and Juvenile Training.— The whole number of these moral machines, as shown by the table,* is seven; whereas, for Glasgow, 84 are required, of 150 scholars each, for one-half of the infant population; 168 also are required for juveniles of the age of six to fourteen, leaving one-fourth of the children at this age to be provided for in private schools. (See Chapter II. p. 56—67.)

Two important practical questions naturally present themselves. First, Will this requisite number of schools ever be provided by the people themselves, or will they ever be provided by the voluntary contributions of the rich? We answer, No. As well may we look for voluntary roads throughout the length and breadth of the land, as a sufficient number of schools being established for the education or training of the poor by voluntary contribution. The experience of

* See Appendix, No. II.

these six Infant Schools, is a sad proof of the absolute powerlessness of the voluntary principle in regard to schools; and, in conjunction with almost every other scheme of philanthropy, has been quite sufficient to shake off any misconceived notions on this point.

A love for truth, and a desire for the extension of suitable moral training for the youth of our own and other large towns, compel us to state the facts regarding these schools, and that consequently we may see the necessity of urging the Legislature for grants of money and endowments for such institutions.

Observing that no means of moral improvement, apart from family training, which was indeed wofully neglected, existed in our large towns, for children under nine or ten years of age, and that even then, only a portion of the better sort could be got to attend Sabbath Schools for two hours on that day, and that the strict parochial improvements, introduced by Dr. Chalmers, in 1819, did not supply this want, Infant Schools, upon Bible principles, were thought of; and, in 1826–7, subscriptions were sought for, and obtained, after much exertion, from persons of all Christian professions, sufficient to fit up, but not to build, a school. A suitable person, acquainted with the system of Infant training, was brought to town, and a school was opened as a model. The Committee was formed of clergymen and laymen of all evangelical professions. This arrangement worked pretty well for about nine or twelve months; but when subscriptions were required to be renewed, so few continued their support,

that congregations were applied to for this purpose, and little or nothing was received. The
ultimatum was this, that with one or two schools
the system must stop, or all the schools must be
taken up by congregations. As none, however,
moved in this way, the Infant System must have
gone down here, had not the parochial churches
taken up the subject. Accordingly, one was
established in St. David's, by those connected
with that parish,—two were established in St.
John's,—one was taken up by the High Church
session, which otherwise, for want of general
support, must have gone down, after accumulating
a considerable debt, which at this moment is un-
paid.

In fact, for three years the Model School itself,
the *primum mobile* for Scotland, and the School in
Drygate, were supported almost entirely by one
or two individuals, so thoroughly averse are the
public to *continued* voluntary subscriptions. The
sessions of St. Andrew's and the Tron parish in
future propose to assist the funds of the Model
School, and the current expenses of the Infant
School Society. The accumulated debt upon the
Model School alone, is £300. The Cowcaddens
School has been established upon the principle of
general subscriptions, which were made all over
the city and suburbs. They fell considerably
short, which was made up by returns from a *soirée*
and musical entertainment. The treasurer is again
above £70 in debt. The school has existed one
year; and whether it can exist much longer, without being attached to a particular congregation,
time alone will determine.

The next practical question is, What class of the community have these moral machines, Infant Schools, influenced? We answer, that, with very few exceptions, it has been those belonging to No. 2. The reasons why, we have already noticed: (see page 42). Thus, if three schools are required for a parish, the first brings out generally the middling class—the second, the lower—and the last, alone, secures that the lowest grade are brought out; after which, the several classes will probably mix in these schools. Our conclusion then is, that our six Infant Schools have scarcely touched that class, No. 3, whose moral elevation we primarily have in view. A complete system of education, will alone thoroughly elevate a people; and that system, we again repeat, must be an intellectual system, not merely upon secular knowledge, but an intellectual, scriptural knowledge, and a practical training to moral habits in real life.

Much has been said about the Prussian system: we see in it much to admire, and some things to shun. With all our faults in education, however, as good schools, here and there, are to be found in Scotland, as in any part of Prussia. What we may take as a lesson, from Prussia, is her admirable plan of Normal, or Model Schools, for training teachers.

In regard to the Protestant schools of Prussia, where the Bible is introduced, a moral elevation may be expected. But as other sects, such as Roman Catholic, are also established, in whose schools the Bible is not taught, a moral result cannot be looked for. So may it be said in regard to liberal France, from whose schools the Bible is altogether excluded. If we must have a religious education in our week-day schools, we must have religious men as schoolmasters; and if we are to have true religion taught, we must have a security, by means of a standard, to which the master can be brought to adhere. Without this security, our schools will dwindle down to mere intellectual schools; but all will be well if the security is continued which we now have, under the Scottish Parochial School system, where the heritors choose the teacher, and determine what branches are to be taught; but the Presbyteries of the Church of Scotland determine as to the fitness for the work, and the religious principles and character, of the master. With this proviso we would then propose, for all additional parochial schools, whether infant or juvenile, which might be established and endowed by the Government, that our new heritors, *the ten pounders*, be the electors, or at least should nominate a committee for this purpose.

In regard to the idea of establishing a national system of education, of a purely intellectual character, without the religion of Divine truth and moral training forming a component part of it, we might show the evil by a reference to innumerable facts. We may look round upon society, and see whether the most highly intellectual, are always the most moral individuals. What was France, during the Revolution of 1789–93? Let the history of its bloody massacres tell as to the fact. We may look at the Hindoo College of Calcutta, where nearly every youth brought up at that purely intellectual seminary, renounces the religion of his fathers, but embraces no other, and is sent forth to the world like a ship without a rudder.

Look at the state of the 56 Egyptian youths, sent lately by the Pacha to Europe to learn different trades. The 36 sent to France, in general still adhere to the religion of Mahomed, or if any have renounced it, they have adopted no religion at all; while the 20 who have come to Great Britain, including four to this city, have nearly, without exception, renounced the religion of the false prophet; and 15 out of these have cordially embraced Christianity, and are maintaining a highly moral and most consistent profession. We shall give the solution in the Egyptian's own words—" Intellectual education will make a Mahomedan renounce his religion, and turn Infidel; but the religion of Jesus, applied to the understanding and heart, can, with the Divine blessing, alone make him a good man."

Out of the 15 who have embraced Christianity, it is not known that one has done so, except when the knowledge of its truths has been pressed upon them by their instructors. What may not yet be anticipated from the land of Egypt, when these interesting and intelligent youths return home, and, of course, form a nucleus of Christian principle and worth!

We have seen, that in the year 1701, when Glasgow contained 12,788 souls, and was divided into six parishes, that in point of pastoral superintendence, it was in equal circumstances with the country districts. As the population, how-

ever, increased, the size of the city parishes became more and more unwieldy, until the parochial minister was no longer the intimate friend
of every family. The people were not to be
satisfied with this state of things; those, therefore, who desired to hear the Gospel, finding no
room in the parish church, very properly built
churches for themselves, and paid the minister
out of the seat rents. This was all very well, as
regarded the better disposed portion of the community; but as to those who cared little for these
things, they willingly absented themselves from
any church, and their children were neglected as
to education. They seldom saw the parish minister, and never the congregational minister, who
had quite enough to do with his own people who
supported him; consequently, the evil has grown,
even amidst many select splendid churches of
various denominations: so that we actually have
a population who attend no place of worship
whatever, and allow their children to grow up in
ignorance, equal to one-third of the whole working community. When we say this of Glasgow,
let it be borne in mind, that most of the large
towns in the empire would be found, we fear,
even in a worse state, if properly surveyed.

The principal cause of all this declension in
religious and educational habits, whilst it has
been progressive, may, at the same time, be termed
self evident; for while the population of Glasgow, since 1701, has multiplied by sixteen, the
parochial pastoral superintendence has multiplied
only by two.

So rapid was the increase of vice and ignorance,

that many mourned over it, but knew not well how to grapple with such a fearful double-headed monster, intrenched through all the ramifications of a disjointed community. The aggressive movements were few, and not organized. But Dr. Chalmers was happily brought to this city, whose genius discovered where the evil lay, and how the power of the old parochial system might be brought to bear with effect upon large towns. His system has been but very partially followed by others,—at the same time, the more closely it has been adopted, the more strikingly apparent have been the moral results.

Every part of the system, which he remodelled, was excellent in itself; but the machine, as a whole, for the purpose of morally elevating large towns, was incomplete. It wanted the early moral training, which masters did not afford in school—which parents did not give at home—and which the altered circumstances of towns and factories rendered it impossible they properly could give. We certainly could have wished that the Rev. Doctor had seen this defect, and proposed a remedy. We have no doubt, however, that half a dozen years' additional experience of the practical working of his system would have proved to him, as it has to us, that the parochial machine was really incomplete; nay, that at present, without these, the minister's influence among the young, especially class No. 3, is utterly powerless; without, however, altering one portion of its beautifully arranged parts, we would now propose to supply the defect, by the system of Moral Training in Infant and Juvenile Schools. Our only claim to be listened to on these points is, that from the earliest period we acted as one of his agents in one or other of the parochial departments, and, to the present day, we continue under the same system.

The parochial system of Dr. Chalmers, or rather, as he says, the country system rendered applicable to towns, is extremely simple—its simplicity, however, which is its greatest recommendation, is the very reason why by many it is rejected, consequently not followed. The Magistrates and Town Council of Glasgow built St. John's church—attached a new parish to it, and translated Dr. Chalmers from the Tron, in order that he might have a full opportunity of proving his system.

We shall give a short statement of its different parts :—

The MINISTER, who ought at once to be the pastor of the congregation, and of a small manageable attached parish, perhaps limited to about 2000 souls. At present, the parochial churches draw their congregations, not from the legitimate source, namely, the parish, but from all parts of the town ; but if an extensive subdivision of parishes took place, and a preference was always given, in the letting of seats, to those resident in the parish, he thinks it might be possible to get the greatest proportion of the congregation from the parish itself—so that the minister, who would visit them through the week, would preach to them also on Sabbaths. Our own opinion is, that four-fifths is the maximum, which, under all circumstances, could be got to attend the assigned parochial district.

280

The ELDER, who ought to have a small defined district, if possible, not exceeding forty families, whose duty, in addition to attending church courts, and promoting church discipline, is to make himself acquainted with every family—be their counsellor in difficulty—visit the sick—and look after the intellectual and religious education of the young, whether of the ordinary poor or the orphan.

The DEACON—whose exclusive office it is to look after the poor, which are paid out of the free-will offerings made at the church-doors, by the congregation. The disjunction of the office of elder and deacon has this important effect, that the office of the former is rendered more scriptural, and what it ought to be—not a secular, but a sacred office. The elder not being a dispenser of a public fund, does not prevent him, if able and so disposed, to give a trifle of his own to the needy, as every Christian would rejoice to have the opportunity of doing; but he is saved the grievous task, of being assailed by applications from the public poor fund *as a right,* and lowering, in the minds of the poor themselves, his Christian visits into that of sordidness. We may mention that there is usually one deacon to every elder's proportion. If the district, however, did not exceed forty families, it would be quite practicable for a deacon to attach himself to two districts. Did our limits permit, it would be easy to show, how this system of managing the poor has a decided moral influence upon the poor themselves.

In regard to the management of the poor, one

gentleman states his experience in the following
manner :—He was appointed a deacon about
the year 1818-19, during the great mercantile
depression and political excitement of that period,
which was a severe trial of the power of this new
system of managing the poor. His appointment
was over a population of 500 souls. The first
object was to visit every family, which he did in
company with Dr. Chalmers, and take down in a
schedule the name of the head of the family, &c.
in the assigned district. This being done, the
following was the result :—

Learning that the minister was taking charge
of the poor of his own parish, and that deacons
were appointed to each proportion, the whole
paupers, and *would-be paupers*, were at once set
upon *the move.* On the very first week he had
probably twenty to thirty calls at his counting-
house ; but it being a rule never to give one farthing on being called upon, without first visiting
the parties at their own dwellings, the countenances exhibited, and *tete-a-tete* conversations
which took place on these first interviews, were indeed highly amusing. The terror of a police-offi-
cer was nothing to the idea of the visit, the scruti-
nizing visit of a deacon. They had got no break-
fast that day, neither had the children—legs and
arms had been broken of late—they would prefer
half-a-crown *just now*, or a shilling, or even a sixpence, rather than suffer the proposed visit.
But all would not do—the principle of no money,
without a previous investigation, prevailed ; and
when to-morrow, or next day, found the deacon,
with his list in hand, plodding his way amid back

entries and trap stairs, and among nominated lodgers, one half of whom were not to be found, or who were downright impostors—the spell was broken. Perhaps some half-dozen required a trifle; and the actual fact was, that it soon became known and current in the district—that no one need apply unless his case was genuine; or if otherwise, they were certain of being found out. Thus, that which at first seemed overwhelming, notwithstanding the badness of the times, with £3 2s. 6d., as donations, and adding two regular paupers to the roll, enabled this gentleman to fight his way through the first *year* of this campaign. But here the campaign ceased; *the would-be paupers*, the intemperate, and the idle, knew their ground, and in future he experienced no annoyance. The real poor were assisted; and during a second and a third year, one hour for visiting, each fortnight or three weeks, was quite sufficient to perform all the duty of managing, in peace and quietness, the poor among 110 families, all of the working classes. The present is but one of the moral aspects in the proper management of the poor: but our limits forbid us to extend.

The whole mystery of Chalmers' system of visiting, then, consists in this, that every man has a little to do, and not too much; and that this little must regularly be performed. One hour a-week, spent in the proportion or locality, will be sufficient for any of the *lay* departments.

Local Sabbath Schools—(In place of the ancient parochial Catechist.)—Instead of opening a Sabbath school, and inviting any who choose to come, from whatever quarter of the city, which plan was found to bring out, or at least to retain, only such of the middling class as had been partially trained at home, leaving the careless, and children of the heathen part of the population, who ought to have been the primary objects of such institutions, altogether untouched—this system, termed the Local System, is intended to confine the attention of the teacher to a small district of forty, or not exceeding fifty families—to take none, for the first time, into the school who do not actually live in the district: in other words, rendering the Sabbath school system strictly parochial.

PAROCHIAL SCHOOLS.—Of these Dr. Chalmers built and endowed four,* by the voluntary contributions of his congregation and friends. Thus, the children of all classes of the community in this parish may receive an excellent English education in these schools, at the low rate of 2s. per quarter, and the higher branches for 3s. to 4s.

If to those five divisions we add these highly interesting and useful institutions, Savings' Banks, we shall have given the outline of the parochial system of Scotland, applied to towns, by Dr. Chalmers. We see in all this, however, no public provision for children under six; and when they attain that age, it is all a teaching of the head, not a training at once of the head, heart, and life: the whole superstructure, therefore, is without the best and only sound foundation,

* The Annfield School (see Chapter VII.) was one of these.

namely, Early Moral Training in Infant and Juvenile Schools. Add these two moral levers, and the machine as a whole, under the Divine blessing, will work in beauteous harmony and with mighty power. Many reiterate, again and again, that parents should train their children. True, they ought; but why refuse them assistance—why ought not parents as well teach their children to read and write; and, besides, if we want to make parents able and willing to perform these important duties, we must begin with the children, who will become the parents of a future generation. Every hour we delay setting up these moral machines for training the young, increases the difficulty, and protracts the evil.

We make no apology for stating this much regarding the country parochial system, applied to large towns, for this is the grand moral machine, and, with the additions we propose, the only machine we know of which can influence or morally elevate the neglected and heathen, which are found so thickly bedded in city lanes. It is possible that class No. 1, and a considerable portion of No. 2, may provide instruction for themselves, but it is impossible that those of No. 3 can; for they are morally impotent, and hitherto every individual or combined influence yet put forth has proved utterly powerless.

From what we know of this system, we think it proper, considering the mighty opposition and prejudice by which some parts of it have been met, to say, that while Dr. C. as a man, is splendid in the extreme, that his schemes and plans are of the most practical kind possible, he exhibits in his own person the rare combination of the most comprehensive views, with the most practical. He is the soundest theorist, and the soundest practical philanthropist. We have often wished, however, that the Rev. Doctor, in promulgating his views to the world, had employed some able friends, who could translate his own ideas into the language of *ordinary* men. There is a glow in the mind and manner of the man, which gives an impetus to all with whom he comes in contact. It is no more than justice to say, that while he was engaged in preaching his Astronomical Discourses in the Tron Church, and regaling the fancy of his auditory with revealed truth, assisted by imagery borrowed from nature—the glassy lakes and murmuring streams—and while his telescopic eye grasped the planetary worlds, and systems upon systems, moving round one common centre, which, for any thing he knew, might be the throne of God, he also took a microscopic view into the filthy wynds and lanes of the Saltmarket, his then assigned parish, and, day by day, was employed plodding his path through every family, and every creek and corner, of that degraded population.

At the commencement of the present chapter, we stated, that so far from large towns and factories necessarily proving sources of vice, they might, by proper management, be turned into an increased power for good; as it must be evident, that while condensed masses of human beings, when improperly trained, or not trained at all, nourish crime—on the other hand, an opposite spirit is more easily infused into a number collectively, than into solitary individuals. However highly in the moral scale, therefore, agriculturalists may be elevated, the inhabitants of a large town may be raised still higher. The sympathy of numbers may be turned into a power for good, as well as for evil. The Infant School is a practical exhibition of the power of sympathy. By the development and training practised there, the whole children, and consequently every child, acquire habits of thinking, feeling, and acting, which under single training could not be acquired.

We have shown how matters stand in regard to families condensed into large towns; we shall now shortly allude to what may be done, and in some instances is doing, for the improvement of factory work-people, in a religious, and consequently a moral point of view.

In twelve or fourteen factories in town, and the immediate neighbourhood, the managers of these works employ young clergymen and city missionaries to give a sermon in the evening, once a week. Libraries are also formed in some of them, containing suitable books for the use of the workers. It is usual to stop the engine a few minutes, perhaps half an hour, earlier than usual, and, in some cases, two-thirds of the workers, old and young, attend these weekly addresses. Much good may be expected from this diffusive influence. In some cases, it is understood to have checked the reckless spirit which was abroad among some of the men, and, externally at least, has been the means of rendering their infidel discussions somewhat less frequent.

PLATE III 28

Parochial Institutions in Towns for each Parish of about 2000 Souls

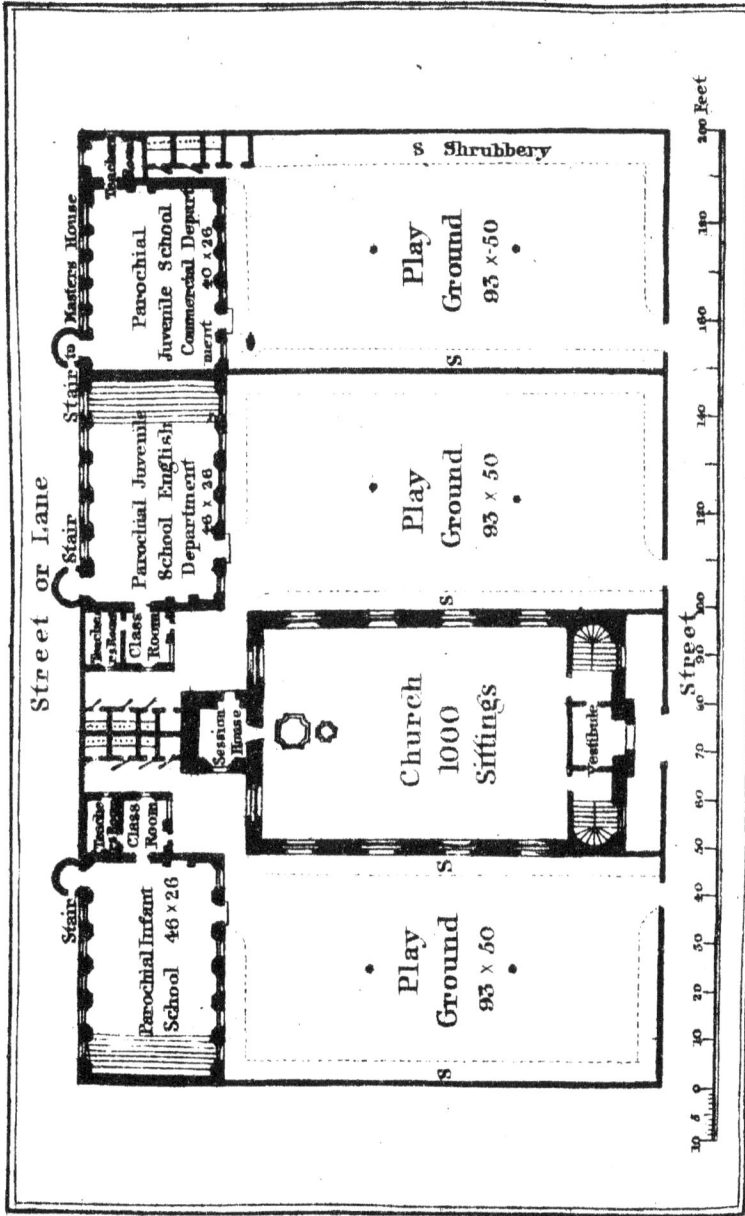

Street or Lane

S Shrubbery

Play Ground 93 × 50

Masters House

Parochial Juvenile School Commercial Department 40 × 26

Stair

Parochial Juvenile School English Department 46 × 26

Play Ground 93 × 50

Class Room

Session House

Church 1000 Siftings

Vestibule

Street

Class Room

Stair

Parochial Infant School 46 × 26

Play Ground 93 × 50

200 Feet

The annexed plate exhibits the combined parochial institutions, which we consider requisite for every parish in a large town, containing about 2000 souls; and if we take our former calculation (see pages 57—63) of 2400, or say the maximum, 2500 souls, such might fill the three schools with 150 scholars each, and also the church of 1000 sittings; leaving one-fifth of the adult population, who may conscientiously differ in form or doctrine, to attend other churches. Also one-half of all the infants from two to six years of age, and one-fourth of the juveniles from six to fourteen, to be provided for privately.

We connect the church with the schools, both to show how ground may be saved, and also, because such forms one of the most important parts of the machinery for moral training.

Give us schools, say some, without churches. We say, Give us both: and if asked, Whether would we have the schools or the church first? We would answer, The church; but we would finish the sentence by adding, that we must also have the schools built within the same year; and both minister and schoolmaster must be partially endowed, or the poorest will continue, as they now are, to be kept out by high seat rents and high school wages.

The question is, Are we to provide for the poor, churches and schools, or prisons and bridewells? We may cast our eye abroad, and wonder, and ask, Is this really an alternative? The following will perhaps throw some light on the subject, and will show the footing on which our plea rests, and that our position is one, not of fancy, but of real and actual necessity. What we mean to analyze, is just one of the twenty or thirty spots, upon which, had we funds at command, we would place such a moral machinery as is now exhibited to view—where there are a sufficient number of adults to fill the church, who worship no where; and also, infants and juveniles growing up in ignorance, sufficient to fill all the three schools.

In one portion of the Barony parish, united with the city, containing a population of 21,000 souls, almost exclusively of the working classes, and where, from the immense size of this parish, people have been left *to the freedom of their own will*, ten Sabbath School teachers, each of whom have attached to themselves a small locality, state the following as the result of their survey in 1833: Out of 454 families, whose residences form continuously three sides of a square, 377 whole families, or five-sixths of the whole, by their own candid confession, do not attend any place of worship whatever. A small proportion in this district are Roman Catholics, and these almost all attend the chapel: those who go no where, therefore, may be stated as nearly all Protestant families. If, therefore, we multiply 377 by 5, and divide by 2, the usual supposed number capable of attending public worship, we have the product 942, which would go far to fill the church of 1000 sittings; but such would never come out, though the church was built in the centre of their dwellings, unless the partially endowed minister was also the pastoral parochial missionary, visiting from house to house, and morally compelling them to come in. Three-fourths of the children also were found not educated at all; and the remaining fourth not half educated. We were present one evening, when 97 children had been collected into one room, of about the age of eight to fourteen, from one-half of said 454 families, none of whom could read, presenting the melancholy product of this moral wilderness. A teacher was appointed to learn them their letters on the week evenings, at a small salary, and to receive one penny per week from each of the children; but their apathy was such, that they gradually dwindled down to about twenty, and from want of public subscriptions, for a time the school was given up. A loud call here, if any where, for early moral training.

Will any man be bold enough to say, that in such a district as this there is no need of something more substantial than private benevolence, which has literally done nothing? Are these, and multitudes of families like these, to remain comparative heathens, and pests to society?—No. Let us give fancy to the wind, and petition the Legislature for that which private subscription cannot, does not, supply.

Whether class No. 3. are more widely diffused amid the ramifications of city lanes, or found in masses, as in this district, such can only be got at and influenced by the combined means of pastoral parochial superintendence, cheap education, and moral training.

APPENDIX.

I.

Weekly Course of Training for an Infant School.

MONDAY MORNING.

10 o'clock.—Obtain order. Hymn. Prayer. Inspect hands and faces. Manual exercise. Chant lesson on Cleanliness. Revise last Monday's lesson on Bible Biography. Hymn.

10½ till 11½.—Marching lesson at lesson-posts. Examine the senior classes in class-room. Farthing table. Count a hundred. Exercises in Marching. Objects.

11½ till 12.—Play-ground. Swinging-poles. Wooden bricks. Take a tour to the Capitals of Europe. Manual exercises.

12 till 1.—Gallery. Revise Saturday's lesson on Prophecies, Promises, &c. Hymn. Natural History. Sing about an animal. Bible story. Hymn. Responses. Ball-frame. Sing Long Measure. Numeral-frame. Mountains mentioned in the Bible. Home.

MONDAY AFTERNOON.

2 o'Clock.—Every child in place. Clap hands and march. Hymn. European Costumes. Sing, "March to the Infant School." Marching lesson. At lesson-posts. Story. Pence table.

3 till 3½.—Play-ground. Swing. Build with wooden bricks. Talk about the Trees and Plants. Imitate sowing, reaping, gleaning, &c.

3½ till 4.—Gallery. Lines on assembling in school. Bible Biography lesson for the day. Hymn. Ring the bells. Hymn. Prayer.

TUESDAY MORNING.

10 o'Clock.—Count, and obtain order. Hymn. Prayer. Carefully inspect the children as to Cleanliness. Manual exercise. Revise the Bible lesson for last Tuesday on Illustrations and Bible History of Animate Nature. Sing an appropriate Hymn. Multiplication and Shilling tables. Objects.

10½ till 11½.—Marching lesson. Examine the junior classes in the class-room. Shilling table. Imitate gentle breeze, brisk gale, hurricane, &c.

11½ till 12.—Play-ground. Swing. Build with bricks. Question one another on the Vegetable kingdom.

12 till 1.—Gallery. Clap hands, and obtain attention. Revise yesterday's lesson on Bible Biography. Sing an appropriate Hymn. Catechise on some animal. Sing about it, or some other animal. Numeral-frame. Anecdote. Hymn. Responses. Geometry. Home; or, perhaps, some take dinner in school. Blessing before meat.

TUESDAY AFTERNOON.

2 o'Clock.—Order. Hymn. Addition and Subtraction. Sing Avoirdupois weight. Responses. Hymn. Marching lesson. Shilling table.

3 till 3½.—Play. March in order round the Play-ground, and sing. Visit the Capitals of Asia. Swing, and build with bricks.

3½ till 4.—Gallery. Order. Manual exercises. Illustrations and Bible History lesson for the day. Hymn. Prayer.

WEDNESDAY MORNING.

10 o'Clock.—Obtain order as before. Hymn. Prayer. Inspect hands, &c. Revise the Bible lesson for last Wednesday on Moral Duties, from Bible Examples and Precepts. Hymn.

10½ till 11½.—Marching lesson. Objects, or Picture lessons. Examine senior classes in the class-room. Scripture Alphabet. Hymn. Numeral-frame. Mental Arithmetic. Sing Long Measure.

11½ till 12.—Play-ground. March round the trees singing. Questions on Animals. Swing and build with bricks.

12 till 1.—Gallery. Manual exercises. Revise yesterday's Bible lesson on Illustrations and Bible History of Animate Nature. An appropriate Hymn. Geography. Sing verses on Geography. Ball-frame. Sing Apothecaries' weight. Brass letters and figures. Responses. Hymn. Story.

WEDNESDAY AFTERNOON.

2 o'Clock.—Hymn. Moral Duties. Hymn. Multiplication. Bible story. Hymn. Marching lesson. Addition. Wine measure.

3 till 3½.—March and sing to the play-ground. Encourage to talk about the trees, &c. Imitate Mowing, Thrashing, &c.

3½ till 4.—Gallery. Bible lesson for the day, on Moral Duties, from Bible Examples and Precepts. Hymn. Prayer.

Thursday, *Friday*, and *Saturday*, are, with variations, carried on in a similar manner. Manual or physical exercise, in one way or other, ought to be resorted to every few minutes during the progress of the lessons; without such, order, obedience, and cheerfulness, cannot be promoted.

II.

We have copied, as annexed, the various sizes of the School-houses and Play-grounds, in order to show that in large towns especially, where ground is high priced, and difficult of being had, contiguous to the densest parts of the population, no arbitrary or fixed plan for Infant School establishments can be given for general adoption. Much must be left to the shape of the ground which can be procured, and other circumstances. Sometimes the school-room may have its gable to the street; sometimes the house may be built on a line with the public street, and the play-ground behind; at other times reversed, with the play-ground in front, and school-house to the back; oftentimes also, a one story house, with a garden, may be had, which can easily be converted into an Infant or Juvenile School establishment. Two things must never be omitted: —1. A class-room, 15 feet by 15; where the children may hang up their hats and cloaks, and where the teacher may occasionally retire during the intervals of school, and, if at a distance from home, take his food, and superintend the children at play. 2. Clean, retired, and separate out-door conveniences for both sexes, each not smaller than six or seven feet within.

The smallest extent of play-ground suitable for a Training School might be stated at 65 feet by about 42. This just permits room for two gymnastic poles, and a narrow flower-border: as much larger than this, however, the better. A school-room of 40 feet long and 24 wide, and ceiling 13 feet high, will accommodate 100 to 120. One of 46 feet long by 26, will accommodate 180.

For the best plan of a Training School, &c. whether Infant or Juvenile, see Plate II.

The Model Infant School is open for parents and strangers each day, between the hours of twelve and one o'clock. The Model Juvenile School, from one to two o'clock, on Monday, Wednesday, and Friday; and on the same days in each of the Infant Schools, Nos. 2, 3, 4, 5, 6. But a note from any of the Secretaries will gain admission any day, and at any hour.

List of Training Schools, now in operation in Glasgow, with their comparative Sizes, &c.

FOR INFANT TRAINING.

	Size of School-room.	Size of Class-room.	Size of Play-ground.	
	FEET	FEET	FEET	
1. MODEL SCHOOL, Saltmarket.—Entry by Steel Street and St. Andrew's Sq. D. Caughie, Master.	57 by 30	18½ by 16½	82 by 32	{ James Ewing, Esq. M.P. *President.* J. C. Colquhoun, Esq. M.P. *Vice-P.* Rev. N. Paterson, St. Andrew's. Rev. R. Buchanan, St. Mary's.
2. *St. John's Parish,* Chalmers Street. James M'Kay, Master.	46 by 26	12 by 9	64 by 46	Rev. Dr. Brown, Minister, *Pres.*
3. *St. John's Parish,* Marlborough street. James Galt, Master.	46 by 26	10 by 9	85 by 43	{ Rev. Joseph Sommerville, Minister, St. John's Chapel, *President.*
4. *St. David's Parish,* High John Street. John Reid, Master.	46 by 26	12 by 12	75 by 30	Rev. J. G. Lorimer, Minister, *Pres.*
5. *High Church Parish,* Drygate Street. Alex. Duncan, Master.	31½ by 21	15 by 7	69 by 45	{ Rev. Principal Macfarlan, Minister, *President.*
6. *Cowcaddens School,* Barony Parish. James Callan, Master.	33 by 21	8 by 8	54 by 42	{ Rev. W. M'Clure, Parochial Missionary, Barony Parish, *Pres.*

FOR JUVENILE TRAINING.

III.

Rules and Regulations for an Infant School, after the Glasgow Model.

INFANT SCHOOLS are intended for the reception of children, from the age of two to that of six years, with the view of imbuing their opening minds with the knowledge of religious truth; of training them up in habits of obedience and good order; and of giving them such elementary instruction, as may prepare them for entering with advantage into Parochial and other Schools.

The only School-book shall be the Bible, from which the Master shall select each lesson for the day, under the following arrangement:—

Monday.—Bible Biography.

Tuesday.—Illustrations and Bible History of Animate Nature.

Wednesday.—Moral Duties, from Bible examples and precepts.

Thursday.—Miracles from the Old or New Testament, and the Parables of our Lord.

Friday.—Illustrations and Bible History of Inanimate Nature.

Saturday.—Prophecies concerning Christ, Bible Geography, Promises, &c.

Under this arrangement the children have each day a new and distinct lesson from the Bible; but, before doing so, the lesson of the preceding day, as also the lesson of the corresponding day of the previous week, are revised upon a mixture of the elliptical and interrogatory plans, as may be gathered from the preceding publication on Moral Training.

Thus, each lesson, as stated above, must be gone over at least thrice; namely, on the particular day, on the day following, and on the corresponding day of the succeeding week. In addition to Bible training, objects and things shall more especially occupy the attention of the children.

The affair of the Society shall be under the direction of

The active management of the Institution shall be under a Committee of   , elected annually from the General   —the Secretary and Treasurer being *ex officio* Members—any four a quorum. Stated Meetings of the Committee of Management to be held quarterly, on the first Monday of January, March, June, September.

Two Members of the Committee of Management to be appointed at each Quarterly Meeting, to meet in the School on the first Monday of every Month, to examine into the state of the School, and to determine in regard to applications for admission. The Members thus appointed shall report their proceedings in a book to be kept for that purpose.

The School to be inspected once a-week by one of the Members of the General Committee, in order; who shall receive notice from the Teacher; and who is requested to record his opinion of the progress of the Scholars, in a book to be kept for that purpose.

The Master and Mistress to be elected annually by the Committee of Management, and to be under their control;—appeals in cases of difficulty being always allowed to the Society. Either party, however, may be at liberty, by giving   months previous notice in writing.

The Master shall open and close the School each day with prayer.

The Master and Mistress shall be specially enjoined, in the daily management of the School, to bring Scripture truth, and sound moral principles, to bear upon the minds and consciences of the little children, with a simplicity and affection suited to their tender years; and to take care that all restraints or corrections, which proper discipline may require, shall be free from *every species* of violence.

Children with any infectious disease, or who have not been vaccinated, shall not be admitted.

The whole School to be swept out every day—the floors washed once a-week—the gallery and seats only on Saturday, so as to be perfectly dry before Monday.

Each child shall pay in advance, 2s. per quarter, or 1s. for six weeks. But should there be two or more children from the same family, only one of them shall be required to pay in full, the others one-half.—Children received only on Mondays.

Parents must send their children with hands, face, and neck, clean washed, their hair well combed, and their clothes as clean and decent as possible.

Children absent two days, or late in coming to the School four days, without a proper excuse, forfeit their right of attendance.

Hours of attendance during Summer, ten till one, and two till four, or half-past four o'clock; and during four months in Winter, commencing the middle of October, ten till one, and two till four o'clock: except on Saturdays, when the School shall open only during the forenoon. Any or all of the children, however, on ordinary days, may remain in the afternoon half an hour or an hour in the play-ground, after the School is dismissed. One of the teachers always to be in the way to superintend in the play-ground. It is understood, that should the parents wish it, any child may bring dinner, and remain within the premises during the stated intervals.

Parents and strangers shall be admitted to visit the Model School each day, between the hours of twelve and one o'clock. Other schools, however, (more private,) only on Monday, Wednesday, and Friday. No individual can be admitted at any other time without permission, in writing, from one of the Committee of Management.

There shall be an Annual Public Examination of the School, on the day of the General Meeting of the Society.

N.B. As a Female Assistant is requisite in every Infant School establishment, a young female of about twelve years of age, with a little training, might suit, provided the Master cannot have wife, sister, or near relative, with him in attendance.

Complete sets of apparatus, of various sizes, both for Infant and Juvenile Schools, may be had at the Model Infant School, Saltmarket.

IV.

Hints on the subject of Local Sabbath School Tuition.

THE following explains in some measure the local system referred to in page 37, and is a paper which, for the last ten years, it has been customary to hand to each young teacher, as a sort of memorandum of the duty required of him :—

It is preferable that a limited, rather than a large number of families, be assigned to each teacher, as few young men have it in their power to spare *much time* for the purpose of visiting, and *that little* having generally to be taken from leisure hours. Forty or fifty families, with proper cultivation, will generally be found to produce twenty-five children, which ought to be considered the maximum for the superintendence of one teacher.

Immediately after Whitsunday, and not later than the middle of June, each teacher ought annually to visit every family in his district, noting down the following particulars under the respective columns of the schedule :—

1. The name and occupation of the representative of the family.

2. The gross number of the family.

3. The number of children between the ages of six and fifteen.

4. The number of children above six unable to read, and not at school.

5. Those at present attending other Sabbath Schools than the district one.

6. Those attending the district Sabbath School.

7. Those not attending Sabbath Schools. From these last, the district school must of course be supplied or replenished.

It will for the most part be found, that those not attending school are proper objects of religious instruction; and no pains or exertion ought therefore to be spared, with a view to secure their attendance.

It is of great importance that no child whatever be received into the school, for the first time, who does not live in the district, as, by admitting strangers into the classes, the teacher has less stimulus to visit his district for the purpose of drawing out those who ought to attend, and who stand most in need of instruction. A rigid attention to this rule, together with frequently visiting the district, is that which gives the local system all its superiority over the general plan.

Those who willingly present themselves as scholars, will generally be found to stand least in need of instruction; while those who can reluctantly be induced to attend, are generally the most ignorant, and, however insubordinate they, in the first instance, may prove, ought at all times to be the primary object of a Sabbath School teacher.

Whilst it is of great importance that no child be received from *without* the assigned district, it is also of importance that, when a family removes from the district, if not at too great a distance, the children of such family should, for their progressive improvement, be induced to continue in the school. But were the local system universal, this defect would no longer exist, as those children who had no deep-rooted attachment to their former school, could be handed over to the teacher of the district into which they had removed.

Every teacher ought to make it a point of conscience, of calling frequently upon those children who do not attend, or who attend irregularly; and besides this, as a further check on the children, when a scholar is not present after the school has been opened by prayer, a message of inquiry to the parents may be influential in obtaining their attendance.

Every family in the district ought to be visited at least once a quarter; the children attending school, of course, more frequently.

Although much time may be usefully employed by a pious teacher in his Sabbath School district, in the various ways which his Christian sympathies may suggest, yet *one hour* conscientiously spent every week, either during the day or in the evening, will suffice for the objects both of forming an acquaintance with the parents, and securing a regular attendance of the children.

We beg to notice, that a number of Sabbath School teachers have adopted with success the system of BIBLE TRAINING : see Chapter VI.

All the addition made to the aggregate number of Sabbath scholars in Glasgow, between the years 1824 and 1832, have been by the powerful influence of the Local System.

V.

LETTERS FROM PARENTS.

THE following Letters are from the Parents of children attending the Six Infant Schools in town. The Masters sent by each child a small printed note, or message, to the Parents, requesting their opinion of Infant Schools, from what they had witnessed in their children's conduct at home. Nearly a hundred Letters were in consequence received, from among which the following are selected; but the difficulty has been to determine which to choose, all being so decidedly warm in praise of the system. In some of the letters a few corrections have been made in the orthography, but none in the style or mode of expression. The originals are in the hands of the Secretary. These parents we acknowledge to be nearly all of the middling class, or No. 2, and not those of No. 3. See pages 261, 262. As being better able to judge, their testimony is of course the more valuable.

LETTERS.

May 18, 1834.—" I have now to state, that I consider, from the great improvement in my own boy, during the short period he has attended your class, not only in acute and correct answers to any questions in general, if simple, but being able to distinguish almost all kinds of animals, and tell their names readily, and many other little particulars of them; this method of teaching being calculated to familiarize children with such subjects, combining both amusement and instruction at one and the same time; and I find him also deriving considerable benefit, by his young mind being stored by many of the most interesting histories of the Old Testament, which are clothed or told in such a way by the Teacher, so as to be easy understood by the children; and although children cannot be expected to remember these things all correctly, still they may receive such impressions in this way as may materially benefit them in more mature years. Under all the circumstances, I think such Institutions may be productive of much good, if followed up by attention on the part of the teachers. I cannot conclude this, without expressing the high sense I entertain of your unremitting care and attention to your tender charge at all times, especially on more than one occasion, when I have experienced instances of your care to my boy, which I feel as an obligation. I have no other way of repaying, than by thus expressing my gratitude to you. Your charge is one of a most arduous character, having not only the training of minds of a very tender nature, but the preservation of bodies of no less tender a character; all of which depend upon you—which, to a reflecting mind, must be no ordinary burden. As to anecdotes of the different animals, or on other subjects, I could relate a number, but which would extend the subject of this small article to too great length; therefore, feeling that I could not do it justice, I rather choose to decline it altogether. But one small thing which occurred shortly since I cannot pass over: Another boy, who was, I dare say, ten or twelve years of age, was along with my boy, and they were examining the pictures in a book, when they came to one which the big boy did not know, but which he alleged was some kind of dog; but he felt at a loss to assign a reason for the lump on its back: when my little boy saw it, he immediately told the bigger one he was wrong, for it was a camel, and began to tell

him some of its properties, &c. But I need add no more
on the subject, having, I trust, said enough to convince
the most credulous of the utility of such Institutions, so
far as the enlargement of the young mind is concerned."

ANN M'F.

May 9, 1834.—" I had formed the most sanguine expectations of its [Infant education] beneficial consequences and
ultimate success; but these expectations, high as they were,
have been more than realized by the observation I have
been enabled to make of its progress at the Infant School.
I consider the system admirably adapted to promote the
health and happiness of the children, to give them clear
perceptions in useful knowledge, and indelibly to impress
upon their minds the value of religious and moral truth.
I consider myself fortunate in being enabled to bestow
upon my boy the benefits of such a system, and consider
myself entitled to return to its Directors and supporters,
and to yourself individually, my warmest expressions of
gratitude for the patriotic zeal and perseverance which have
been evinced in its promotion." J. M'K.

" In compliance with your request:—Our little boys
repeat some of the history of Joseph and his brethren,
and of Jesus being in the common-hall, and a crown of
thorns on his head. Their mother says, that the wages is
saved in the washing of their clothes. I approve of the
institution." D. C.

May 8, 1834.—" In compliance with your request, I
would beg to say, my opinion of Infant Schools is, that
they are of the greatest advantage to children, both as
regards moral and religious instruction. Having often
been struck with remarks made by my boy, who has been
with you for some time past—a number made from the
Scriptures, also from the animal and feathered tribes,
along with the fine feelings they possess towards others—
giving Scripture for the reason not to offend; and if
offended, not to retaliate,—I will trouble you with an
anecdote or story. In taking a walk with them in the
Green, he talked much of the vegetation of spring and

autumn : when we came in view of Clyde, he asked me if I could walk upon the water? I said, ' No person could walk on water;' he then said that our Saviour could walk upon the water, and that Peter saw him. Having a neighbour of the name of Peter, I said, ' Surely no.' He then said, ' No Peter——, but Peter the apostle, who denied our Saviour three times, and the cock crew;' and gave a pretty fair account of the circumstance. Also, I being badly one night, he was very much concerned, and said, ' Father, were I to pray to God, would he come and make you better?' and a number of similar questions : all of which I attribute to the instructions given and impressed on the mind by you." J. B.

May 10, 1834.—"I have always had a favourable opinion of Infant Schools, as I am of opinion, that impressions made upon the infant mind are generally more lasting than any other ; but I am certainly more deeply interested in the propagation of infant knowledge, since I have observed the great benefit that my daughter Helen has derived from it. She must have every thing explained to her that she does not clearly understand. Before she went to the Infant School, her habits were rather of a dull, retired nature ; but, since that period, both her body and mind have undergone a great change for the better ; she has acquired a degree of information, which surprises all who converse with her, and which she could not have acquired under any other mode of teaching. I cannot recall to mind any of her sayings worthy of notice, but I can say that every day of her life furnishes me with fresh proofs of the great utility of Infant Schools. For your devoted attention, and heartfelt interest in the cause, I beg to return you my warmest thanks, and also to the Managers and Directors of the Institution." JESSY R.

" In giving my opinion of the advantages that children receive by attending the Infant School, they are numerous. It keeps them off the streets, where they can learn nothing that is good, but in danger of being hurt, and many other evils which too often occur. They learn to be agreeable with their school-fellows, lively and cheerful. And there is a knowledge of animals and countries infused into the mind, which they will retain while they live. And there is a knowledge of the Scriptures, of their duty to God and man, imbibed into their young minds, that will never be eradicated." W. ———.

"As a parent, I acknowledge I am in duty bound to acknowledge myself very much obliged to you for the care and attention paid to my infant child. Be assured I am aware of the trouble she, and a number like her, must be to you. Indeed, I cannot conceive how one who is a stranger can have patience to put up with the follies of a child, when I see oftentimes the most indulgent parent's feelings roused almost to madness at the follies of their own child. Yet your good patience can bear, and at the same time instil into their youthful minds such useful instructions that never can be eradicated out of their minds. I allude to incessant active exercise, then to moral goodness of character, connected with religious instruction. How pleasant to hear a babe sing praise to its heavenly Father, and then pray for its kind earthly parents' welfare! This, Sir, as a mark of my esteem, binds me to wish you and your family health and prosperity, and all the comforts this earth can afford."

J. ———.

"I greatly approve of Infant Schools. Although I had a dozen children, when I have but one, if my circumstances would allow, I would have them all into it; for they are away from all vice, and good morals instilled into them. There is but little that our boy hears or sees, but he can give a little description of when he returns from school." JESS ———.

"In giving my opinion as to the progress my boy has made under the Infant system, I may say, in the first place, I have always considered the Infant system the best that ever was thought of for improving the rising generation. Under this impression I sent my boy, when just about two years of age, to the Infant School, then under care of Mr. ———; he being, at that time, a very delicate child, and always had been. This being the case, and the child being only weaned, after a week or two I kept him from the school for a few months; and when I sent him back, and has attended the school ever since, being about twenty-one months, and what he has learned in that time has gone far beyond my expectations; and this is not an only case, for I have known them that surpass him, and I have heard of many that gave like satisfaction to their parents. I am convinced that this system may be the means, under the blessing of God, of carrying instruction home to the parents; for it is surprising how they detect sin at home, by telling them how God sees them, and where sinners go, &c.; and it is astonishing how correct they repeat the Scripture stories and other Bible information repeated to them by the Master,—the sacred and other songs composed for the school, how well they sing them to their different tunes. Thus while their young minds are stored with the best of information adapted to their capacities, they receive a taste for and a knowledge of music. Well may we apply to this system the language of Scripture, and say, 'Bring up a child in the way he should go, and when he is old he will not depart from it.' I am sorry the system is not much more popular, and more generally patronized by the public, than it is. This arises from ignorance and prejudice—the one from ignorance of the system, and the good it has done; the other from prejudice, that it is injurious to the health, &c. I have already said that my boy was delicate before he went to school; with the exception of when he had the measles and hooping-cough, he has had better health since he went to school than he had before. I do not mean to say that his health would not have improved had he not been at school, but it shows at least that his health has not been hurt by the school; but I am of opinion that the system has a tendency rather to improve, than otherwise, the health of the children, from the cleanly and regular habits, useful, but innocent exercise, of the system."

R. ———.

May 9, 1834.—" In compliance with the request of the Secretary of the Glasgow Infant School, I am happy to state to you the following facts; as Colin is most about my house when at home, and he and I have more conversation toge-ther than any other person in the house, his father has left it to me to write:—Colin F. was sent to the Infant School about two years ago. He was not then three years old; and at that time I had only had the charge of him about three months, and had not commenced giving him any particular instruction on sacred things; but, in a few weeks after he was placed under your charge, he could talk to us about heaven and hell, knew what characters went to each respective place, and that Jesus was the only Saviour of sinners. He could also speak of the great Creator of the world—how that He had made all things, and knows all things—and can do any thing and every thing—that we should love him better than any one; that we should love God's day, love the Bible, love the church, and love every body. He often surprises us with his knowledge of the Scriptures—he can give us a pretty correct account of a great many of the historical passages both of the Old and New Testament—he can talk of the sufferings and death of Jesus Christ, of his rising from the dead, and ascending up into heaven, and that He shall in like manner descend; that the archangel shall sound the trumpet, and the dead shall all be raised, and that the righteous will rise first. About six months ago, when reading to him one Sabbath of the creation of the world, and of God's resting from all his works on the seventh day, he said, 'Mother, Jesus was wearied with his journey, and rested on Jacob's well.' I asked him, 'Who came to Jesus when he was there?' He replied, 'The woman of Samaria;' and he an-swered me question after question, until he gave me a correct account of the Saviour's interview with the woman of Samaria. I asked him where I would find that beauti-ful story, as he called it. He instantly replied, 'In the fourth chapter of John.' One afternoon, soon after that, when he came from school, he told me that two ministers had been put in bridewell. Not knowing what he meant, I asked what they had been put there for. But we soon understood him, when he told us how they sung praises to God, and the prisoners heard them; and the jailor, see-ing the doors open, thought they had run away, and he was going to kill himself; but they cried, ' Do thyself no harm ;' and he brought them out, and washed their stripes, and so on.   He often delights us with his knowledge of many other passages of Scripture, too numerous to mention; and I will conclude with the following anecdote :—A person employed by his father, whom we were reproving for deviating from the truth, Colin, with an audible voice, looked him in the face, and said, ' Do ye no ken that all liars shall have their portion in the lake that burns with fire and brimstone ?—the Master tells us that.'   When he hears the Bible read, and when he is in the church, he will often be whispering to them that are nearest him, ' The Master tells us about that.'   Indeed, he has learned so much useful knowledge in the Infant School, that I could entreat every parent to send their children to Infant Schools."

JANET F.

"With regard to my own little girl, it would be unreasonable to think that she should have made much progress in the short period of eight weeks; but she has certainly derived as much good as I expected.   Besides acquiring a few things by rote, your instructions appear to have made some impression on her infant mind, for she occasionally makes inquiries, in the artless simplicity of children, concerning the moral government of God—a subject which forms the foundation of a virtuous character."

J. ——.

"It is a duty which I owe myself, as well as you, to acknowledge the progress which my grandchild has made under your care.   I mean not only what he has learned regarding the different quarters of the globe, and the different species which inhabit them, which is very great, and beyond what I could have expected; but more particularly what he has learned regarding the evil of sin, and his knowledge of the Scriptures generally, and the effect this knowledge appears to have on his young mind.   In support of which I will state two cases.   One day there was an ass standing with a cart of coals, the owner being up some closs, I suppose ringing his bell, when a boy said to mine, ' Let us take a lump of coal, as there is no one sees.' 'No,' says my grandchild, 'there is One in the skies who sees, and will send us to the bad place if we do that.' The other, he being badly some time since with the small-pox, a friend said to him he would give him a pie. 'No,' said my grandchild, 'I would rather have my master, for he would tell me of my Father which is in heaven, for I think I am going to Him.' Now, Sir, such instances as these are no less satisfactory to us, the parents, than they must be to you, the master; for, while they show the blessed fruits of the system, they, at the same time, show the hold you have on their affections; and, while I am bound to acknowledge my sense of you as a teacher, I am confirmed in the opinion I always had, that the system under such teaching is the best that ever was devised for the rising generation, and may be the means, under the blessing of God, of doing much good, both to children and parents." WIDOW ———.

May 8, 1834.—" You have requested my opinion of Infant Schools. I have only to state, that as I have never had an opportunity of witnessing the plan, and as my child has only had a few weeks' tuition upon the system, therefore I can but say little on the subject. However, I have heard much to their praise, by persons who have had their children in these schools. I have also been delighted with some little things that my own child has recited to me. My wife is well pleased with the progress she is making; and I must say we are both enthusiastic admirers of the system." G. B.

May 9, 1834.—" Agreeable to your request, I have no hesitation in affirming, what I have often done before, that I regard Infant Education as the most effectual mode which has yet appeared in forming and training the infant mind in the paths of virtue, piety, and benevolence; and had I fifty children, I would send them all to the Infant School." R. S.

May 9, 1834.—" In returning answer to your note, I have only to say, that I approve very much of Infant Schools. My daughter, though unable to read, can say the alphabet by heart to me, and says she likes to go to the school, to hear about Jonah and the whale's belly— Samson, who killed a lion—the man punished for having gathered sticks on the Lord's day," &c.　　　Mrs. W.

May 8, 1834.—" My little girl, Elizabeth, is two years and two months old; she has been three months in the Infant School, and I consider she is much benefited by her attendance.　She can sing some songs; she knows a perpendicular and a horizontal line; and is altogether much improved.　I have therefore every reason to believe, that such Institutions must be of the greatest service."　R. H.

" It was with favourable opinions of the usefulness and practicable utility of Infant Schools, that first induced me to place under your tuition two of my children.　Keeping out of sight all pecuniary considerations, which cannot be a drawback upon the principles or practices of Infant Schools, I have every reason to consider them great and noble public seminaries, for the early instruction of the infantile and youthful minds of the rising generation.　Aware of the immorality and hideous obscenity of all large commercial cities and towns, I think it a duty incumbent on all heads of families, to bring forth the intellectual and reasoning faculties of their children at an early age, so that they learn the ways of truth and righteousness, and be a barrier and safeguard against the vices and immoralities to which youth is prone.

" My children, for their age, are all that a fond and doting father could wish or expect from them, since they were placed under your tuition.　Their infantile gambols and rehearsals of an evening, after the day's instruction, are pleasing and delightful, and their manners and polite breeding, fully display the paramount benefit of the system practised, to further and advance the young and thoughtless minds of the infant race."　　　D. S.

May 8, 1834.—" As I had long been sensible of the benefit which the rising generation might derive from the institution of Infant Schools, I put my little girl under your tuition at the age of three years.　She has now been a year with you, and the progress she has made has fully realized my warmest anticipations. She has received a knowledge of Bible history, suited to her tender capacity; her memory has been improved by the exercises submitted to it; her voice has been modulated, and her ear cultivated by the admirable method of turning the lessons into verse, and making them be sung to popular and sacred melodies. I am sorry that the richer classes should be so little alive to the advantages to be derived from these admirable institutions, and am surprised to perceive that several who have written in favour of them, should have taken it for granted, that the children of the better classes have no need of attending them. A moment's reflection, however, will be sufficient to show that the benefits to be derived from Infant Schools are no less applicable to the one class than to the other. No mother, however much time she may have it in her power to bestow upon her children, can have them continually under her eye; they must in a great measure be left to the care of servants, in all probability of limited education or vulgar manners: and no one will, for a moment, hesitate to admit, that they would be better employed under the care of a zealous and efficient teacher, than in hearing idle conversation, or in listening to tales which debase the mind, or terrify the imagination.

" I may mention, as it is a thing of which I am very proud, that my little girl, who is only four years old, amuses herself in the evenings with singing the pretty airs she hears at school; and does so with a precision and truth which astonish and delight us.

" In the hope that the public will appreciate the labours of those gentlemen, who have so philanthropically commenced these Institutions in this city, and cordially second them in their work of love—I remain," &c.   W. R.

May 7, 1834.—" In answer to your letter, I feel much pleasure in stating it as my opinion, that Infant Schools will prove themselves to be of the utmost importance to society, in regard to their moral and religious instruction; and I would warmly support and recommend such institutions, as being calculated, under the Divine blessing, to be productive of much good to the children in after-life; and particularly a school under such management as yours hath been since its commencement. I would be happy, would time permit, to go farther; but I will conclude by saying, that my daughter is not seven years of age, and I am above forty, and I must confess that I have learned some things of her that I did not know before." D. M.

May 9, 1834.—" I highly approve of Infant Schools. It puts early knowledge into their minds, and it keeps them off the streets, and from harm's way. How pleasant it is to hear the little ones reciting their little pieces that they have got by being at Infant Schools! Great deal could be said as to the usefulness of Infant Schools. I must confess my children have got much benefit in being put to Infant Schools." J. M'G.

May 9, 1834.—" It is my conviction, that Infant Schools are of more benefit than the public are aware of. My children, by your unremitting attention, have been much benefited, particularly Andrew: the Scripture truths and natural history which he has acquired, are more than I could have expected." R. S.

" I would cheerfully comply with the wishes of your Secretary, had I any thing of consequence to communicate; but as my boy has only been with you for a few weeks, little can be said regarding his progress. He seems, however, to enjoy the school-exercises much,— they afford amusement and instruction to the rest of our children; and I think he does not learn mere sounds, but understands their import. The other day he wished to point his mother to a window in a house opposite, and did so by telling her that it was an *oblique* one. So far as I can judge, such institutions are admirably adapted to develop the mental energies of children." J. H.

May 8, 1834.—" I am convinced that Infant education is one of the grandest schemes that ever was invented, as it tends to enlighten the mind, and gives them a knowledge which, in former ages, would have been considered supernatural.   My oldest child one evening said to me, it was a great sin to tell lies; and that God knew every lie that a child told.   She can answer questions with a correctness which would ashame them of greater years.   May you, through the blessing of God, be long spared to be the instructor of a portion of the rising generation."   D. S.

May 9, 1834.—" In compliance with your request, I give it to you as my opinion, that Infant Schools are of great utility, inasmuch as they acquire knowledge, both natural and moral, more than it is practicable to do at home, even considering the family to be of a pious cast; because there, their young minds are familiarized to Bible truths and anecdotes, which do not often come into practice at home.   As an instance of this, I put a question to my little boy, ' Can you tell me any story to-night?' He answered, ' I can tell you about the three Children, and Daniel, and Joseph.'   I asked him what kind of man Daniel was.   ' He was a good man.'   ' How do you know he was a good man?'   ' Because he prayed to God often.'   ' What did the wicked men do to him for praying to God?'   ' They cast him into a den of lions.'   ' Did the lions eat Daniel, as the wicked men expected?'   He answered, ' How could they eat him, when he prayed to God!'   I might enumerate a few others; but this may suffice upon this head.   After being a considerable time in school, while he was amusing himself one evening over his psalm-tunes, I was agreeably surprised to hear him go over some notes which were familiar to my ear, and in a little I realized the notes simply, but correctly, of New Portugal and Oldham; also another long metre tune.   In consequence of this practice in school, though he cannot read, yet in family worship he sings very correctly, and even in church, as it regards the music.   One Sabbath evening, after going to bed, he commenced one of his favourite tunes, set to the following words in school:—

' Let manna to our souls be given,
The bread of life, sent down from heaven.'

And when he had gone over it, he bawled out, ' Mother, is that not beautiful?'   In his songs of natural history, he both sings and acts with great energy, especially upon the several parts of the usefulness of the cow, as well as of all the other animals." J. T.

May 9, 1834.—" In reference to your requisition of the 5th current, sent by my little boy, John, who has been under your tuition for a considerable period, I have no hesitation in stating, that it is my decided opinion that Infant Schools, conducted in the same manner, and with the same ability, as the one under your charge, must prove a great blessing to the community. Such institutions merit public support; and in so far as my humble efforts will go, they shall not be wanting. The religious truths from the Sacred Record, the innocent anecdotes, from which useful morals can be drawn, and the general information—all given in so simple a form, and so congenial to the infant mind—will leave impressions on the generality of your interesting auditory, that will never be effaced by time, but ' will grow with their growth, and ripen with their years.'

" I may mention, as a small anecdote of your young charge, John, that upon being asked the other day what he would like best to have, a question not uncommon among heroes of his time of life, answered he had not yet made up his mind, but this he was certain, that he ' *would rather have wisdom than gold.*' Yesterday I happened to say something that he did not consider was proper; he checked me in a modest manner, by simply asking if I knew what *repentance* was? I answered in such a way as to discover his views on this subject: when he answered, that it came from God, *and if I would go to the Infant School,* you would give me its meaning more particularly.

" I beg your acceptance of my acknowledgments for your attention to my two children under your charge, and hope you will be long spared to continue in your useful public labours." W. M'K.

May 9, 1834.—" The note I received from you two days ago, I have much pleasure in answering. The bearer, James W——, is my cousin, but has lived with me for about two years past, and of course, during that time, I have had ample opportunity of observing his disposition and mental capability, and been able to compare the change that has taken place in his mind, both previous and subsequent to the time he entered your Infant Seminary. Now, I am quite of opinion, that since he went under your care, the development of his mind has been accelerated, and his powers of observation much improved. In what way this has been effected I do not attempt to account for; I merely state the fact. I am sorry I do not recollect any thing worthy, in the shape of anecdote, to mention to you about him. There is a second benefit he has decidedly derived from the school—a great improvement in his speech. This has been a faculty of late development in him, as well as in all others of his family. He now speaks much better than he would have done had he been kept at home. I may mention another benefit, and, although last, I do not think it the least he has received; namely, a great improvement in his health. Formerly he had to be kept very much within doors, and his complexion became white and delicate, and his spirits flat; now he is lively, more florid, and in first-rate health. This improvement, of course, is the result of the exercise he is allowed to take in the play-ground."

J. S.

May 9, 1834.—" I have had no opportunity of witnessing the proficiency of the more advanced scholars attending any of the Infant Schools; yet, from what I have observed in the case of my daughter, who has attended the Infant School for a few weeks only, I am convinced that the system is one attended with the most beneficial results, and amply deserves the encouragement of parents and guardians of youth.

" During the short time my daughter has attended your school, I have observed a very marked improvement in her manners and general activity; besides, her mind seems to be gradually opening up to the comprehension of subjects above the capacities of children generally. This I attribute to the winning mode of instruction adopted in Infant Schools."

J. W.

May 9, 1834.—" My opinion of Infant Schools is, that they are of great use, and will be productive of much good. This was not my former opinion, till I had one at school, and saw the progress he has made. I sent him with no other intention than to keep him out of mischief at home, and that we might know where he was ; for as he was so careless, I considered he would not learn any thing: so on that account I did not pay any attention to what he was doing, till one night I heard him repeating some things to his mother—she requested my attention, and I am happy to inform you, my astonishment was not small, when I heard him repeat hymns, and other very interesting little stories, both correct and distinctly; and, indeed, we can speak about little but what he has some knowledge of, whether Sacred, Natural History, or Geography, which must be very useful for the child, and very interesting for the parent." R. S.

May 8, 1834.—" Although little accustomed, and but ill qualified, to communicate my ideas in writing, yet I cannot withhold my approbation of an Institution, of which I have had some opportunity of judging, and which I have long considered as well adapted for the moral, physical, and intellectual improvement of the rising generation.

" We must keep in view, in the outset, man as a social, an active, but a depraved creature, whose powers begin to be developed at a much earlier period than we have been accustomed to believe. As a social being, we know that imitation is the first and grand source from which he receives his principles of action. As an active creature, he cannot be stationary; but, as depraved, he must make progress in evil, if left to his own unaided efforts.

" With regard to the first, I conceive that Infant Schools, from the mode of classification of children of a similar age, and the endless variety of exercises in which they are called to engage, to be well adapted for securing their attention, and promoting those principles of imitation and emulation, that lie so deep in our nature; and also to engage the affections, without which little good can be expected.

" As to the second, I consider Infant Schools as highly beneficial, in directing the energies of the mind into a proper channel; and, particularly, that happy method of combining amusement with instruction, (which is so conspicuous in your system,) is certainly calculated both to expand the mind, and invigorate the body.

" With regard to the third, we must ever bear in mind, that he needs the renewing influences of the Holy Spirit, without which all our efforts will prove abortive in endeavouring to raise him to that rank, as a moral and a spiritual being, for which he was designed: in this he is entirely at the disposal of sovereign mercy, and mercy has no respect to qualifications in its objects; yet mercy has respect to certain means of communication and knowledge of the true character of God, as he is revealed in his word; especially through Jesus Christ, is indispensable; for we cannot believe in him of whom we have not heard. And as this is a principal part, as certainly it should, of the Infant System, in early directing the mind to the doctrines, precepts, promises, threatenings, and examples, of the word of God—if this be accompanied with earnest, persevering, and believing prayer on our part, we have every reason to expect the Divine blessing.

" With regard to its effects, which I have witnessed, I must speak with caution, as we are extremely prone to be sanguine, and even partial, with our own children. One thing, however, I can affirm, that you have completely succeeded in gaining the attention of my little boy: to keep him from school would be a great punishment indeed. With regard to his improvement, I think I may say it has been considerable. He has got some of the rudiments of arithmetic, natural history, geography, algebra, and some of the other sciences: in these he has outstript his father. He cannot indeed tell

' How many miles it's to the moon,
How many rake wad drain the ocean toom;'

Yet he can speak fluently of the temperate, torrid, and frigid zones. He can squat on the earth like a New Zealander; he can tell you the names of all the principal towns in Europe, and indeed in the world. He talks of quadrupeds, reptiles, and insects, minerals, metals, &c. &c. and seems to have considerable knowledge of the properties of these things, both animate and inanimate; and although he asked me, above a twelvemonth ago, when at Kirkintilloch, knowing that we had sailed north, ' Father, is this the torrid zone ?' yet I believe he would laugh heartily now at such a question. He amuses us at home with his little hymns, stories, and anecdotes; and all these in general have a moral tendency. I was a little struck, last Sabbath evening, in observing that he had made more progress in knowledge than his sister, who is two years older than he; and, indeed, he put a question to me from the Old Testament history, which I could not answer.

"Another thing I would remark, that I think he has made as much progress even in the art of reading, (which your worthy Secretary said, at last public examination, was no necessary or component part of the system,) as he could have done in the same length of time in any other common reading school; and when it is considered that he is little more than six years of age, and has only been eighteen months at school, his progress is certainly greater in general knowledge than he could have gained at any other school. With regard to some objections I have heard urged, one of them is, that it has a tendency to lead the child's affections away from his parents; I think it might with as great propriety be said, that it has a tendency to withdraw the affections of the parents from the children.

"Infant Schools have been an interesting era in the history of education; and the gentlemen who have founded them, and who continue to support them, certainly merit the sincere thanks of the public. And that you, Sir, may be helped to fill that place of high respectability in which you are placed, is the sincere desire of—Yours," &c.

J. Y.

ANECDOTES.

THE father of a little boy stated to me, regarding his child, that when he came home, he was always sure to tell the Bible lesson they had during the day, and would give him no rest till he had it read from his father's large Bible —after which he would endeavour to tell him all he heard about it in school.

The mother of another little boy told me, that having occasion to reprove one of her family for telling a lie, no sooner had she done, than little 'John, our infant scholar, instantly marched up, and placing himself beside his brother, did all in his power to convince him of the sin he had committed—at the same time repeating to him several very appropriate texts of Scripture.

The mother of a little girl being one day unwell, and confined to bed, no sooner had the child returned from school, than she ran to the bed-side, and tapping her mother on the cheek, in the most affectionate manner, inquired if she was any better? The mother answered, No; when the little girl immediately informed her that Jesus was the best Doctor, because he could not only save the body, but also the soul!

While one day superintending the play-ground, I observed a very little child at great pains to get an insect into his over-all. I waited with patience to see the result, when the little fellow bore it along, and placed it upon the flower-border, and then marched off to his amusement. I was, however, anxious to know his reason for all the pains he had bestowed on the insect, when he boldly replied, that he was afraid they would tread upon it, and kill it.

One day, having missed a favourite pink, I was very anxious to know who had taken it, and having assembled the children in the gallery, I informed them that I had lost the varied pink, and that one of the children must have taken it: after a great deal had been said against the sin of stealing, a little girl stood up, with tears in her eyes, and the pink in her hand, and said, " Here, Master; here's the pink, and I wont touch the flowers any more."

A little boy one day found a farthing on the street, and

would give it to no one, till he had first brought it to school, in order to ascertain what should be done with it.

A mother informs me, that her little girl remarked to her one Sabbath morning, when doing something which she thought not proper to be done on the Sabbath, "Mother," said the child, "did you ever read about the man who gathered sticks on the Sabbath-day, and what was done to him?"

An Infant scholar, on observing her mother one day have a great deal to do with her brother, who was very obstinate and disobedient, asked her if she would "tell Robert about Absalom, and what the Bible says about the child that mocks his father, or disobeys his mother."

The same little girl, on hearing a man one day express an oath to her mother, said, "O, man, you are like Shimei! do you know the Bible says, 'Swear not at all?'"

A little boy being told by his mother to strike his sister, who had taken his plaything from him, instantly replied, "O, no! I would rather pray for her; because the Bible says, 'Be not overcome of evil; but overcome evil with good.'"

A little boy one day being observed crying at *piece-time*, and on being asked what made him cry, answered, that a thief had stolen his roll when coming to school. No sooner had the little fellow told his tale, than another little boy starts up, and says, "Here, Master; give him the half of mine, for I got the half of his yesterday." "And why," I inquired, "did he give you the half of his yesterday?" "Because a thief stole mine too, walking along the street."

A woman called upon me one morning, and expressed, in very warm terms, how satisfied and thankful she was at the *moral* and *religious* improvement of her little girl, whose age I think might be close upon five years. She said that the regularity and attention of the little creature in the duty of prayer might put them all to the blush. As a proof of her fondness for prayer, her mother told me, that the elder members of the family, who wrought in a cotton establishment, were obliged to rise at five in the morning, and that the little girl woke at the same hour, arose, said her prayers, and lay down again till the usual time of rising.

One day, while occupying a spare hour in digging the flower-border around the play-ground, I was surrounded by a group of little children, attracted by the novelty of the employment, and who, with all the eagerness of young naturalists, stood watching the insects that were thrown up in every spadeful of earth, crying out, as they appeared, " O ! the millepede ! the millepede!" (Maggy-mony-feet) ; or, " O ! the worm ! the worm ! Master, don't kill the poor worm !"—When one of the children, a little girl, came close to me, and, in her own lisping and imperfect accents, said, " Master, didn't God make the little flowers ?" " Yes," I answered, " He did ;" and, glad of such an opportunity, I began to lay down some things about the wonders of creation. " Master, doesn't God see us just now ?" she observed again. " Yes," I replied. " And I'm sure he knows what we're saying," she added. But, leaping away again, in obedience to the impulse of an untutored mind, she asked, " Wasn't it God that made the skies too?"—but what followed struck me as astonishing in infant capacity—"Master," said she, " I'm sure God didn't make a *tiny* ?"* No, I answered ; when she immediately added, " No ; but he made the iron." I recollected that some days before I had been speaking upon a similar subject ; but I never mentioned any thing about the *tiny*, the iron, or who made it. On the child's part, it must have been reasoning from induction.

A little girl, four years of age, attending the Infant School, seeing her mother weeping over a little sister, who was dead, seemed anxious to comfort her mother, by telling her, " that she should not cry after Janet was dead— that she ought rather to be glad, because all good children when they die will go to Jesus Christ."

" The second account is with regard to two boys we had who were at a Sabbath Evening School. The attention of the teachers was attracted towards them, from the ready answers which they gave to the questions which were put, and especially the correct knowledge they had of Bible biography. The teacher, not knowing how they could excel others in a general knowledge of the truths of

---

* A small tin vessel for children.

Scripture, asked them what school they were attending during the week. ' The Infant School,' said the boys."

I have heard parents say, that frequently, when their children return from school, they ask questions of various kinds, to which they are not at all times prepared to give an answer. On this account, they are obliged to think upon the questions, that they may be able to answer the inquiries of their children, and by this means their own knowledge is increased.

The teacher of a Sabbath School, in the vicinity of an Infant School, finds as his experience, that those children who have been previously trained in an Infant School, are much more orderly in their behaviour, and much easier interested in the exercises of the school, than those who have not enjoyed that privilege.

Cleanliness.—A mother mentioned to me, some time ago, that the fees paid by her for her boy had been saved in the article of soap.

Obedience to Parents.—A mother informed me lately, that before her son went to school, he was exceedingly disobedient to her and his father; but that since going there, he has become quite a new child.

Truth.—The parents of some of the children have repeatedly told me, that an approximation to deceit at home is immediately detected.

Prepares for higher Schools.—Parents have repeatedly told me, that their children, who had entered the Juvenile School, made greater progress than their other children, who had never had the benefit of Infant Training.

A boy, nearly three years of age, seeing his father unwell, after being put to bed along with him, he began to address him in the following manner:—" Father, are you going to die?" " No, William," said the father. " But if you were to die, would you go to a bad place?" The parent asked the boy where he would like him to go. " To heaven, and Jesus Christ."

A little boy, when at prayers, before being put to bed, having prayed for his "father," the unusual expression roused the mother to inquire, "Who had told him to pray for his father?" " He told her that it was his master;" and said also, " that God would give us any thing we want, if we ask it right from him."

A parent, who has two children attending school, has often told me, that he cannot understand how his boys love one another so well now, as, previous to their being sent to school, there were so much quarrelling and fighting between them, that their mother had enough to do to keep order in the house ; but now, instead of quarrelling, they seem so fond of each other, that should their mother speak of beating one of them for any fault, the other will cry to the mother to forgive him.

Another parent has often told me, that she was very much surprised to see how easily her youngest girl, attending school, would check the eldest of the family, for the smallest fault, almost before she could perceive it herself.

FINIS.

Printed by W. Collins & Co.
Glasgow.

www.ingramcontent.com/pod-product-compliance
Lightning Source LLC
Chambersburg PA
CBHW062035090426
42740CB00016B/2917